D.H

Tra
Your
Ancestors

Trace
Your
Ancestors

by

Estelle Catlett and Peter Verstappen

Contents

Part 1

Who Were Your Ancestors?

1

Looking for your Ancestors

This book assumes that you have no knowledge at all of family history research, that you are a complete but enthusiastic beginner. It will take you step by step through the process of tracing your own family history. I would ask you to read Part 1 of the book through first so that you will have some idea of what you are about to undertake, then to return to the beginning and follow the suggested assignments through, chapter by chapter.

Who are you? You are the present day accumulation of all the genes, characteristics and hereditary behaviour of your ancestors. Have you ever wondered who your ancestors were, where they lived and what they did? What they looked like?

Heredity is not exclusive to anyone. We all have ancestors and we all have sagas to tell. Everybody can enjoy this hobby. The dustman and the duke, the ordinary person as much as royalty is able equally to research his or her own family history. It is not an area exclusively owned by the nobility although, of course, in the writings of history, opinions as to whose families matter the most will always differ.

Over the past 40 years the growth of this leisure activity, which seems to reflect a romantic nostalgia for the past, has astounded professional researchers. This development has been both beneficial and stimulating. Men and women work at their researches, introducing into what used to be a recreation a certain amount of professionalism. Information has spread worldwide and the chances of finding out more about remote branches of your family are increased because your distant relative, hitherto unknown to you, has also been working away researching his family history and you can exchange your knowledge to each other's benefit. Even more exciting is that it has become worldwide, perhaps because of the increasing ease of communications made available to us by our electronic age.

In order to research your own family history you will have to be a detective, looking for clues and sifting the evidence available. Perseverance, luck, careful correct copying and note taking are all essential. There can never be a guarantee of success, but you will always find it a challenging and satisfying hobby. It takes time and is a slow process but it is well worth all the effort put into it. With persistence and a degree of luck you will be able to trace your family roots back to the late 1700s and possibly even further. I experienced an extreme example of luck recently when I required the assistance of an American researcher. Using my list of professional researchers, covering the whole of America, and the 'pin' method I wrote to an unknown genealogist in the State where I required a search. The work was quickly and efficiently completed and when the documents were sent to me the letter accompanying them also told me that my professional colleague had an ancestor with the same surname as myself (my husband's family surname) whose family originated in Kent in England. The name is unusual and I was able to confirm that my husband's family did indeed originate in Kent. I am now awaiting a copy of my American colleague's own family tree to see if we can make a connection somewhere. The patron saint of genealogists must have guided my 'pin' that day.

If you can one day show your family a well presented and interesting history they will be delighted. Do not doubt it. You will also gain great satisfaction and pleasure from a job well done and have something to pass on to your children who may well be bitten by the bug and continue the research. It is endless. As members of your family are born, marry or die, so the information to add to your research grows.

Before you start, go to the library and borrow biographies of famous people. You will find them interesting to read and they will give you some ideas on how to start and what you are looking for. Your own family history is as interesting as anyone else's, whether famous or not. There are also Family History Societies in existence. Go to a meeting of your local society – your library will probably know where and when they meet. They will welcome you as a newcomer and give advice and you will meet people who have the same interest as yourself.

How and where do you start? First talk to your family and tell them what you are doing. Write to your cousin in Australia or your aunt in Scotland. It may be that someone else in your family is engaged in family history research and has done some of the work for you. They will produce all sorts of bits and pieces which may prove useful (if not immediately then perhaps later when they slot into a space and confirm some piece of research which you have been following).

Gather up all the information you can from your family before you start. It may provide clues and help which will save you a great deal of time. Old letters, postcards and birthday cards in particular are very helpful. Articles from newspapers, letters from abroad, wills and diaries can provide dates and names that you are looking for.

Before it is too late, talk to your older relatives and make a note of what they tell you. There is nothing that old people like to do better than talk about 'the old days'. They will, while reminiscing about past events and places, reveal much information to help you. They may need gentle prompting as to exact names, dates and occasions. Don't be afraid to ask them, encourage them and they will be a mine of information. Personal knowledge will often reveal unknown relationships but they must always be checked and supported by documentation if your family history is to be based on fact.

If you find it difficult to write quickly and keep up with what is being said, invest in a small personal tape recorder, the type which is not intrusive, which you can hold in your hand or lay on a table. They are not too expensive and you can save all the information to go through at a later date when you have more time. Some people may object to the use of a tape recorder and 'dry up' but most will soon forget its presence and talk freely. Your only difficulty will be to change the tape quickly enough so as not to miss anything that is being said.

A word of warning, do not take everything that members of your family tell you as fact. They may choose not to tell you about one particular person whom they disliked or with whom they quarrelled or who they consider is a disgrace to the family. There may have been incidents in the past which they do not wish to remember. Memories are often hazy as to dates and places. They are also coloured by happy or sad experiences. Memory plays funny tricks. We all have some things we would rather forget. It may be those very things that you will need to know. Everything should be checked where possible by following up information given. If several members of the family tell the same story it probably is true, but not always. It may have been handed down by tradition and the facts changed by each story teller to suit the occasion. It is for you to discover the answers.

Some families have family bibles in which generations of names and dates have been recorded. Possibly one of your older aunts or a grandparent has it pushed away in a cupboard. Although it is not on display, they will not want to part with it. You may have to copy the entries. If you do, make sure you copy them exactly, even if you think the spelling is incorrect. If you have difficulty reading the handwriting ask other members of the family if they remember any of the names. If you can persuade the owner to part with the bible for a short time, take it to a shop to have the relevant pages photocopied. Most towns have 'copy shops' charging a small sum per page for copies. If you return the bible promptly the owner will know you are to be trusted and may produce other treasured documents for you to see.

Old photographs and photograph albums can be a source of much information. Very often notes of the people in the photographs or places and dates where they were taken will be found written on the back. If there was an enthusiastic photographer in the family who kept their work in an album, they probably wrote all the details beside each picture. This could prove a great source of information.

When you have gathered all the available details you should have many pages of your notebook filled, or several small tapes waiting to be played at your leisure and you will probably have renewed acquaintance with a few distant relatives who were no doubt very pleased to hear from you. Family history research can result in many happy reunions with those we thought were lost to us and introductions to those we did not know existed.

It is no use jumping into the middle just because you have some odd pieces of information about distant relatives. You can only start with the information about which you are certain, so begin with yourself and work back into the past. If you have an uncommon name or a family name that is passed down from one generation to another, then it will be much easier, but you may find that your name, which you thought was unusual is in fact very common in some other part of the country. This may be a helpful point of reference but could lead you on a time-consuming and wasteful exercise unless you are sure there is some connection.

Remember to keep ALL the notes that you make, even those on scraps of paper and the backs of envelopes. You never know when they may come in useful. It is also essential to make a note of where you obtained the specific pieces of information in case you ever need to check the notes you made or refer again to a particular book or documents. Cite the exact source of the information and give all the data you have at the time you may make your notes. If you copy information from the family bible, it is not sufficient to mark your notes 'from the family bible'. You may not remember who has possession of the bible or where it is housed. Make a full note of the date on which the notes were taken, in whose possession the bible remains and the address. It is particularly important to make a note of your sources of reference when visiting registries, libraries, museums or newspaper archives. You may have spent a great deal of time tracking down the information. If you know where you found it, the next time you need to refer to it a great deal of wasted time and frustration will be avoided if you know where to look. The following are examples of good and bad reference notes. For the purpose of these examples you are the family historian 'John Smith'.

BAD	GOOD
'Letter from Aunt Annie'	Letter from Mrs. Annie Goodall dated 27 January 1985 to John Smith (family historian). Letter now in possession of John Smith filed under reference G/29.

BAD	GOOD
'Family Bible'	Copied by John Smith, 19 January 1994 from family Bible record of Arthur Smith of Harrogate b. 2 November 1867. Bible in possession of Harold G. Smith of 22 Grace Street, Harrogate. Original entries in Bible handwritten, authors unknown. Photocopies in possession of John Smith filed under reference S/6.

BAD	GOOD
'Book in Guildhall Library'	Information copied 2 March 1993 by John Smith from book 'Gleaning History' by S. R. Green. Published by Fish & Sons. Book available at Guildhall Library, London. Library reference No. 86/B7.

BAD	GOOD
'A death certificate'	Information copied by John Smith 6 May 1995 from death certificate of Constance Ellen Harris d. 29 October 1899. Original in possession of Alice Cross (daughter of C. E. Harris) of 22 Cramery Road, Northampton. Photocopy in possession of John Smith filed under reference H/219.

All families do not have 'skeletons in the cupboard' nor a banished 'black sheep' but it is much more interesting if they do. Not many people can boast a highwayman or an illegitimate Earl as a distant ancestor, but you may be surprised by the occupations and connections of your forebears. I have met many who through their research claim a family association with the royal family, the Churchill family or one of the great families of Europe, however tenuous the link may be. Most families, however, even if they have a tradition of being town dwellers will find roots somewhere in the countryside.

A little like a jigsaw puzzle, start at the outside edges and work inwards as you find the pieces that fit together. It may take a long time to find the one piece that will enable you to proceed further but do not give up. You may lose your way and feel discouraged. You may decide to give up the research for a time, possibly a few months, or even years. It doesn't matter, it is always there for you to return to. The chances are, however, that once you start you will find it difficult to stop. It will be your own personal serial or 'soap opera'; you will feel compelled to know 'what happened next'.

One more thing to decide before you go any further is which branch of your family you are first going to follow. The further you go the more branches your family tree will have and those branches will divide into smaller branches and eventually into

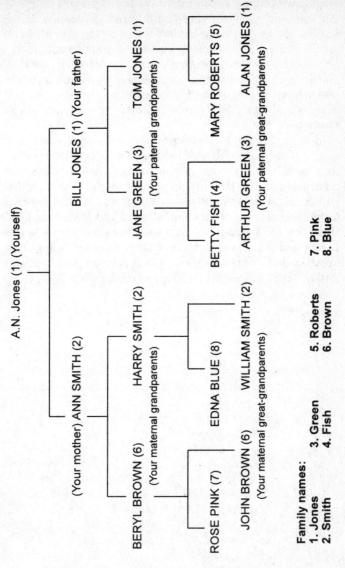

Fig 1. Family Tree as far back as your great-grandparents.

Family names:
1. Jones
2. Smith
3. Green
4. Fish
5. Roberts
6. Brown
7. Pink
8. Blue

15

twigs, each bearing a name and a relationship to the others. If you start with yourself, your family name will usually be the same as that of your father. Before they married, your mother's family name was different from that of your father, so that immediately you have two family names to follow. By the time you get to your grandparents you will have four family names to research and when you reach your great-grandparents you will have eight different family names. The diagram (Fig. 1) gives an illustration.

Most people follow their father's family name when they start, following through with the male line only. This is called the paternal line. If you follow your mother's family, that is your maternal line. It is easier to start on your paternal line since you will be following only one surname. Any other names gathered at the same time can be kept and followed later in your research. If you come to a sudden stop with your paternal line because you cannot find the next clue, leave it for a while and follow your maternal line, or branch off on to your paternal grandmother's family. There will always be plenty of other trails to follow.

2

The General Registry

When you have gathered all the existing information from your family, store it safely and start at the beginning with yourself. Do you have a copy of your own birth certificate? Get it out and look at it. What does it tell you? It gives you the following information:

1. Your date and place of birth.
2. Your name.
3. Your sex.
4. Your father's name and surname.
5. Your mother's name and maiden name (her surname before she was married).
6. Your father's occupation.
7. The name and description of the person giving the information of your birth and their address.
8. The date of registration.
9. The district in which you were registered.
10. The sub-district in which you were registered.
11. The county in which you were registered.

If you were born in England or Wales after 1968 your birth certificate will also show the birthplace of both your parents and the previous name of your mother if different from her maiden name. If, for instance, she had been widowed or divorced and remarried then her previous married surname would also be given.

Your birth certificate as a starting point gives you a great deal of information. Armed with that information you are on your way to a thrilling journey into the past.

If you do not have a copy of your birth certificate you can obtain one from the Registrar of Births, Deaths and Marriages. There are separate registries for England and Wales, Scotland, Northern Ireland and the Irish Republic. All the addresses are given in the Appendix to this book.

Write to the Chief Registrar giving as much detail as you can. Your full name, exact date and place of birth. If you know your father's full name and your mother's maiden name give that information. In England and Wales if you are able to go to the Registry to make the application yourself a copy certificate will cost less than if you request the Registry staff to make a search on your behalf and you can collect the copy within two or three days. If you have to write, the cost is considerably more for each certificate and it can take as long as three weeks before you receive that elusive document. Charges and length of waiting time vary from registry to registry.

Registration of births, deaths and marriages in England and Wales became compulsory on the 1st July 1837. In Scotland registration commenced on 1st January 1855 and in Ireland in 1864. All entries in the Register are indexed alphabetically and by searching the indexes you should be able to find the details and obtain the certificates you require. It should therefore in theory be easy to trace your family history at least back to the dates of compulsory registration with little difficulty. It should be, but it is not always so. That is what makes it so interesting. If it were a matter of simply going to the registries with a list of names and dates it would soon become repetitious and boring, but somewhere along the line you will 'lose' someone and you will have to start looking elsewhere. That is when you become a detective and when the information you have gathered from your family can be used as a reference.

If you live in or near London and your first searches relate to people who lived or are living in England and Wales, it is well worth a visit to the Office of Population Census and Surveys at St Catherine's House, part of which houses the index search rooms for Births, Deaths and Marriages. You will, over the course of your research, return many times. Your first visit is always exciting but can be bewildering if you do not know what to do or where to look. Provide yourself with a good notebook – the type used for shorthand or an exercise book – and plenty of pencils with a pencil sharpener with its own box for the pencil shavings. Many registries, libraries and archives do not allow the use of ball point pens and insist on the use of pencils only. If you make a practice of using pencils everywhere, you can't go wrong. A useful 'travel pack' to take with you when carrying out any form of research should contain pencils, pencil sharpener and eraser, a magnifying glass (particularly useful when researching early original documents) and plenty of small change for use in copying machines where they are available. On your first visit to St Catherine's House allow yourself a whole day so that you have plenty of time. Wear casual clothes and comfortable shoes, you will be standing most of the day.

As you enter St Catherine's House through the revolving doors, on the right is the enquiry desk and to the left are the security personnel. In front of you are the search rooms. There is no entry fee and no search fees to pay if you carry out your own researches. There are attendants who will direct you if you cannot find what you are looking for, but they are not usually available to assist individuals with their own personal searches.

The first thing you will realise is that you are not alone in your interest in family history research. The Registry is always full of people looking for their ancestry. You will hear Australian, American, West Indian, Canadian, Indian, Scots and Irish accents as well as English. The Registry is always crowded with both professional and amateur searchers of all ages. Not all family historians are maiden aunts, retired colonels and house-wives, many are young. The one thing they all have in common is enthusiasm. In the summer holiday months the number of searchers is increased by visitors from abroad and students on holiday. Most, but not all, researchers are friendly. They are all absorbed in their own research, but sometimes do not object to being asked for advice – they may even offer it! A delighted cry of 'found it' can often be heard when a dedicated but tired searcher's patience is rewarded. Sympathetic smiles and nods of encouragement will greet that lucky person. Do not be intimi-dated by obviously experienced searchers – they were all begin-ners themselves once.

Before you start your searches, walk through the Registry so that you know where things are. The Registry is divided into three large rooms. Each room has banks of shelves containing many volumes which index alphabetically all the entries con-tained in the registers. The first search room contains red indexes for births on the right and black death indexes on the left. A side room off the death indexes also houses some birth records. Walk forward to the end of the room, up a few steps and to your left are more death records. In front of you is the desk where you can collect certificates which were previously ordered and the Supervisor's Office where they will deal with any specific enquiries. To the right are the cashiers' booths where certificates are ordered and paid for and the desk where application forms for certificates can be obtained. At the end of the cashiers' booths are swing doors. Immediately through those doors to the left are the toilets. Walk down the corridor and turn left by the telephones for the green marriage indexes. Directions are clearly marked. Also in that area are the Miscellaneous records.

You will not be allowed to see the original registers. You must search the indexes to find the details of the entry that you require and then apply for the certificate. The volumes in each search area are housed in banks of shelves each three shelves high. The upright at the end of each bank of shelves is clearly marked showing the dates of the volumes contained and between the banks of shelves are long desks at which you can stand, where the volumes can be rested while you search. There are no seats, so be prepared to stand in fairly crowded conditions. There is a small section with seats and low desks provided for disabled people. The volumes are large and heavy and some have canvas handles on the spine to assist when taking them from the shelves. The earlier volumes are handwritten, the later ones are typewritten or printed.

In each section (births, marriages and deaths), each year is divided into quarters: March, June, September and December. The quarters are divided as follows:

March quarter entries	January, February, March
June quarter entries	April, May, June
September quarter entries	July, August, September
December quarter entries	October, November, December.

Each quarter is divided alphabetically so that for some years, when there were more births, marriages or deaths, there are more volumes. For some years there may be only four volumes: March A–Z, June A–Z, September A–Z and December A–Z. In others each quarter may be divided into several volumes such as:

20

March A–F, March G–L, March M–R, March S–Z,
June A–D, June E–K, June L–R, June S–Z,
September A–E, September F–P, September R–Z,
December A–K, December L–R, December S–Z,
giving a total of fourteen volumes for that year.

Birth Certificates

As an example, let us look for your birth certificate in the red volumes. You know your name, date of birth and roughly where your birth occurred. First find the bank of shelves showing the date you require and walk along until you come to the exact year. Remember there are three rows of shelves, only the middle shelf is at eye level. Look for the quarter in which your birth took place and then the volume containing the letter of the alphabet with which your surname begins in that quarter. If your name is Joan Shepheard and you were born in August 1920 you would look for the volume marked 1920 September S. If you are Henry Arthur Brown born in April 1908 you would look for the volume marked 1908 June B.

Take the volume from the shelf (you may have to wait if someone else has that volume out) and put it on a space nearest to you on the desk. You will have to fit in with the other searchers; spaces are jealously guarded. Look through the book until you come to the page showing the surname you require. The pages are alphabetically indexed at the top left hand and right hand corners so that you can quickly find the page you need. The indexes will show the name of the persons, the district where registered, the volume and page in the register as follows:

Surname	District	Volume	Page
Shepheard Joan	Barnsley	9a	666
or			
Brown Henry Arthur	Hackney	21	271

The district of registration is the local area registry or county registry and is not always the exact place of birth. It is as well to know the names of the surrounding towns or boroughs in case you have a fairly common surname.

Remember also that registration of an event may not necessarily take place on the same date as the event. In the case of a birth the time allowed for registration is forty-two days. Registration could therefore have taken place some time later, so that if you are looking for an event which occurred in September it may be recorded in either the September or the December quarter. The only thing of which you can be certain is that it could not have been recorded in the June quarter before the event took place.

Once you are sure you have the right person, and if you start with yourself it should not be too difficult, copy all the information into your notebook taking care to get the numbers and letters of the volume and pages correct.

Try another exercise with your father's birth. You will need to know his full name, date and place of birth. Information as to the maiden name of the mother is only required for births registered after the September quarter of the year 1911. The important details are the volume and page so make sure you get the numbers correct. One digit wrong and you will not get your certificate, or you may get the wrong one – an expensive and time-consuming mistake. You are now ready to make the application for a copy of the entry in the register. Go to the desk in front of the cashiers' booths where you will find supplies of application forms. The application forms for a full birth certificate are coloured pink and are numbered CAS 51. Instructions for how to complete the forms are clearly printed on them. Complete box A as in Figure 2 opposite and box B exactly the same as box A. Sign the form and print your name and address in block capitals. If you have any difficulty, an attendant may be able to assist you.

Take your completed form to a cashier together with the fee. If you are able to collect the certificate yourself the cashier will give you a receipt and will tell you when you can return to collect the certificate which is usually within three days. Do not lose the receipt. Receipts are issued in different colours and are used to identify your certificate when you collect it from the front desk. If you wish the certificate to be posted you will be given an envelope to address to yourself and will probably be told that the delay will be about two to three weeks. In practice certificates sent by mail usually take about ten days.

Death Certificates
A death certificate will give the following information:

1. Date and place of death.
2. Name and surname.

When you have found the entry, **copy the names and particulars from the index into the spaces A and B below in BLOCK CAPITALS**

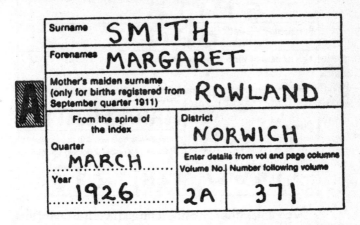

Surname	SMITH
Forenames	MARGARET
Mother's maiden surname (only for births registered from September quarter 1911)	ROWLAND

From the spine of the index	District
	NORWICH
Quarter	Enter details from vol and page columns
MARCH	Volume No. | Number following volume
Year	
1926	2A | 371

Now complete the rest of the form and take it to one of the

Fig. 2 Application Form for a Birth Certificate – Example of Box A
Completed for Birth of Margaret Smith, January 1926

3. Sex.
4. Age at death.
5. Occupation.
6. Cause of death.
7. Name of Informer.
8. Qualification of Informer (relationship to deceased).
9. Date of registration.

Certificates issued for deaths after 1969 will also give the date and place of birth of the deceased, the maiden name of a woman if married and the usual address of the informant. In particular the date and place of birth can be very helpful.

The indexes of the death registers can be searched in the same way as those for births. From 1865 the age at death is given in the index so that if there are two people with the same name the age of death can help to pinpoint the one you are looking for. If you know roughly how old the person was when they died and

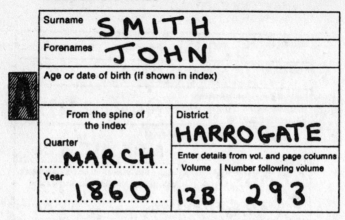

When you have found the entry, **copy the names and particulars from the index into the spaces A and B below in BLOCK CAPITALS**

Surname	SMITH
Forenames	JOHN

Age or date of birth (if shown in index)

A

From the spine of the index	District
Quarter	HARROGATE
MARCH	Enter details from vol. and page columns
Year	Volume	Number following volume
1860	12B	293

Now complete the rest of the form and take it to one of the

Fig. 3 Application Form for a Death Certificate – Example of Box A
Completed for John Smith who died January 1860

the age of death shown is many years different it is probably the wrong person.

The application forms for death certificates are numbered CAS 52 and are coloured lavender. They should be completed in the same way as the applications for birth certificates by completing boxes A and B and the other requested information. (Figure 3, above.)

Marriage Certificates

A marriage certificate will give you the following information:

1. Date.
2. Names and surnames of the bride and groom.
3. Ages of the bride and groom.
4. Descriptions (spinster, bachelor etc.).
5. Professions.
6. Addresses.
7. Name of the fathers of both parties.

8. Occupation of both fathers.
9. Names of witnesses.

The green indexes are searched in a similar manner. One advantage is that you can cross check that you have the correct marriage by looking in the same quarter under the names of both the bride and groom. If the volume and page numbers are the same for each, you have the correct marriage entry and can proceed to apply for a copy certificate on the green printed application forms. If the marriage took place from 1984 onwards, no quarter is shown on the index volumes. There is a column beside the names headed 'REG' and that reference should be entered on your application form instead of the quarter in the special box provided. ('REG' is an internal reference used by the Registry.)

If you are married, look for your own entry, if not look for that of your parents. All you need to know are the names of the groom, the maiden name of the bride, the date and place of the marriage. The place is not quite so essential since if you have both names you can cross check that you have the correct entry and the index will give you the district of the registry. Make an application for the marriage certificate of yourself or your parents on the green coloured form numbered CAS 53, completing box A and box B as shown in Figure 4 (overleaf). The details given on that certificate will provide you with information which will enable you to continue your searches.

Additional records contained at St Catherine's House are for births and deaths at sea, records kept by British Consuls abroad since 1849, some Army records for personnel as well as their families since 1761 and Royal Air Force returns commencing in 1920.

A two-tier charging system for postal applications operates at St Catherine's House, whereby a researcher will be charged a lower fee when quoting the exact index volume reference for the certificate required. If a search is involved, a higher fee will be charged. The object of this two-tier system is to encourage the use of microfilm copies of the St Catherine's House indexes which are now widely available for use in local record offices and libraries. The OPCS publish a free small but useful booklet giving instructions about how to use the facilities at St Catherine's House.

This chapter has assumed that you have experienced no

When you have found the entry, **copy the names and particulars from the index into the spaces A and B below in BLOCK CAPITALS**

Now complete the rest of the form and take it to one of the

Fig. 4 Application Form for a Marriage Certificate – Example of Box A
Completed for Marriage of Robert Brown and Joan Smith, February 1936

difficulty in finding the entries you require. In the next chapter we will discuss how to proceed if you cannot find the entries for which you are looking. We will also find out where the information can lead and where to search if your family comes from Scotland or Ireland.

3

Other Registries

In addition to the indexes for births, marriages and deaths, St Catherine's House holds other indexes housed under the subject name of Miscellaneous.

These cover British subjects who were born, married or died abroad including deaths in the air and at sea. However, they only cover those events when they were registered at the nearest British Consulate. In addition there are some Army registers. These events are not fully indexed and are not a complete record, but should be considered when looking for a 'missing' relative. The volumes in this section are on shelves in the same area as the death registers. Each is labelled showing the contents, such as 'H.M. Ships Marriages 1849–1889' and 'Deaths in the air 1945–1970'. There are about 18 of these volumes all containing different information. The indexes are colour coded similarly to the general indexes, red for births, green for marriages and black for deaths.

Also on the Miscellaneous shelves are indexes for Foreign Registers kept by British Clergymen abroad, some of which are very old, the oldest being 'Belgium, Baptisms and burials 1817–1850.' The countries covered by these registers which include births, marriages and deaths are Belgium, Burma, China, Denmark, India, Japan, Mesopotamia (Iraq), Palestine (Israel), Portugal, Roumania, Russia, Sweden and parts of France, Germany, Holland and Italy. They cover various years, some spanning from 1840–1947 and relate to some of the British living in those countries, but by no means all of them. Copies of all these certificates should be applied for on the blue forms provided at the desk near the indexes. The forms are printed in red (births), green (marriages) and black (deaths) and are completed in a similar manner to those for the general entries. Some of the overseas indexes are not on the shelves. If you cannot find the one you require, ask at the front desk. You will be given a pass and taken to the overseas section by an attendant where you can see all the overseas indexes.

Records of still-births in England and Wales commenced on 1 July 1927. Application for special permission has to be made to the Registrar General if a copy of the record is required.

Copies of entries from the other Miscellaneous registers are applied for on special forms and by special procedures. Help in completing these forms should be sought from one of the official assistants on duty.

Adoptions

There were no official adoption certificates before 1920 and the records at St Catherine's House commence on 1st January 1927. Indexes for adoption certificates show only the adoptive name and the names of the adopting parents. They do not give the name of the person before adoption. They do give the correct date of birth and are therefore similar to a normal birth certificate, except that the surname shown is not the name at birth. Some children were adopted by close relatives in which case the surname could possibly be the same, but the certificate would not reveal this.

Only an adult adopted person can obtain a copy of the original birth certificate showing the name of the natural parents. A substantial amount of information is required in order to obtain such a certificate. The date of the adoption, the court where the order was made, the full names and surname of the adoptive parents and the name of the child (adoptive surname). For adoptions up to and including 12th November 1975 an adopted person requiring their original birth certificate would have to see and be counselled by a social worker before the information was made available to them. For adoptions after 12th November 1975 the person has a choice whether to be counselled or not. Written application must be made.

Scotland

Family historians whose families have roots in Scotland have an advantage over those whose records are in England and Wales.

Scottish civil registration did not commence until 1st January

1855 but their record keeping was much more thorough than that of England and Wales. All the certificates of births, marriages and deaths contain more information than the English certificates.

Birth certificates give, in addition to the information on the English certificates, one important addition, the date and place of the parents' marriage. This enables the searcher to obtain a copy marriage certificate for the parents without having to search the indexes quarter by quarter, year by year from the date of the child's birth to find the marriage date. Marriage certificates give the names of both parents of the bride and the groom, not only that of the father as on their English counterparts. Death certificates give the names of both parents of the deceased. All this additional information is most helpful and saves a great deal of research time.

The first birth, death and marriage certificates, issued in 1855 contained much additional information. The birth certificates give the parents' ages and birthplaces and the number of other siblings living and deceased. The marriage certificates give the places of present residence and the usual residence if different of both bride and groom and details of any previous marriages. The death certificates give the place of birth, details of marriage, burial place and all living and deceased siblings. Sadly, for genealogists and family historians, as the volume of work grew the inclusion of this additional information was not continued after 1855.

Scottish records are held in New Register House, Edinburgh. For an inclusive search fee (see Appendix) the researcher has access to the indexes from 1855 for births, marriages and deaths, and divorces from 1984. Also available are old Parish registers pre-1855 and the Census records from 1841 to 1891.

Each researcher is given a numbered seat at a desk. All indexes are on computer and searching is very easy. Instructions for use are given at each terminal and the computer will offer various recorded spellings for each name. There is also a very useful cross check for female marriages and deaths as these are indexed under all known surnames, i.e. maiden surname, previous and present married names.

Original records are not open for inspection but most are available on self service access microfiche or microfilm so you can check you have the correct entry before ordering and paying for copy certificates. You can also get photocopies or make accurate copies without purchasing certificates or photocopies if you prefer. (Remember to cite your sources!) This helps you to continue your researches, making full use of your time at the Registry. For instance, if you find a correct birth certificate this will give you the names and ages of both parents; a marriage certificate will give you the names of both sets of parents. Note this information and return to the indexes to search for the relevant page and volume numbers. One visit could uncover several generations.

When you have found your entry in the computer index, complete the relevant (colour coded) order form. Take the microfiche or microfilm that you require and replace it with your order form, first detaching the counterfoil on which you should have noted the entry number that you wish to search. You can remove three fiches or two films at a time. After use, put them in the relevant trays for filing. If you require some minor records, fill in an orange order form and put it in a request tray. An attendant will bring the register to your seat number.

The attendants are very knowledgeable; they can often point you in the right direction if the record inspected proves to be the wrong one and will help you to master the equipment.

Before visiting New Register House it is advisable to book your seat in advance by letter or phone. The Registry issue very informative free literature (which can be obtained by post) showing what records they hold, their charges and times of opening, which will help you plan your visit in advance. There are, of course, charges for copy certificates; these are less if you search the indexes yourself but you may find that the assistance of the Registry staff is worth the extra charge. You may only use pencils here; they sell them in aid of a local charity to anyone who forgets to bring one.

A genealogical search room will shortly open in Glasgow. This will be linked by computer to New Register House in Edinburgh and, as there, bookings will have to be made in advance and a search fee will be charged. (See Appendix.)

Ireland

If you go to Dublin, I suggest you visit the Genealogical Office in Kildare Street before you visit the research centres. This offers an excellent consultancy service where for £20/hour a professional genealogist will assist you and give advice on where to search and what is available. An appointment can be made in advance to avoid wasted time.

Civil registration in Ireland commenced in 1864 and the indexes are kept at the Registrar General's office. A charge is made for the privilege of searching the indexes. There is a small comfortable search room with separate tables and all the indexes are housed in that room. There are usually two very helpful clerks on duty.

Birth certificates in Ireland give the date and exact place of birth, the name of the child, the full name, occupation and residence of the father, the maiden name of the mother and the name of the person present at the birth. Marriage certificates give the names of the parties, date and place of the marriage, the place of residence of the bride and groom and the names of their fathers. Death certificates only give the name of the deceased, the age and the date and place of death. The original records are not open to inspection by the public, but once you have found what you think is the correct entry you can pay a lesser fee for a photocopy of the entry. The copy will be brought to you in a short time. Once again you have only spent a small sum to find out and not paid the full fee for a certificate as you would in England and Wales. When you are sure you have the correct entry the full fee can be paid and the certificates ordered and supplied while you wait. It is therefore possible to carry out your searches and obtain your certificates without waiting too long, enabling you to further your searches the same day. The fees payable are in Irish punts, English currency is not accepted in Dublin. If you wish to send a remittance to Ireland, you can obtain a bank draft or Irish currency from most banks. If you send currency, use registered post.

Northern Ireland
All the original registers and records for Northern Ireland which commence with the partition of Ireland in 1922 are kept in the General Register Office, Belfast. The Belfast registry also holds some records for the northern counties of southern Ireland (the counties of Cavan, Monaghan and Donegal). This is because before partition these counties were part of Ulster. Birth certificates will give you the date and place of birth, name, sex; full name, occupation and usual residence of father; maiden name of mother, date of registration and name and residence of inform-ant. Marriage certificates give the date, names and ages of both bride and groom together with their residences at the date of

31

marriage and their occupations, the names of the fathers of the bride and groom and their occupations. Information on death certificates is similar to that given on the English certificates. The Belfast Office has a unique system to assist family history researchers. Appointments have to be made in advance and the office will usually take only one researcher each day. For a comparatively small fee per day, the researcher is given an assistant and 6 hours free range of all original documents held in the Registry. One day's searching can give you details of a whole family. There is also a fee for copy certificates. However, if you do not seek copies for your records you can, provided you are meticulous, copy the original documents into your notebook and dispense with copy certificates. Unfortunately, due to staff holidays this Registry is normally closed to genealogists during the summer from July to September, an important point to remember. However they will issue copy certificates by mail if requested to do so. The Registry will also carry out a one name five year search of their records for a small fee.

The Isle of Man
Here again, if your family originally came from the Isle of Man and even if they moved on around the world which many Manxmen did, all the records are held in close proximity. Compulsory registration commenced in 1878, and all the research can be carried out at the Registry, which is on the first floor of the General Registry building in Douglas. The information available from the certificates is similar to that shown in certificates from England and Wales. There are no search fees and the helpful staff will produce the indexes and also the original registers once you have found the entries you require. Copies of the certificates are obtainable on payment of a fee.

The Channel Islands
If you need to research records in the Channel Islands, civil registration began in 1842 and some of the early documents, particularly pre-20th century, may be written in French. No personal searches of the Jersey registers may be made, but postal enquiries should be addressed to the Librarian at the Société Jersiaise who will charge a search fee. Personal researchers may use the Société's excellent library which contains a wealth of local and genealogical material. None of the records held in

Guernsey are open for public research and only postal enquiries are dealt with. Application should be made to the Registrar General in Guernsey for records for Guernsey and the other Channel Islands. A telephone call to the Registry will give you details of the amounts charged for copy certificates and searches.

You will, by now, have realised that all the registries adopt different methods. The least helpful to family historians being the largest at St Catherine's House.

All the registries will supply copy certificates by mail provided you can give them sufficient information and send the correct fee with your application. In the case of birth certificates they require the full name of the person, the date and place of birth and the name of the parents. The maiden name of the mother is only required for entries after September 1911. For marriage certificates, the date and place, full names of both parties and the names of the fathers if possible. For death certificates, the full name of the deceased, place and date of death. If the person was married the full name of the spouse is also helpful. Charges vary from registry to registry. The Registry at St Catherine's House issues a leaflet giving the fees and charges for all the other registries, but a telephone call direct to the registry in question will elicit their requirements as to fees and save time and correspondence.

Most registries do not have the facilities for protracted correspondence and are unable to deal with detailed written enquiries. If incorrect applications are made, they will be returned with a printed form stating what is wrong, usually by the method of ticking the various printed options.

Each certificate you obtain will lead you further in your researches. A birth certificate will give you the parents' names, including the mother's maiden name, the address at which they were living, and the father's occupation, enabling you to search the Registry indexes for the marriage of the parents, and the Census returns for the address which could reveal ages and other family members.

A marriage certificate will give you the names of the fathers of the bride and groom and their occupations, the addresses of both parties, their ages and occupations from which you can search the Registry for the birth dates of the bride and groom, and the Census for addresses which should give details of their parents such as ages and any others of the families present at the Census count.

A death certificate will give you the age, occupation and address of the deceased, the maiden name if a married woman, the name of a spouse and the name and relationship of the informant. This information can lead to a date of birth, a date of death of the spouse if the deceased was a widow or widower and an address for the informant – certainly a point worth following in the Census records.

The more certificates you obtain, the more you will be able to evaluate the information they contain in relation to further research.

4

Keeping Your Records

What is the main objective of the family historian? It is exactly the same as the professional historian. To record the historical events and genealogy of a family, offering the reader a well documented presentation, interesting not only to the historian and his family but to anyone who chooses to read it.

Record keeping is sometimes felt to be the most difficult area of family history research. Family trees often have gaps and no cross references so that clear identification of individual members of the family and their relationships is not possible. Careful methodical recording not only helps you to clarify and direct your own thoughts, but can act as a guide showing where to commence your next searches. It is also an important requisite if your researches are to be of assistance to future researchers. It is important to record both negative and positive searches so that you can remember where you were *unable* to find some piece of information and do not duplicate the work. It also gives direction if you stop at any given point and do not follow up the result of a piece of research. You will know that there is material there to follow up later.

Now that you have amassed a fair amount of material the time has come to decide how you will store and record it and how you should prepare your first family tree. If you have never worked in an office, where filing and collating information are routine, don't be daunted by what may seem to you an endless amount of paper work. While you are recording and sorting all the information you have collected it will begin to fall into some sort of order and you will understand what you are trying to do.

The main points to bear in mind are that you wish to achieve:

1. The recording of all the information gained, in a system giving easy access to that information.
2. The safe storage of original documents in a system easily displayed.
3. The preparation of a simple easily followed family tree.

A visit to any office stationer will give you some idea of the many methods of storage and information recording now available. Rigid plastic boxes and card index cabinets, folders, box, concertina and pocket files, plastic document holders and display envelopes, loose flat files and photograph albums. The possibilities are many and varied. The cost varies widely also, therefore a great deal should not be spent until you discover the method which you find easiest and which will fit into the space you have available.

Recording the Information
How are you going to keep your records? Chronologically (date order) or by name? The answer is both, by using a system of cross references. The easiest method is to use a card index system which can also be colour coded, using the same colour cards for each family which will make it even easier for quick access. For your main family (probably your father's surname) the cards can be white, for your next family (probably your mother's family surname) the cards can be blue. You can use any colour combination you choose. If you prefer to use only one colour of card you can use a system with coloured marking pens, highlighting connecting members of one family by drawing a line through the names, using a different colour for each family.

Cards, ruled or plain, together with plain and indexed guide cards in various colours to be inserted between the groups can be purchased in several sizes and you will soon discover the best size for you. Rigid plastic boxes with hinged lids, which hold approximately 1000 cards, to fit the various sizes of cards are readily available, as are larger index cabinets with movable divisions. If you are going to adopt the card colour coding system, a card box for each colour might prove the best method with which to begin. If you are using the marker system, one large cabinet with colour coded divisions could be used. It is essential that all boxes and files be clearly labelled showing the contents.

If you do not wish to commit yourself to a particular card size when you first start your records, clear plastic food boxes with different coloured lids in many sizes are available and are less expensive than the custom made boxes. They can be used quite effectively to store your card index system. Even more economical is the use of strong cardboard boxes with lids. If you wonder why I emphasise that your storage boxes should have lids, the reason is that paper seems to gather dust wherever it is stored. While over the years your cards may look a little dog-eared from constant usage, if they are kept in covered containers they will keep cleaner and will not have to be renewed so often.

As you sort, evaluate and record the information you have gathered, you will need somewhere to keep the original notes you have made. These can be kept in box files, one box to each family, the notes kept in either alphabetically indexed sections or simply in chronological order inside the box. Alternatively, they can be kept in concertina files or individual pocket or wallet files. The pocket or wallet files which can be purchased in different colours to match your colour codes and are reasonably priced may be the best when starting.

When you have decided on the card size and method you are going to use, as an exercise, start with yourself and record all the information that you have. In order to save time and space, there are standard genealogical abbreviations for frequently used words which are used universally as follows:

b.	*born*	div.	*divorced*
bapt.	*baptised*	dau.	*daughter*
bur.	*buried*	unm.	*unmarried*
d.	*died*	=	*married*
m.	*male*	f.	*female*

Two other words frequently used in genealogy are 'spouse' meaning marriage partner either male or female and 'siblings' meaning brothers and sisters in the same family.

Always write the date in full; do not use abbreviations or numbers for the months. Abbreviations for January, June and July (Jan., Jun., Jul.) can be confusing, and September has not always been the ninth month. Dates should be recorded with the day first, followed by the month and the year – 27th January 1899.

Using your white cards, or whatever colour you have chosen

for your family name, begin by recording the name cards with the following information on one card:

Top line	–	capital letters	your name
second line	–	b. (for born)	date of birth
third line	–	at	place of birth
fourth line	–	married	date of marriage
fifth line	–	at	place of marriage
sixth line	–	father	name of father
seventh line	–	mother	maiden name of mother

If you are unmarried put 'unm' beside your name and don't include the lines referring to the date and place of marriage.

If you are married, continue:

eighth line	–	spouse	name of husband/wife
ninth line	–	children	names and sex of children

Beside your name in the top right hand corner of the card put your reference number 'W1' (1 for the first name to be recorded and 'W' for white). If you use only white cards your reference should show the colour of marker used for each family, i.e. R1 (red), B1 (blue), G1 (green), etc. If you have family names that you intend to follow at a later date you could give them the reference 'M' for miscellaneous and need not give them a colour. Additional information such as when and where baptised can be included on the back of the card. You can also record a note of where your copy birth certificate and any other documents are held. It may be necessary, as you gather more information, to use more than one card for each person, but provided you use your reference numbers and file all the cards for one person together this will prove no problem.

From this information you can prepare more white cards. Your father:

Top line	–	capital letters	his full name	'W2'
second line	–	b.	date of birth	
third line	–	at	place of birth	
fourth line	–	married	date of marriage	
fifth line	–	at	place of marriage	
sixth line	–	father	father's full name	
seventh line	–	mother	mother's name	

| eighth line | – spouse | maiden name of wife |
| ninth line | – children | names and sex of children |

Your own name as connecting link will appear on the ninth line and you can put the number 'W1' beside it to show where further information can be obtained concerning yourself.

As you proceed making and numbering cards you can put the references beside all the connecting names. Put as much information as you have on each card. As more information comes to light the cards can be updated. As you go further back in time, you might enter on the back of the cards a note of where the information was obtained. As emphasised in previous chapters it is essential to cite your sources of information. When you have had some practice of record making you will be able to decide what information you wish to include on each card, but a general rule is to record as much as you know about each person. Cards should be kept for each individual encountered.

The following illustrations are a set of name cards for my own family which I started many years ago as a beginner, only the surnames are changed (Figures 5 and 6). I have remained faithful to this system of recording which I find gives quick and easy access to all available information. From these samples you will see how the reference numbers at the top of each card appear on other cards so that you will have easy access to any person by referring to the numbers and finding the cards. You will also see the reason for numbering each person recorded. In many families male children are named after fathers or grandfathers and female children after grandmothers or favourite aunts. Some families have a tradition of giving the firstborn son the same name through the generations and Scots families sometimes give a son his mother's family name as first name. So, unless there is a clear identification of each name, the records could soon become muddled and difficult to follow.

If you are using a separate box for each family, the cards can be filed numerically, using the reference numbers. Alternatively if you are using one box for all your cards you can file the cards alphabetically by surname. As a cross reference a set of cards can be prepared on a chronological basis, filed in date order. These will not require reference numbers, but will, of course, show the reference numbers of each person beside the names. Samples of these cards are also given (Figure 7).

These index cards are for your own use and will form the

```
SMITH, LESLIE GEORGE                      W1

b.            1 January 1923
at            County Borough of West Ham
married       27 March 1949
at            County Borough of West Ham
father        SMITH, CHARLES WILLIAM (W2)
mother        ROBERTS, JEANNIE REBECCA (R1)
spouse        CARTER, ESTHER (B1)
children      Anthony (W13), Susan (W14)
```

(a)

```
Occupation – Link Man, Royal Opera House,
                Covent Garden

Served British Navy (Chief Petty Officer)
      1940 – 1945

Birth & Marriage Certificates, Navy Discharge
    Papers, Photographs (Book 2)
```

(b)

Fig. 5 **(a)** Front of index card for Leslie George Smith
       (b) Back of index card for Leslie George Smith

basis of the information shown on your family trees and in your written history. If you are asked how you know that a distant relative was deported to Australia for stealing a loaf of bread, your index cards will tell you where you obtained the information and where any documentation is stored.

It is important at this stage to start a general information and address book or card index. The book can be a loose leaf ring binder with two sections, one divided alphabetically for addresses. Or you can continue to use a card index system. Enter in alphabetical order every address you need and even those you think you may not need again; relatives, registries, record

```
SMITH, GEORGE WILLIAM JOSEPH          W3

b.          23 April 1878
at          Dartford, Kent
married     19 November 1898
at          Dartford, Kent
d.          25 December 1939
at          Dartford
father      SMITH, WILLIAM CHARLES (W4)
mother      DEAN, SARAH ANN (M6)
spouse      SHARPE, EMMA JANE (M5)
children    Susan (W7), Eliza (W8),
            Charles William (W2),
            Ann Sophia Dean (W9)
```

(a)

```
Occupation – Journeyman

Lived Mount Pleasant House, Dartford,
    Kent all his life

Bapt. St. Mark's Church, Dartford, Kent

Birth, Death & Marriage Certificates
    (Book 1)
```

(b)

Fig. 6 **(a)** Front of index card for George William Joseph Smith
     (b) Back of index card for George William Joseph Smith

offices and archives, bookshops, family history societies, parish councils and cemeteries. I recently received a letter from an unknown person in Australia seeking my help in tracing a document. He had been given my address by someone I met at a genealogical conference many months ago. My address, taken

```
1922

24 June    Married

           SMITH, CHARLES WILLIAM (W2)
           ROBERTS, JEANNIE REBECCA (R1)
```

(a)

```
1878

23 April    b.   SMITH, GEORGE WILLIAM
                       JOSEPH (W3)
```

(b)

Fig. 7 **(a)** Chronological index card for 1922
         (b) Chronological index card for 1878

by someone I would probably never meet again, had proved useful to her. Genealogists and family historians are inveterate note takers, hoarding any snippets of information like squirrels hoarding nuts for the winter!

Any other information such as opening times of libraries, the cost of documents, where to buy certain items, can be entered in the general information section. You will soon learn to distinguish what sort of information will be helpful and which you wish to record.

At this stage of preparing your family history patience and

meticulous attention to detail are required. If record making appears a tedious exercise at first, persevere. It will soon become second nature and you will enjoy completing your cards, adding information as it is obtained. Your diligence will also be rewarded when after several years' work you are still able to return to your first notes and find information without difficulty.

Storing Original Documents

Copy birth, death and marriage certificates, original letters, photocopies, photographs and precious elderly papers need to be stored so that they do not suffer damage but can be easily displayed for they will play a major supporting role when you show your family history. Once again a visit to a stationery suppliers will enable you to evaluate the various methods available. Books of clear plastic pockets are available in many sizes and with a range in the number of pockets they contain. The covers, usually with an outside pocket for a label, come in several colours and can be used to fit in with your colour coding. Where documents such as certificates need to be read on only one side, two can be placed back to back in one pocket. Letters, if written on two sides of a page, can easily be read. The plastic pockets can be turned like the pages of a book and will protect the documents. An index of contents can be placed in a pocket provided on the inside cover or in the first pocket if preferred. These documents can be filed chronologically, starting with the present day and working backwards or with the earliest documents you have and working forwards to the present day.

For each person you may have a birth, marriage and death certificate, a baptismal certificate and several other documents. A photocopy of a bible entry, newspaper items referring to a 21st birthday celebration, giving the names of those present (very useful if you are able to make the family connections). Keep all the documents relating to one person together placing them in the pockets in chronological order, thus building a picture of their life and times. It is these certificates and documents which will put the meat on the bones of your family history and bring the people to life. The reference numbers and colour codes can be used in the index to link the documentation with the information cards. The following illustrations are sample index/contents pages showing the documents which can be displayed (Figures 8 and 9).

CONTENTS

1. Fragments of history – The Smith Family (author unknown)
2. Handwritten Parliamentary Return – Smith family with initialled note "DS 1815"
3. Memorandum handwritten by William Charles Smith 1867 with handwritten family history
4. Receipt 1900 – William Charles Smith
5. Letter 1878 – Sarah Ann Dean
6. Copy Memorandum – handwritten by William Smith
7. Extract from Charles William Smith's Manuscript Book
8. Handwritten note re Smith of Dartford (author unknown)
9. Smith family tree – letter E. Smith (undated)
10. Handwritten notes re Smith family (author unknown)
11. Handwritten Smith Family Tree (author unknown)
12. Letter 1894 – Jessie Smith
13. Letter 1894 – Rev. R. S. Graves
14. Smith place names with note Rev. R. S. Graves
15. Handwritten note re Smith family (author unknown)
16. Handwritten note re Smith family 1907
17. Letter 1912 – Frederick Appleton
18. Handwritten copy of The Parish Registers of Dartford made by Charles Smith of Barringdon Street
19. Letter Margaret F. Smith
20. Drawing Smith family crest (artist unknown)

Fig. 8 Example contents page for plastic pockets

The information where the documents are stored can be entered on the index cards as a cross reference.

Photographs can be kept in conventional photograph albums

CONTENTS

1. Census Return – Dartford District 1851.
2. Census Record – West Ham 1871.
3. Marriage Certificate – William Charles Smith (W4)/Sarah Ann Dean (M6)
4. Death Certificate – William Charles Smith (W4)
5. Copy Will and Grant of Probate – William Charles Smith (W4)
6. Birth Certificate – Samuel Charles Smith (W5)
7. Death Certificate – Samuel Charles Smith (W5)
8. Marriage Certificate – George William Joseph Smith (W3)/Emma Jane Sharpe (M5)
9. Copy Will and Grant of Probate – George William Joseph Smith (W3)
10. Copy Will and Grant of Probate – Emma Jane Smith née Sharpe (M5)
11. Marriage Certificate – William Smith (W6)/Ann Perkins (M8)
12. Marriage Certificate – George Henry Roberts (R2)/Sarah Jane Dowsett (M1)
13. Birth Certificate – Charles William Smith (W2)
14. Photographs – 6 Constance Street, Silvertown, West Ham (W2)
15. Photographs – Mount Pleasant House, Dartford (W3)
16. Photograph – Wedding: Charles William Smith (W2)/Jeannie Rebecca Roberts (R1)
17. Photographs – Burial plot showing memorial column and enclosure rails, Highgate Cemetery: Samuel Charles Smith (W5), George William Joseph Smith (W3), Emma Jane Smith née Sharpe (M5), Susan Smith (W7) and Eliza Smith (W8)
18. Map and booklet – Highgate Cemetery
19. Photocopy – pages 'Past and Present' relating to West Ham

Fig. 9 Example index page. This one shows cross-references to index cards

or the new type of album with loose leaf pages each with its own clear plastic cover. The photographs are placed on the stiff pages under the covers and are easily moved and changed round. Each photograph should be clearly identified. If of a person, the individual should be named and their reference number shown.

If a photograph of a house or a monumental inscription, details should be given and a reference number of the person to whom the picture relates. Photographs can be kept in the folders with other information if preferred. A plastic pocket will hold several photographs. Details can be written on a piece of card inserted in the pocket. A small piece of double sided sticky tape or a tiny spot of 'Blu-tack' will hold the pictures in position, but they will be movable when required. If a card slightly smaller in size than the pocket is used this will give support to flimsy photographs. Photographs and information can be placed on each side of the card, making the most economic use of a plastic pocket.

A computer or word processor can be a great help in keeping and collating your records – you can keep a great amount of information on 1 or 2 disks. It is possible to buy genealogical programs, some of which are very comprehensive and will enable you to prepare and print family trees and charts. Others will collate family relationships, ages, birth and death dates and index source material, etc. Some very sophisticated programs will even allow you to add photographs. Information relating to computer programs and their uses is given in some family history books and magazines. The Family Tree Magazine devotes a whole part of each month's issue to the use of computers and programs.

5

Your First Family Tree

Preparing your first family tree from the information you have gathered requires patience and experiment. It will probably be necessary to try several drafts before deciding on the size, style and shape you wish to adopt. The amount of detail recorded will be up to you and will depend upon the depth of your researches, but a simple family tree will be helpful and will encourage you to go on with the work.

It is rare for a family tree to be complete in every detail; too many individuals appear without full information. Relationships are not always clearly defined, but if your tree is based upon the information contained in your card index, with the reference numbers shown by each name, missing information can be checked from time to time and when obtained added to the chart and the card. It is important to include the reference numbers since if you prepare a chart for each family name you will then have a cross reference to show where the family relationships lie between the families by referring to the numbers given to each person.

It is impossible even to contemplate recording every name on a single chart. I have known a researcher use a roll of wallpaper, but even that gave insufficient room and was very difficult to read since it meant rolling it up from one end until the name required was reached and the rolled ends kept snapping together if they were not held strongly apart.

How and where you store the charts will play a part in deciding the size. They can be stored flat in a drawer or rolled and held by elastic bands. Rolling the charts gives more storage room, but makes it necessary to pin them out on a board for easy reading. A chart for each family could be prepared on size A3 (17" × 12"/43cm × 30cm) paper and a display book with plastic pockets used. The charts could then be placed back to back with thin card between to support them, two in each pocket so that a book of 20 pockets could hold 40 charts. The charts could be shown chronologically commencing either with the earliest known name or your own name. The final family tree (following only your paternal line) might be framed and hung in a prominent position in your house. It could be handwritten for you by a calligrapher in special lettering with names in different colours and line drawings of associated houses or places.

It is possible to purchase printed family charts in many sizes, some fanciful and some plain, coloured or black and white. The Society of Genealogists offers a choice of several as does the Federation of Family History Societies. Genealogical magazines contain advertisements for many different styles of chart. A chart with a printed tree – usually an oak – with the main family name on the trunk of the tree and spaces for names on the branches. A large circle with a space in the middle for the main name and segments for each family radiating outwards. The choices are many and varied as is the cost. If you join your local Family History Society or visit the Society of Genealogists you will, no doubt, see the charts prepared by other members which may help you to decide on your final size and design.

Your first family tree or chart should, however, be a simple record of your findings, using the abbreviations given previously and should concentrate on one family only. As you progress, further charts can be prepared for each family with the reference numbers showing the links between the families. It is easiest at this stage to start with the present day and work back into the past although you may elect in your final chart to start with the first known person of the family and work forwards to the present day.

A reasonable size sheet on which to draft your first chart is 17" × 12" (43cm × 30cm). This should give you ample room to display four generations. Paper this size and in varying qualities can be purchased from stationery suppliers and is known as size 'A3'. An alternative size is 13" × 8" (33cm × 20cm) known as 'foolscap'. Lay the paper in front of you with the longest side at the top and the shorter side running vertically from top to bottom. Arm yourself with pencils, a 12" (30cm) rule and an eraser. It is preferable not to use biro or permanent ink when first drafting your chart. It is easy to go over the pencil work with ink when you are satisfied with your first efforts. Before starting, rough in the blocks where you think the names will come on the paper in order not to waste too many sheets on your drafts.

The following measurements are based on using the size A3 paper. Begin by blocking in the areas where the information is to be written. Against the left side of the paper, 5" (127mm)

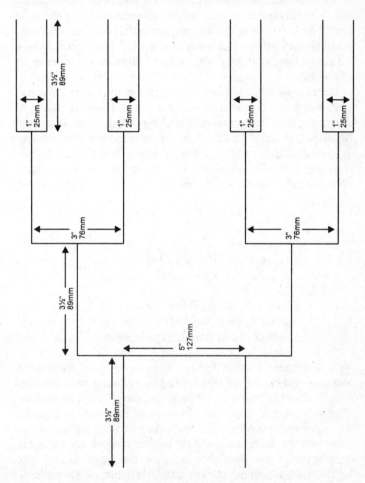

Fig. 10 Dimensions for the family tree outline

49

downfrom the top draw a horizontal line 3½" (89mm) long. Two inches (50mm) below that draw another horizontal line 3½" (89mm) long. Against the right hand edge of these lines, 3½" (89mm) down from the top of the page draw a vertical line 5" (127mm) long with horizontal lines of 3½" (89mm) each at the top and bottom. This will give three areas where your own name and those of your parents will be written. Follow across the page in a similar manner, dividing each area created by two. When you reach the right hand side of the page you will have four blocks marked out down the page. As you need more blocks, they will become smaller. Keep the horizontal lines at the same length of 3½" (89mm) all the way across the page but reduce the vertical lines first to 3" (76mm) and then to 1" (25mm). Figure 10 shows how your page will look and gives the measurements of the lines.

Begin at the left hand side of the paper in the middle. Write in your name, with your reference number in brackets beside it, above the first horizontal line and the details from your card immediately under the line. If you are married write the name of your husband/wife on the second horizontal line with the details underneath the line. The following samples follow the index card examples shown in Chapter 4.

> SMITH, LESLIE GEORGE (W1)
> b.: 1 January 1923
> at: County Borough of West Ham
> married: 24 March 1949
> at: County Borough of West Ham
>
> CARTER, ESTHER (B1)
> b.: 2 November 1927.
> at: London Borough of Hackney

You will require space for six lines under your own name andunder all the names of your father, grandfather and great-grandfather since this is the family name you are following. You will require space for four lines of information beneath the other names. Move across the page to the right and put your father's name on the next top horizontal line with his details under that line. Move down the page to the next horizontal line and put in your mother's name with her details under the line.

SMITH, CHARLES WILLIAM (W2)
b.: 1 August 1900
at: Dartford, Kent
father   married: 24 June 1922
at: West Ham, Essex
d.: 15 May 1972
at: London Borough of Newham

ROBERTS, JEANNIE REBECCA (R1)
b.: 23 April 1899
mother   at: County Borough of West Ham
d.: 4 February 1975
at: London Borough of Newham

Now you have two generations of your paternal line on paper, follow through across the page using the same method of horizontal and vertical lines to guide you. Add the third generation, your grandparents, and the fourth generation, your great-grandparents. The second main line will show your maternal grandparents and great-grandparents.

If you have roughed out the blocks first you should find the measurements given fit the paper size. If you use different sized paper you may find that you have left insufficient room to accommodate all the names and need to start several drafts until you reach a satisfactory result. Figure 11 shows how your chart should look, with the names, references and details clearly shown. If there is information missing, you can put a question mark to denote that fact. If you wish to remind yourself of missing information that is to be researched you can mark the space with a small coloured sticky spot which can be removed when the information is inserted. These coloured spots can be purchased in packets in most stationers. In order to avoid confusion, I usually use small gold spots, a colour different from any of my family reference colours.

Looking at the chart you will see that although you wish to keep the chart to one family name, other names have been included, but the main family name being followed is always at the top of the page. You can then prepare similar charts using the same method for any other families researched. Although you will probably concentrate on one name when you start, information about other connected families will be gathered so that family charts can be started for each connecting family and

SMITH, CHARLES WILLIAM (W2)

b.: 1 August 1900
at: Dartford, Kent
married: 24 June 1922
at: West Ham, Essex
d.: 15 May 1972
at: London Borough of Newham

SMITH, LESLIE GEORGE (W1)

b.: 1 January 1923
at: County Borough of West Ham
married: 27 March 1949
at: County Borough of West Ham

CARTER, ESTHER (B1)

b.: 2 November 1927
at: London Borough of Hackney

ROBERTS,
JEANNIE REBECCA (R1)

b.: 23 April 1899
at: County Borough of West Ham
d.: 4 February 1975
at: London Borough of Newham

Fig. 11 Sample Family Tree.

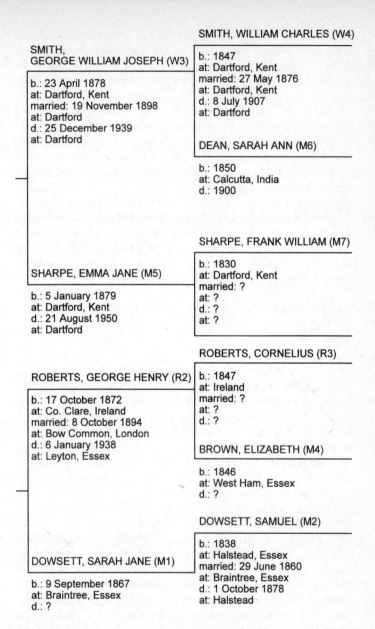

SMITH, WILLIAM CHARLES (W4)

b.: 1847
at: Dartford, Kent
married: 27 May 1876
at: Dartford, Kent
d.: 8 July 1907
at: Dartford

SMITH, GEORGE WILLIAM JOSEPH (W3)

b.: 23 April 1878
at: Dartford, Kent
married: 19 November 1898
at: Dartford
d.: 25 December 1939
at: Dartford

DEAN, SARAH ANN (M6)

b.: 1850
at: Calcutta, India
d.: 1900

SHARPE, FRANK WILLIAM (M7)

b.: 1830
at: Dartford, Kent
married: ?
at: ?
d.: ?
at: ?

SHARPE, EMMA JANE (M5)

b.: 5 January 1879
at: Dartford, Kent
d.: 21 August 1950
at: Dartford

ROBERTS, CORNELIUS (R3)

b.: 1847
at: Ireland
married: ?
at: ?
d.: ?

ROBERTS, GEORGE HENRY (R2)

b.: 17 October 1872
at: Co. Clare, Ireland
married: 8 October 1894
at: Bow Common, London
d.: 6 January 1938
at: Leyton, Essex

BROWN, ELIZABETH (M4)

b.: 1846
at: West Ham, Essex
d.: ?

DOWSETT, SAMUEL (M2)

b.: 1838
at: Halstead, Essex
married: 29 June 1860
at: Braintree, Essex
d.: 1 October 1878
at: Halstead

DOWSETT, SARAH JANE (M1)

b.: 9 September 1867
at: Braintree, Essex
d.: ?

completed as the information comes to light. Probably the next chart will concentrate on your mother's family name. Once started, most family researchers do not concentrate solely on their paternal line, nor try to research all their ancestors, but follow a few of the families as the intertwining details are gathered. Turning to the sample chart in Figure 11 you will see that you can learn quite a lot of information about the male lines of the Smith and Roberts families, that three generations of Smiths were born in Dartford in Kent and the Roberts family originated in Ireland, where they married and died, but little about their spouses and nothing about any other siblings.

If you wish to prepare a chart showing more detail of one family only, it is necessary to commence with the oldest known name. If you use this method, brothers and sisters, not shown on the previous chart can be shown. Using the same size sheet of paper – A3 – start by putting the name in the centre at the top of the page. The following chart can be prepared commencing with the great-grandfather shown as the last entry on the previous chart. Write in the name and details as follows;

SMITH, WILLIAM   =   DEAN, SARAH ANN
CHARLES (W4)   (M6)
1847–1907   1850–1900

Draw a short vertical line from the middle under the equals (married) sign then a horizontal line at the bottom of the vertical line. You can then show all the children of William Charles and Sarah Ann Dean by drawing short vertical lines down from the horizontal line and inserting their names, dates of birth and death, starting with the eldest on the left hand side. If they married you can also show the names of their partners. Figure 12 shows a grid without the names but with the relationships. Follow the male lines which will always have the same family name. The children shown on the second horizontal line will be the second generation and those on the third horizontal line will be the third generation. Brothers and sisters of each generation will be shown and their children will be cousins. The names on the fourth generation will be the great grandchildren of the first name at the top of the page. Details of the female line may be entered, but not followed if there is insufficient room on the page. If you wish you can highlight your own line through the chart by using a different colour to write the names and the actual lines drawn from one generation to the next. It is quite difficult to plan this style of family tree to fit the space available,

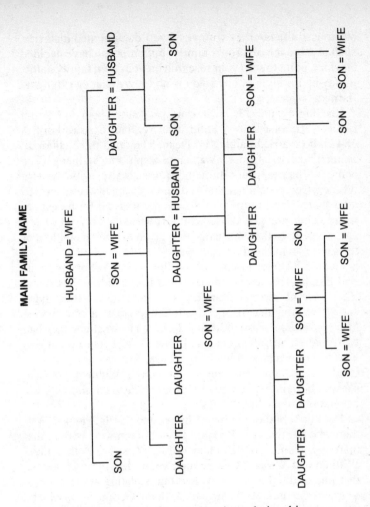

Fig. 12 Grid without names but showing relationships.

particularly if you wish to show as many of the family as possible. This could include brothers, sisters, uncles, aunts and cousins all belonging to the same family and is a chart which concentrates more particularly on one family name than the previous style of chart shown. Drafting this form of chart will take careful planning, using long and short vertical and horizontal lines to make best use of the space. Figure 13 shows a family tree prepared in this form. It is the form of family tree most often used for families with very well documented histories, such as a branch of a royal family, but once you have decided at which point to stop your research on your own family name, it may be the style of chart you wish to have handwritten and framed.

Reading Figure 13, what can you learn about the Smith family? The first known Smith was William Charles born in 1847 who married Sarah Ann Dean. They had three children: Samuel Charles, George William Joseph and William. (The name William appears throughout this family, with the two brothers George William and William presumably being named after their father. In the past, it was not unusual for parents to name a child after a deceased child who had died at a very early age. Sometimes the same name was given to several children of the same parents until one survived.)

George William Joseph, whose line we are following, married Emma Jane Sharpe and they had four children. Susan and Eliza have no birth or death dates. Checking with their index cards, we find that neither lived longer than a few weeks. Charles William married Jeannie Rebecca Roberts and they had two children one of whom was Leslie George (our researcher) who has also included his own spouse, Esther Carter, and his children, Anthony and Susan. Anthony's children are also shown, bringing us up to the present day and showing six generations of the Smith family.

The third child of William Charles and Sarah Ann was William who married Ann Perkins. Two children were born of that marriage, Samuel William and William George. Both Samuel William and William George died young leaving no issue, so that line of the Smith family died out. Looking at the dates of death of Samuel William and William George it would be reasonable to assume that they both died in the 1914–1918 war. This information would be shown on their index cards or in original or copy documentation.

Ann Sophia Dean Smith, daughter of George William Joseph and Emma Jane, sister of Charles William, married Peter Hodge and the family line of Hodge is followed. The reason for the inclusion of this new family name becomes clear when Ann Sophia Dean's grandson, George Hodge, marries Susan Smith, the granddaughter of her brother Charles William, thus bringing two branches of the Smith family together again.

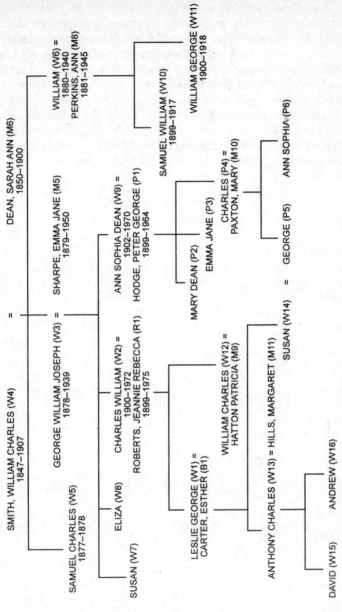

Fig. 13 Smith Family Tree.

57

Both forms of family tree, Figures 11 and 13, give information about the Smith family and are complementary. They can be filed in a display book facing each other in two of the plastic pockets so that they can be read in conjunction showing a substantial amount of the history of the Smith family. (If you are using a genealogical program on a computer, this will prepare a family tree for you.)

This short analysis of the Smith Family Tree shows how much we know about the family. When we have even more detailed information we can proceed to the writing of the history using our index cards, notes and family tree to guide us.

6

Where Do We Go From Here?

Most beginners are able to find their own birth certificates and those of their parents, but what do you do if you are unable to get any further? If you cannot obtain the certificates you need to start you on your trail, what do you do?

Using your own birth certificate as a sample, go back to the beginning to look for clues and try to find your parents' marriage. If one of your parents had an uncommon surname, look for that name first since you will have less searching to do. If both have a fairly common name like Smith or Jones, concentrate on your father's name first. Usually your parents were married some time before your birth date – but not necessarily so. When you look into your family history, be prepared to learn many things you did not know – and for some shocks. You may unearth some family skeletons but your curiosity is natural and tracking a family history can reveal that some of our ancestors lived different or eccentric lives. How brave they were and worthy of admiration when they defied convention in a day and age when social behaviour which we now take for granted was considered outrageous and a scandal. You also have to take into account that registration may have taken place at a later date or in a different place.

Starting one year before your birth look for your father's name in the marriage indexes, systematically searching the indexes back from that date. When searching the indexes in this way, prepare your notes carefully so that you do not miss any volumes. Write the names of the parties to the marriage at the top of a page in your notebook. Underneath the names write the dates of each year, one line for each year. Underneath each year write the quarters and the books in each quarter. As you search, cross off each volume in turn. You only need look in the particular index which includes the first letter of the name of the person you are looking for; for example, if the name was Smith you would not look in A/K or L/R. In this way you will not make a mistake and miss one volume, easily done when you might be searching through ten years, giving at least 40 volumes and probably 50 or 60 to search. You will become quite practised and fairly quick. However, be thorough, don't be tempted to skip through too quickly causing you to miss the vital names. The following illustration shows how to keep a note of your searches, following only five years of which four years have been searched:

Smith, William Charles = Dean, Sarah Ann
Smith, William Charles

1873			
March	June	September	December
A/K L/R ~~S/Z~~	~~A/Z~~	A/L ~~M/Z~~	~~A/Z~~

1874			
March	June	September	December
~~A/Z~~	A/K ~~L/Z~~	A/R ~~S/Z~~	A/M ~~N/Z~~

1875			
March	June	September	December
~~A/Z~~	~~A/Z~~	~~A/Z~~	~~A/Z~~

1876			
March	June	September	December
A/R ~~S/Z~~	~~A/Z~~	A/G ~~H/Z~~	A/K ~~L/Z~~

1877			
March	June	September	December
A/Z	A/K L/R S/Z	A/Z	A/R S/Z

(The ones crossed out are the ones which have been looked at.)

The first time you try this form of searching you may feel frustrated and tempted to give up but the more you carry out these searches the easier it will become.

When you find what you consider to be the correct entry, remember with marriages that you can cross check by looking for the marriage partner. If the volume and page are the same you have found the correct entry. The indexes from 1912 onwards give the name of the marriage partner in brackets which will give you an instant cross check.

If you are unable to find your father's name in your searches, look for your mother's name. In all cases make sure that you have the correct spelling and the correct first names. Many people are known in their family by names which are not the names under which they were registered. It can be quite surprising to learn that your mother who was always referred to as 'Cissie' by your father appears on her birth certificate as Alice Jane. If your father gave the information at the registration of your birth he may have given 'Cissie' as her name. If you have brothers or sisters and you know their dates of birth get a copy of their birth certificates and compare them with your own. They may show slight differences in spellings or names. Look to see who was the informant of the birth. If it was your mother on one of the certificates, her name is more likely to be correct on that one.

If a person had two first names such as Henry George but preferred the second, he may never have used his first name and always called himself George. He may have given the name by which he was known on his marriage certificate which could be different from that on his birth certificate. This did not invalidate the marriage. If they were married and the marriage registered, the marriage was valid even if they used a different name. Ages are often incorrect on marriage certificates, particularly if there was a marked difference in the age of the bride and groom or if the bride was under age and married without the consent of her parents.

If you are unable to find the marriage entry, consider other questions. Were they married overseas or even at sea? If so search the Miscellaneous Indexes, or Marriages at Sea. The Army records can also be a possible area for search. If no marriage can be found, be prepared for the fact that there never was a marriage to be registered and turn your search in another direction.

If you are looking for a birth entry consider the following question: are you looking in the right quarter or even the right year? Once again systematic searching, over a period of years either side of the year you think it is, might well be necessary. It is possible for several reasons that the baby was registered in the maiden name of the mother. If a first name had not been decided upon when registration took place the child would have been registered as 'male Smith' or 'female Smith' and would appear at the end of the entries for Smith. Don't forget the Miscellaneous indexes for babies born abroad. Many births in the early years of compulsory registration were not in fact registered so be prepared for that fact and search elsewhere.

There are also very often mistakes on death certificates since the informant may be a distant relative or a friend giving the information from hearsay. Check the information you have against all the other notes you have made concerning that person. If a widow remarries, the name on her death certificate will be her new surname. Once again don't forget the Miscellaneous indexes for deaths abroad and deaths at sea.

Even with an uncommon surname it is possible to find more than one entry coupled with the same first name. If you find an entry with the name you are looking for, continue your search in case there is a similar name in the same period. If you find a number of entries with the same name and you are not certain which one is 'yours' you can apply to have each name checked against the particulars you have supplied. If you are looking for the birth of Charles Smith you may give as many 'checking points' as you can. His parents' names, George William Smith and Emma Jane Sharpe, the date of birth, the place of birth as exactly as possible, and the occupation of the father. The Registry will then, for a fee per name, compare each index reference you give against the checking points given. The form on which to request this search is on the reverse of the application forms for birth, marriage and death certificates. The form asks you to state also whether you wish the Registry to stop at the first entry which agrees with your 'checking points' or whether they should continue checking every index reference you have given them. Checking fees are payable for each item checked, whether the search is successful or not. A fee is also payable for the certificate if it is issued. If no certificate is issued, only the checking fees are charged. An information sheet relating to checking is available. The number of this form is CAS/Ref.

Other points to consider if you are unable to trace your missing relative are that the copy certificate you have received from St Catherine's House on which you are basing your search has been incorrectly copied from the original register. A name badly written in the original register could easily be misread by the person preparing the copy you have received. A name like 'Joan Crook' could easily be transcribed as 'Jane Cook'. The original registrar might have misheard what was said at the time of registration. All these things, some of them working together, can be very confusing for the family historian, but must be taken into account when a 'lost' relative cannot be found. If you are relying on addresses shown on the certificate as confirmation, 'Hart Street' could easily become 'Hurd Street'.

The original birth and death registers are held by local registrars and it is possible to search at these local registries. You might find it easier to do this since you will not have to travel so far and you may have several members of one family in the same area. It is advisable to enquire by telephone whether it is necessary to make an appointment and whether you need to book a microfilm machine. Local registries also have different times of opening and closing. A telephone call will help to avoid a wasted journey. Local registrars do make a charge for searching their indexes. Most marriage registers, if the marriage took place in a church after 1837, are still held by the present incumbent of that church, or have been transferred to a local Record Office. An enquiry at the church would give the information as to where the original registers are now kept. Registers of civil marriages and marriages other than the Church of England are held by the local registrar.

If you search the original registers and find that a mistake has been made by the person copying that register and you have an incorrect copy certificate, you can return that copy to St Catherine's House, pointing out the error and requesting a correct copy. However, if an incorrect entry is made in a register, whether it is a spelling error, an incorrect name or age, or even sex, there is no provision in law for the entry to be corrected, it can never be altered. If a male child is inadvertently entered as female, in the eyes of the law he is female for ever. The registrar might be persuaded to make a note in the margin of the register that an error has occurred, but this would not be shown on any copy certificates issued. If you have any doubts about spellings, ages and names, ask in the family and check the notes you have made from the information you have gathered. It is possible to have several different spellings of a family surname over the generations, in which case other information is necessary to back up your view that the person included in your family history is entitled to be there.

Remember that everybody makes mistakes. Registrars, clerks and officials are no exception. They did and still do make mistakes. If you think you have found one, write to the local registrar or person responsible. Be polite but persistent, do not blame anyone, simply point out the error. If you cannot get a satisfactory answer, try further up the line of responsibility or ask for an interview to explain what you have found. You may be able to get the matter put right, or, if not, an acknowledgement in writing that a mistake has been made which you can use to support your own findings in your records.

If you are unable to proceed with your family history because you really cannot find a way through to the next generation, seek professional help. It is not always as expensive as you might think and a little help is always welcome. There are many professional genealogists and researchers, as in all professions, some good and some bad. Your local County Record Office will have a list of names and your local Family History Society may be able to help. Many advertise in genealogical magazines and there is an Association of Genealogists and Record Agents who have strict requirements for membership. In all cases ask for a list of their fees and charges. Most charge by the hour for work done plus expenses. If you decide to employ a professional agree a limit to the amount you wish to spend, requesting that when that limit is reached they do no more work without consulting you. As an example of using professional help, if you wish to obtain some certificates from St Catherine's House without making a visit or paying their high fees charged for a search, a professional searcher given the names and dates will search the index and obtain a certificate for you. You will have to pay the normal cost of the certificate plus postage and for the time taken. Very often this is less costly than writing to St Catherine's House direct, particularly if you require several certificates at the same time, and it is almost certainly quicker. Another way a professional can help to save time is by collecting certificates that you have yourself ordered when at the registry, but which you cannot return to collect two days later. Most professional researchers visit St Catherine's House regularly and could for a small fee collect the certificates and mail them on to you, so that you do not have to wait the two or three weeks taken by the Registry to mail certificates to you.

It is difficult to recommend a professional researcher since one person may find a researcher particularly helpful and another experience difficulties with the same person. However, I have listed several researchers in the Appendix to this book who I have found consistently careful and reliable. I take no responsibility if you choose to use their services but hope you will not be disappointed.

7

Census Returns

The Census is basically a head count of every person living in England and Wales, Scotland, Northern Ireland, the Channel Islands and the Isle of Man on a certain day and is taken every ten years (except in 1941 during the Second World War) commencing in 1841. In addition to the names and ages of each person, other information is requested which makes the Census returns one of the most important sources of information for the family history researcher. The Census is compulsory, every house is visited and every person documented from the babies one day old to the oldest in the land, giving a wealth of material for research.

The returns are released to the public after a hundred years. At present the years available to the public for research are 1841, 1851, 1861, 1871, 1881 and 1891. The 1901 returns will be open to the public in 2002 and the 1911 returns in 2012.

Last time new returns became available, a long queue of anxious and excited researchers formed outside the Census Office overnight in order to be the first to obtain the information they were seeking. Whereas genealogists and family historians were once the only people interested in the Census returns, historians and sociologists have now become aware of the value of the Census and frequently use them as a basis for research into Victorian society and as a comparison to support their theories and researches relating to the present day.

The Census Office is part of the Public Record Office and the new Census rooms were opened in July 1990 in the basement of the Public Record Office in Chancery Lane. The Census Office issues a small but very informative seven page leaflet (with two maps attached) Number 58, entitled 'How to use the Census Rooms'. Send a self-addressed foolscap-size envelope to the Public Record Office, Chancery Lane, London, WC2A 1LR, requesting a leaflet before your visit.

To find the Census rooms, enter the Public Record Office by the main entrance in Chancery Lane and follow the very clear signposts along the corridors and down the stairs to the Census rooms. Security is very strict at the PRO and you will be asked to show the contents of any bags you may have with you.

At the bottom of the stairs is a small desk where a security officer will ask you to sign a visitors' book, giving your name and address; you will be given a plastic pass on a chain with a number on it which you will also enter against your name in the visitors' book. A quick glance through the page offered for your signature will reveal that researchers at the Census rooms come from all over the world. No other requirements are made of searchers, no readers' permits are required and no fees are charged. As with all archives, opening times may alter and it is always safer to telephone to check for any changes before setting out on a wasted journey. The plastic pass will give you the number of the microfilm machine which is allocated for your use. Most searchers put the chain over their heads and wear the plastic card like a necklace, leaving hands free for work.

At the end of a long corridor is the entrance to the Census rooms. Near the security desk is a cloakroom where you must leave any coats or bags – you are allowed to take only one small bag, notebooks and pencils into the Census rooms. Only pencils may be used, so do not forget to take your 'travel pack'. Pencil sharpeners are, however, provided.

The first room on the left of the corridor is a 'rest room'. There are chairs and low tables and a drinks vending machine. Here you may relax if you need a break and eat any food you have brought with you. If you intend spending a day in the Census rooms (and you will probably spend many once you start your research) take a packed lunch with you to make the best use of your time. I have to admit that I find searching the Census returns a rewarding and fascinating part of family history research. Food and drink may not be consumed in the research rooms but time spent in the rest room will not be wasted since you may well learn more from other searchers to assist your research. Family historians are always willing to share their experiences and knowledge when they have the time.

The original records are not available to the public but can be seen on microfilm; your plastic card will give you the number of your machine. There are seven rooms of machines; at the entrance to each the numbers of the machines in that room are shown. There are over 200 machines available, provided on desks in rows, each with its own seat, and they are quite simple to use. There is not much space between the machines, but there is sufficient room on the desk beside your machine for your notebook.

The film, which comes in a box, is on a reel which fits onto the spindle at the front on the left of the machine, runs under a frame and is threaded up onto an empty film reel on another spindle on the right. A handle on each spindle enables you to wind the film backwards and forwards and to stop at any point. There are two switches on the machine, one to turn it on and a light switch. The picture on the film is thrown up onto a screen on the machine and can be regulated and brought into focus by turning a small wheel. If you watch the person using the machine next to you for a few minutes you should find it fairly easy. The information leaflet Number 58 gives clear illustrated instructions on how to use the machines.

If you have put the film in backwards, do not be deterred, just take it off and turn it round. Handle the film carefully, try not to put your finger marks on it and try not to drop it. If you do, you will have the trouble of rewinding it by hand since the film, if dropped, tends to unwind itself very quickly despite all your efforts to catch it.

Using a microfilm machine requires concentration and can be quite tiring for the eyes and the back of the neck because of the angle when looking at the screen, particularly if you are either taller or shorter than average. In addition, some of the films are difficult to read since they are films of handwritten documents. The writing can be difficult to decipher in some cases and the film makers were not always careful. Films can be too light or too dark. A short rest away from the machine at regular intervals is refreshing and gives renewed energy.

It is not possible to book a machine in advance so it is advisable to go to the Census rooms early. In the summer months a queue may form and the security officer will give you an idea of how long you might have to wait for a machine. It is not much use popping into the Census rooms if you only have a limited time to spare.

The first room leads into the 'Reference Room'. Here you will find the reference books which will help you find the numbers of the films (the 'piece references'). Census returns are not indexed by names, but by villages, towns, districts and counties. London, the Greater London area and some other large cities are indexed by streets, making the research easier. The basis for your research will be the addresses on the birth, marriage and death certificates you have obtained, those you have been given by members of your family and found during your original research amongst family documents. Those on the certificates will also have a precise date and your research will begin in the Census year nearest to that date.

There are separate sets of books, colour coded, for each of the years 1841, 1851, 1861, 1871, 1881 and 1891 and for London. Each year has a main index of place names showing which number book to look in to find the reference number of the film for the place you wish to research. The reference numbers consist of letters and numbers. Clear instructions on how to use these indexes are displayed on the walls in the reference room and are very easy to follow. In addition, there is a desk where attendants will explain how to find the reference numbers.

If you are unable to find a place name in the index books it could be because of changed boundaries or spelling. Ask the attendants for help, explaining what you are looking for – they are very helpful. Sometimes other researchers, if you explain you are a beginner, will give you assistance, but do not presume on their good nature, their time is as valuable as yours.

If you have several addresses to research, look up all the reference numbers while you are in the reference room, which will save you several journeys back to this room. Always make a careful and correct note in your notebook of the 'piece reference'. You may need to return for further research another day and it will save time not to have to look through the indexes again. It will also assist others in your family if they wish to help with the family history research.

When you have made a note of all the film numbers you require, make your way out of the reference room to the micro-film machine reading rooms. As mentioned above, the entrance to each room shows the numbers of the machines in that room.

Films are in cabinets in most reading rooms and are available on a 'help yourself' basis. The cabinets are clearly marked for each year and the drawers are marked showing the 'piece reference' numbers contained in each drawer. At the side of your machine is a black box the same size as the boxes in which the films are kept. This box is your marker and shows the number of your machine. Taking your marker with you, go to the set of drawers which contains the films you require. Take the film you require and put your marker in its place. This helps you to find the place when you return the film and also allows other researchers to know that that particular film is in use. When you find an entry you are looking for, copy it in detail, leaving nothing out. Other occupiers of the premises, visitors or lodgers, may be members of the family, in-laws or cousins with different surnames.

When you have finished with your film, rewind it onto the main spool and return it in its box to the cabinet. At the same time, remove your own marker from the cabinet. You can continue in this way to search all the films you wish to use. When you have finished, return your last film to the cabinet and leave your marker beside the mircofilm machine, ready for the next searcher.

If you wish for photocopies of the relevant Census returns, these can be obtained from the photocopying room. There are instructions on the wall in that room telling you how to obtain the copies and how much they will cost. Read those instructions before you start your research so that you will have some idea of what to do. The attendants in the photocopying room will deal with your request. Some of the very old returns do not make very satisfactory copies, but the attendants do their best to give you a fair copy.

The 1841 returns are the least informative, giving only the names of the occupants of each house, shop, hospital, work-house and all occupied buildings on the night of 7th June 1841. Ages are not specific except for those under 15 years of age. Over 15 years the ages are rounded up or down to the nearest 5 years. Divisions between families are shown and between houses and also occupations, but relationships in which you are interested are not shown. There is a column showing 'where born' in which initials are used. 'Y' means 'Yes, born in county of present residence', 'N' means 'No, not born in county of present residence', but no indication is given of where actually born. 'I' means 'born in Ireland', 'S' 'born in Scotland' and 'F' 'born in foreign parts', again giving no specific place of birth.

The returns for the following years are much more informative giving detailed information very helpful to the family historian. The details given in the years 1851 onwards are the names, the head of the house and the relationships to the head of the house of every other person present at the time of the Census, whether they were married, their ages, occupations and exact places of birth. The 1851 and 1861 returns show those who were blind, deaf or dumb and the 1871 and 1881 ones also indicate those who were idiots and lunatics.

Although people were supposed to answer the Census questions truthfully, they did not always do so. Do not, therefore, rely entirely upon the information found in the Census returns, check it against all the other information you have. Ages were often incorrect. If you are able to follow a female relative through several Census returns, you may find that she remains the same age over a period of 30 years or mysteriously grows younger. I had one relative who in 1851 gave Scotland as his birthplace, in 1861 England and in 1871 decided to give Scotland again. Such discrepancies can be confusing, but put together with all the other information you have gathered, will sort itself out in the end and you should be able to decide which is the fact and which the fiction, but not always. There will always be question marks against some of the names in your family history.

When you have finished your research, gather up your notes and collect your coat and bags from the cloakroom. Return your plastic pass to the security officer at the desk where you first signed in and follow the signs to the exit of the PRO.

Scotland

The Census returns for Scotland can be seen at New Register House, Edinburgh. A search charge is made and it is necessary to book in advance by letter or telephone in order to reserve the microfilm machine. This does, however, eliminate a queue and the films are provided very quickly. The original Census records including those of 1891 are also available to researchers.

The original Census returns for Scotland had to be sent to England and were then returned to Scotland. Unfortunately, parts of the 1841 Census for the County of Fife were lost at sea on their way home and are not available in any form. If yours were lost, there is no alternative but to give up using the Census for that line of research.

Ireland

Census records in Ireland can be seen at the Public Record Office in Dublin. These records have suffered losses caused, not only by fire, but also by deliberate destruction based on a decision made by the government, as in the case of the 1861 and 1871 records. There are, however, many Census records still available to the family historian and you may well find what you are seeking.

The Isle of Man

The Census records of the Isle of Man are available at Chancery Lane and the Reference Library of the Manx Museum. A useful piece of information given on these records is the place of birth of the person recorded. If the person was born off the island, the country of birth is given.

The Channel Islands

The Census records for all the Channel Islands are available at the Chancery Lane Census Office on microfilm and can be searched as described above. The Census records for Jersey are also available on microfilm at the Central Library in St Helier in Jersey.

Why are you at the Census Office and what are you looking for? The Census returns give a great deal of information about where families lived, what they did, and family relationships. This will be the first time during your researches that you will see official records of different branches of your family in groups. Up to now the certificates you have obtained have been either for one person or for two people if a marriage certificate.

When you look at the Census returns for your own family, take time to look at the surrounding houses and buildings, the occupations and names of neighbours, the sizes of the families. All this will begin to give you an idea of the environment in which they lived and the lives they led. In cities many families herded together in single dwelling houses, others occupied large houses with servants. Workhouse inmates are shown as well as hospital patients. Occupations can also give an indication of the area in which people were living. Very often people engaged in the same or ancillary occupations grouped together and lived in one street. Street names were occasionally changed to reflect this. Fathers who had a trade taught their sons. Following through the ten year cycles, sons grow up, take over their fathers' occupations and themselves become 'Head of the house' although if a widowed mother is left she will sometimes be given as the 'Head of the house'. Apprentices lived with their masters and many city dwellers let rooms to lodgers. In rural areas different branches of the same family lived near to each other and you could find a lead to take you on to another branch of the family.

Between one Census return and another, you may lose some-one. Check the information given. They may have moved away or they may have died. If they died, their spouse would be shown as widow or widower. This would give you a clue to the date of death if you do not already know it. It must have been between the dates of the two Census returns. This would pinpoint the date more closely and possibly save much time searching the death records. Look in the adjacent streets for their names. They may have been visiting a neighbour at the time the Census was taken. The other alternatives are hospital, school, or prison. Remember that house numbers, street names and boundaries may have changed between two Censuses. If you have noted the names of neighbours on previous Censuses and they are still in occupa-tion of adjacent houses then your family must have moved away. If all the families have disappeared they may be recorded elsewhere under a different street name.

Search each return from 1841 onwards, gradually assembling a picture of the family, its occupations and movements during those years.

Take a look at the marriage certificate of your grandparents or great-grandparents which you should have found without too much difficulty by following the instructions given in previous chapters. Once again using my Smith family as an example, we have the marriage of William Charles Smith and Sarah Ann Dean which took place in Dartford in Kent in 1876. The certifi-cate gives the actual place of residence at the time of the marriage of both the bride and the groom. The groom was living at 1 Mount Pleasant Road, Dartford, and the bride at Chalk Row, Dartford. Taking the nearest Census date, 2 April 1871, we can request the microfilm for each house. Hopefully Sarah Ann Dean and William Charles Smith or at least one of them were living with their parents in their family homes at the time of the marriage. If they were not, their families may be living there or may have only recently moved there. A search of the previous

Name of Street, Place or Road and Name or No. of House	Name and Surname of each Person who abode in the house, on the Night of the 30th March 1851	Relation to Head of Family	Condition
21 Millfields Road	HENRY DANIEL	Head	Widower
	ELIZA DANIEL	Dau	Unm
	JOHN FOX	Lodger	Unm
	FRANK WILLIAM GREEN	Lodger	Unm
	ELEANOR CROSS	Serv	Mar
23 Millfields Road	SUSAN BERKLEY	Head	Mar
	HENRY HOLCOME	Son	Unm
	ALICE HOLCOMBE	Dau	Unm
	BENJAMIN BERKLEY	Son	Unm
	CHARLES BERKLEY	Son	Unm
25 Millfields Road	THOMAS SMITH	Head	Mar
	MARY SMITH	Wife	Mar
	JOAN BANKS	Niece	Unm

Fig. 14 What you might see in the 1851 Census return

1861 Census for the same address will give the answer. If it is the family home the Census return will give us the names of their parents and other information, taking us back one generation further and possibly even more.

The Census returns for 1871 show that Sarah Ann Dean was

| Age of | | Rank, Profession or Occupation | Where born | Whether Blind or Deaf and Dumb |
male	female			
57		Manager at Bank	Norfolk, Norwich	
	27		Middlesex, London	
24		Bankers Clerk	Surrey, Old Kent Rd.	
40		Porter in a bank	Herts, Watford	
	30	Housekeeper	Kent, Dartford	
	38	Shop manageress	Middlesex, Hackney	
16		Scholar	Middlesex, Hackney	
	14	Scholar	Middlesex, Hackney	
12		Scholar	City of London	
8		Scholar	City of London	
39		Coalman	Middlesex, Tottenham	
	35		Northumberland, Newcastle	
	19		Northumberland, Newcastle	

living with her parents at Chalk Row, Dartford. Her father
Alfred Dean was the head of the house, his age was 46, sex male,
occupation Army, and that he was born in Dartford. Her mother
Ann is shown as 'wife'. Her age is 43, sex female, occupation
housewife and place of birth Maidstone. All the children of the
family are shown including Sarah Ann – daughter – age 21
unmarried – whose occupation is shown as seamstress. An

interesting point is that Sarah Ann and two of her brothers were born in India, probably while their father was in service in the Army – a point well worth following. In addition to the family there is an entry for Alice Brown, a servant, and William Cross, a lodger.

The birth certificate of George William Joseph the son of Sarah Ann and William Charles, dated 1878, shows them living at 81 Mount Pleasant Road, East Hill, Dartford. A search of the 1881 Census for that house reveals all the family of Sarah Ann and William Charles, thus filling gaps in your family tree and spreading the branches further.

Sometimes you may be lucky enough to find visiting relatives or in-laws which can carry your research further. Figure 14 is an example of what you might expect to see in the Census returns.

The enumerators used abbreviations to save time and room on the forms when making their entries. Some of the more common abbreviations are:

Ag. Lab.	– Agricultural Labourer
App.	– Apprentice
Dom.	– Domestic servant
H.	– Head of household
Lab.	– Labourer
N.K.	– Not known
Serv.	– Servant.

Most abbreviations are easily deciphered but if you have any doubts about the meanings ask one of the attendants.

If you feel that you need a sight of the next two Censuses after the cut-off year to further your research, a request for a search can be made. The Census Office will require an exact address and the name of the person. They will search for only one address and not the surrounding properties. It is essential, therefore, to get the address correct. If your family is living in the house next door, that information will not be given. There is a special form on which to apply for this search and the applicant must be a direct descendant or be acting on their behalf. The applicant must also confirm that any information given will not be used for litigation purposes. The only information the Census Office will supply if the search proves positive is the age and place of birth of the named person or persons.

This form of search is quite expensive and the fee has to be paid in advance. If no entry is found there is no refund. A leaflet giving details of this service is available from the Chancery Lane Office. If you have come to a dead end in your research it may be worth paying the search fee in order to get started again. At this early stage in your work it should not be necessary to go to that expense as there are so many other avenues to follow if one is blocked.

8

Parish Registers

When you have exhausted all the research sources offered by civil registration records, where can you look for pre-1837 information? There are many pre-registration sources. The details gained from your Census research and copy certificates can lead you to probably the most important which are the Parish Registers.

Parish Registers, which were handwritten, contain records of baptisms, marriages and burials and were instituted in 1538 by Thomas Cromwell, during the reign of Henry VIII. They relate to the established Church of England. However, all the earliest registers have not been preserved, and you may find that the records of the parish in which you are interested start much later. The information given in each register was at the discretion of the parish clerk and may vary from parish to parish and from year to year in each parish. A diligent and conscientious clerk would give the maximum and a lazy clerk the minimum.

The parish registers were normally in the charge of the vicar or incumbent of each church, but in 1979 a law was enacted to ensure the protection and preservation of parochial records. If a local incumbent was not able to keep the documents in a suitably safe environment the records had to be deposited elsewhere in a record office covering the diocese of that church. The usual place was the County Record Office. The diocesan Record Offices also have the power to request that any parish registers still held by a local incumbent be deposited with them on loan for a period of one year. Under the 1979 Law, County Record Offices may not make an inspection charge for parish registers deposited with them, although they may have a general search fee and a fee for use of microfilm and microfiche machines. Incumbents are allowed to charge a fixed inspection fee. Incumbents are legally bound to allow any registers they hold to be inspected, but they have no duty to search the registers themselves in response to requests by letter. However, many will do so but although they may be willing, they may not be experienced or efficient researchers. They may miss just the point that you are seeking to confirm. If you seek their assistance a donation to the church funds sent with the request would probably be appreciated.

If you wish to inspect a parish register, first enquire from the local Record Office whether they hold that register. If they do not, they will be able to advise the name and address of the incumbent who does hold that register, or any other place where it is held. If you require the name and address of the present incumbent of any parish church, this can be obtained from Crockfords Clerical Directory which should be available in your local reference library. If the register is still held by the incumbent, write (enclosing a stamped addressed envelope for reply) or telephone in advance of your visit, requesting an appointment and listing the registers you wish to inspect. This will help the incumbent and also save time, which may be limited. Make a list for yourself, chronologically, which is the way the registers are kept, and by name. Include the surnames of all the families you are researching, cousins, in-laws and any other relatives so that you can make the most use of your visit. Do not forget the ever important notebook and pencils, magnifying glass and money to pay for copies and fees. Make a very careful and exact copy of the records you find, together with a note of the source and references in case you wish to return for further research. Follow exactly the names, spellings, and dates even if they are different from what you expected to find. Copy all the references to your surname however remote the relationship might seem, they may well fit into your family tree somewhere on a distant branch. In some Record Offices you can obtain photocopies of the pages of the parish registers, which can be added to your supporting documents file.

Bishops' Transcripts
Commencing with the year 1597, a full copy of each parish register had to be sent to the diocesan Bishop each year. Many of the Bishops' Transcripts, referred to by family historians and

genealogists as 'BTs', are easier to read than the original parish registers and are available at County Record Offices sometimes on microfilm or microfiche. There are also some BTs commencing in 1561 but these are not comprehensive. All the BTs for Wales are held in the National Library of Wales. Bishops' Transcripts are by no means complete records since parish clerks did not always comply with the instructions given. In addition mistakes were made by the parish clerks in transcriptions from the registers, and full returns were not always made. They may be helpful however, if original parish registers have been lost. Many Bishops' Transcripts were lost or destroyed, including those for the diocese of St Paul's Cathedral, lost in the great fire of London in 1666. BTs should be used as an aid, and any entries found should be checked with the original parish registers if possible.

The Calendar

It is important to know that before 1751, following the Julian calendar, the church year began on Lady Day 25 March and ended the following 24 March. The Gregorian calendar then came into use giving 1 January as the first day of the year and 31 December the last. In order to catch up with the alterations in the calendar, in 1751 25 March became the first day of the year and 31 December the last, giving 1751 only 9 months. In 1752 the year commenced on 1 January and ended on 31 December, but 14 September followed 2 September leaving out 11 days. In 1753 and from then onwards the year began on 1 January and ended on 31 December. When recording entries between 1 January and 24 March for the years prior to 1750, both the old and present day style of dating should be shown. E.g. 23 February 1731 should be shown as 23 February 1731/1732, the historical date being 1732 but the church date being 1731. (This applies *only* to the dates between 1 January and 24 March.)

Kings and Queens

Some early documents do not give an exact date, but refer to a time in the life of the reigning monarch. E.g. 'on the twelfth day of August in the ninth year of the reign of our Gracious Queen Elizabeth'. This requires a little extra research into the exact date the monarch in question ascended to the throne. The reign of George IV commenced on 29 January 1820, making the year 29 January 1820 to 28 January 1821 the first year of his reign, and 29 January 1822 to 28 January 1823 the third year of his reign. The practice of dating documents using what are known as regnal years was not used during the Interregnum or Commonwealth years (1649 to 1660) and ceased after the reign of Queen Victoria whose first year as Queen began on 20 June 1837. After the restoration of the monarchy, at the end of the Interregnum, the reign of Charles II was backdated to the death of Charles I and was deemed to have commenced on 30 January 1649. In the Appendix I give the dates of the commencement of each reign up to and including Queen Victoria.

The Marriage Act 1753

In 1754 an Act promulgated in 1753 by the then Lord Chancellor, Lord Hardwicke, was enforced. The Act, which covered England and Wales, was designed to reduce the number of clandestine marriages. It standardised the performance of marriages and the entries to be made in parish registers. Parents or guardians had to give consent to marriages of minors. Banns had to be called or marriage licences issued before a marriage could take place in a church or chapel, failing which the marriage had to be entered in the register on printed forms, thus providing more information for the family historian. The Act did not affect those of the Jewish or Quaker religions who were allowed to marry within their own religions provided a proper registry was kept. Roman Catholics were not excluded from the Act. This Act led to clandestine but legal marriages taking place over the border in Scotland where the consent of parents to a minor's marriage was not required. If you are unable to find a marriage record you are seeking in a local parish register, don't forget Gretna Green in Scotland where many marriages took place. A couple might then return to their parish where no record of their marriage existed, but the birth of their first child might show in the parish register, leaving the family historian with a missing piece of the puzzle. Until 1929 boys were allowed to marry with parental consent from the age of 14 years and girls with consent from the age of 12, so do not be surprised at the dates of marriages compared with birth dates. In 1929 the minimum age for marriage for both boys and girls became 16 years. These points should be taken into consideration when searching for marriages.

During the period of the Civil War and the Commonwealth that followed, between 1641 and 1660, bishops were abolished and the keeping of registers was abandoned by many parishes. Licences were not issued and marriages were performed under

Civil Law by authorised ministers, J.P.s and magistrates. There is therefore a fairly large hole in the run of parish registers.

It is essential to search all the registers of a parish, commencing with the latest and working back to the earliest. Make a note of all entries relating to surnames connected with your family. Do not assume that you have a complete record from one parish register. Families moved about then as they do now. They could have left the parish before all the children were born, or come to the parish from another bringing some children baptised elsewhere with them.

Baptism

The information in parish registers relates to baptisms – not births. If a child was not baptised there will be no record of the birth in the parish register. There are a number of reasons why a baptism did not take place. The parents could have been non-conformists, Quakers, Jews or Roman Catholics. A baptism could have taken place in a nearby parish if, as was common, a young wife returned to her mother's house for help with the birth of her child. A child born in a city to country born parents may have been taken back to the country parish for baptism. Not all baptisms took place near the time of the birth. Sometimes if a child was born early in a marriage the parents could not afford the baptism fee. As they prospered and the families grew, a whole family could be baptised at the same time after the birth of several children, in which case their respective ages may be given. Some baptisms refer to adults and not children. If you are doubtful, try to check elsewhere. The BTs might help. Illegitimate children were often baptised and reference made in the register to their illegitimacy with, occasionally, the father also named.

The information given for a baptism will be the date, christian names of the child, parents' christian names with the father's surname (mother's surname for an illegitimate child), where they lived (village or town), profession of father and by whom baptised.

It was not compulsory to give the age at baptism and often that information was omitted, making it difficult for the family historian to find an exact date of birth from parish registers. It was the baptism which was important at that time, not the age of the person being baptised. It may be necessary to try to find evidence of exact dates elsewhere if possible, from monumental inscriptions, family bibles, other family documentation or entries in the parish registers relating to other members of the family. Dates and ages were not so important in parish registers which were meant to be records of religious events.

Marriages

Marriages are more likely to be shown in parish registers than are baptisms, since most were performed by the church, although not always in the expected parish. From 1754 onwards the banns had to be called or licences issued. Banns had to be called in the parish of the proposed bride and groom and the marriage could have taken place in either parish. It was only necessary to have been a resident in a parish for three weeks to enable a marriage to take place. One or other of the couple could come from a distant parish or a travelling couple could have decided to remain in a parish for the purpose of marriage and then moved on again. If you are unable to find the entry in the groom's parish, look for it in the bride's parish where the marriage was more likely to have taken place. Banns were usually entered in a separate banns book, but could be entered in the marriage register separately from the marriages. If a marriage was by Licence (which gave permission to marry without the calling of the banns) the fact would be recorded in the register. An application for a Licence would have been for a Licence bond or Allegation and either made to a Bishop or an Archbishop's office. If a register entry shows a marriage by Licence, search for the Bond or Allegation which will give further genealogical information. If there is one, obtain a photocopy for your documents file. Marriages by Licence became quite the fashion in all walks of life, although the licences themselves no longer exist since they were given to the bride and groom when issued and have been lost through the ages.

A marriage entry in a parish register will give the names of both parties, the occupation of the groom, the names of their respective parishes, and their status (spinster, widow, bachelor, widower). If the bride is shown as a widow, remember that her surname will be that of her former husband and not the family surname, leaving you with further research. If either or both of the parties to the marriage were minors and the marriage was by consent of parents or guardians, that fact will be shown. This would show that the consenting parent was alive at the time of the marriage, another piece of useful information. The names of two and sometimes three witnesses are also given in the register.

These are of particular interest as they could be other members of the family. If the same name as a witness appears at other marriages in the register this may have been a professional witness or the parish clerk. It is worth checking the surrounding marriages if only to eliminate that name from your researches.

Burials
The information in parish registers relates to burials – not deaths, although burials usually took place within a few days of the death. Once again the deaths of non-conformists, Quakers, Jews and Roman Catholics will not be entered. The information given in relation to a burial is often only the name and age of the deceased and the date of burial. Other information shown might in the case of a female be 'widow or wife of . . .' and in the case of children 'son or daughter of . . .'

Parish Register Copies
Many parish registers have been copied, with some copies available in printed form. The printed copies can be seen in County Record Offices, libraries and the Society of Genealogists in London. Local family history societies sometimes hold copies relating to the parishes in their own areas. These should only be used as an aid since as with all transcriptions they do contain errors and omissions but they are helpful as a guide where to look and what records exist. Also held at the Society of Genealogists is 'Boyd's Marriage Index' which, in a series of volumes, indexes marriages in several counties from 1538 to 1837. Copies of this index on microfilm can be seen in some County Record Offices, and reference libraries.

Parish registers can, like the Census returns, reveal the way of life followed by our ancestors. How large families were, how they moved about, how long people lived. A sudden increase in burials one year could indicate an illness sweeping through a parish or a bad winter. There is much more to be learned from parish registers than names, dates and places.

Other Registers
If your ancestors were followers of a religion other than that of the established Church of England, they were known as non-conformists or dissenters and were excluded from many laws, such as Hardwicke's Marriage Act of 1753.

Roman Catholics

Registers of births and marriages were kept by Roman Catholic churches and some still remain in the possession of the priest in charge of local churches. Some registers are held in the Public Record Office or have been deposited in local County Record Offices. Roman Catholics were frequently buried in local parish churchyards and their burials were recorded in the general parish registers. If you wish to trace an ancestor of the Roman Catholic religion, contact the archivist of the Roman Catholic diocese concerned. He will know the present whereabouts of the parish registers. Alternatively, The Catholic Family History Society (see Appendix) may be able to help you with your research.

Jews

Jews lived in many parts of England, but the largest community was in London. Most synagogues kept records of their congregations. Some Jews paid for their children to be included in local parish registers. If such entries were made they stated 'son or daughter of a Jew'. There are many such entries in parish registers of City of London churches. Marriages were not always recorded, but brides had to be given a marriage contract and often deposited copies with the synagogue. Burials were recorded in the records of Jewish burial grounds. For information of the records available, write to the synagogue in the area in which you are interested, asking what documentation is available. There is also a Jewish Museum in London where original records can be seen.

Quakers – The Society of Friends

Of all the non-conformists, the Quakers kept the most extensive and informative records. Some have been deposited at County Record Offices and some at the Public Record Office. Before being deposited, many of the original records were transcribed and are held by the Society of Friends. The records have been indexed and upon payment of a fee can be seen at the Library of the Society of Friends in London.

Protestant Non-Conformists

Baptists, Methodists, Presbyterians, United Reform Churches and Congregationalists, all kept records of the births, marriages and deaths of their congregations. Here again some records have been deposited with local County Record Offices and some with the Public Record Office. Many remain with the local congregations. Write to the local chapel or church asking for information as to the whereabouts of the documents you are seeking. There is a Baptist Historical Society in London, a Methodist Archive Collection in Manchester, and a Presbyterian Historical Society in London.

Huguenots

Huguenots were French, but many also came to England from Holland or Germany. They settled mainly in London, Bristol, Canterbury, Colchester, Norwich, Plymouth, Rye, Sandwich and Southampton. Their records have been deposited in local County Record Offices and the Public Record Office. If there was no local French church, baptisms were carried out by the local parish church and the records appear in parish registers. Deaths generally are not documented except for those that occurred at the London Huguenot Hospital. Check with the local archives to see what is available or contact the Huguenot Library in London.

Scotland

The Parish registers in Scotland can be seen on microfilm at New Register House in Edinburgh. A search fee is charged and it is necessary to make an appointment as in the case of searching the civil registration records. However, since all the records are under one roof, one day may cover a great deal of research.

Not many parish registers survive before 1700. There are more registers for Glasgow and Edinburgh than for country areas. The information given for baptisms often includes the maiden name of the mother which is helpful. Some registers have been indexed and transcribed. The Society of Genealogists in London holds copies of some areas of Scotland on microfilm.

Ireland

Many parish registers in Ireland were deposited in the Irish Record Office in Dublin and were destroyed by fire in 1922. Do not be put off by this generalisation concerning Irish records. Many records were transcribed and copied locally before they were sent to Dublin and some were not sent to Dublin at all. Copies of most of the parish registers are available in Dublin at the National Library. There are registers for both Catholic and

Protestant churches. The Catholic registers are usually written in Latin and some help may be required in translation.

Original registers are usually held by local parish priests and parish clerks and the usual written approach can be made. Try the local parish priest by writing, setting out clearly the information you are seeking. You cannot expect a busy parish priest to do your research for you, or he may not have the expertise, but a polite request accompanied by a contribution to the upkeep of the church may bring a very helpful response. There are many parish registers on microfilm and some local Family History Societies have detailed information concerning their parish registers.

While on the subject of Ireland, if you have any form of enquiry and you know the parish concerned, it is always a good idea to write to the present parish priest. He is usually very knowledgeable about his own area and its history or can point you in the right direction. A written request accompanied by a reply paid envelope and a donation to church funds often produces a great deal of information concerning the history of a family.

Isle of Man

Copies of parish registers on microfilm or microfiche can be seen at the reference library of the Manx Museum. Original parish registers are held in various places, but an enquiry made to the local church or the Museum will enable you to find out where they were held and what is available. The usual stamped addressed envelope is not of much help since the Isle of Man have their own postage stamps. A postal order to cover the cost of postage or an International Reply Paid Coupon can be used.

The Channel Islands

Parish registers in the Channel Islands are mostly still held by the incumbents of the local churches in Jersey, Guernsey and the other islands. Write first to the present incumbent to ask which records they now hold or whether they know where the records you are seeking are held. The usual stamped addressed envelope is not of much help since the Channel Islands have their own postage stamps. An International Reply Paid Coupon available from your own post office should be used.

If you are directed by your searches to other religions, always write to the local church, chapel or meeting house (with the usual stamped addressed envelope for reply) stating that you are compiling a family history and what records you are seeking. If they do not hold the records themselves they will almost certainly know where they have been deposited or be able to direct you where else to apply.

9

Wills, Probate and Monumental Inscriptions

Wills provide a very important source of information for the family historian since they often contain references to several members of the family, even when they are excluded, giving their full names and relationships to the deceased person, known as the testator (male) or testatrix (female). The name and address of the person asked to administer the will, executor (male) or executrix (female), would also be given. If a beneficiary was a distant relative or one who had moved away, the address might also be given. A will could also introduce you to a previously unknown member of the family or show a connection with a distant branch. If there was no will, but property (the estate) was left, a member of the family or several of them together could apply to be executors by means of Letters of Administration which took the place of a will. In this case the full names and addresses of the proposed executors together with their relationship to the deceased would be given. A will could also give guidance as to the place of burial where a tombstone or monument might give the names of other members of the family and family relationships.

Many people, even the poorest, made wills, some of them being 'deathbed wills' dictated to a close friend or church representative just prior to death. Women bequeathed their 'best bonnet with the blue ribbons', 'my large copper pan' or 'my second best grey woollen skirt'. Men bequeathed 'my milking cow with calf', 'one shilling' or 'my heavy working coat'. Blankets and feather beds were frequently bequeathed as were single items of furniture such as chairs, dressers and beds. It may seem an odd thing to say, but wills can bring your ancestors to life in many ways. The value of the goods bequeathed can indicate how highly the testator thought of the recipient. Lists or inventories of possessions indicate the wealth of the family and sometimes its standing in the community. I recently assisted a local archive to sort and catalogue a bundle of early handwritten wills, most of which had not been inspected before. The time spent on this work was most rewarding, bringing to light the environment in which people were living. One will was made by a widow who had been a shopkeeper and the inventory attached gave the total contents of the shop, which was a general store, together with all the prices. As I read the will, I could see her in my mind's eye weighing bags of flour and oats, measuring off yards of blue sprigged muslin and lavender silk and dispensing molasses and rum. Another will gave minute details of all the dresses bequeathed by an obvious lady of fashion to her daughters and friends.

Family quarrels can be referred to. Members of the family can be included or excluded by name giving their relationship to the testator. Next of kin could contest a will if they had been excluded, thereby delaying the execution of the bequests. It became the custom to leave a small amount, usually six pence to a disliked relative so that they could not object, giving rise to the saying 'cut off with a sixpence'.

Before 1882, when a woman married, her possessions and property became the possessions and property of her husband and at her death she had no right to bequeath any of her belongings. Therefore before that date not many women made wills, unless they were widows. In 1882 a law was passed giving married women rights over their own possessions and from that date you may find wills by both male and female members of your family.

Figure 15 is a copy of a will of William Catlett of Sittingborne, one of my husband's ancestors, proved in the Prerogative Court of Canterbury in 1647. It was written by him in 1646 and a death bed codicil was added in 1647. William obviously tried to remember everyone he could think of and mentions no less than thirty four people by name as well as the poor of five different parishes. This will gives many relationships and some parishes where people lived. It is also of assistance in tracing family members since it clearly identifies married women by their maiden and married surnames. The occupations of some beneficiaries are also given. As you will see, this will provides many hours of research if all the names and relationships are to be followed and checked in parish registers. Even those mentioned without giving the relationships have to be checked in case they are family members or for the purposes of elimination if they are not.

Fig. 15 Copy Will of William Catlett.

Copy Will of William Catlett, 1646

William Catlett of Sittingborne co. Kent gentleman dated 15 March 1646.
To poor of Sittingborne £5.00, of Milton £5.00, of Fong 40/–, of Bapchild 40/–, of Podmersham 40/–.
To Edward Gurland of Sittingborne clerk £5.00. To Mr. Lane of Bridgar clerk £5.00. To Mr. Picard clerk of Bapchild 40/–. To my niece Dickerson of Faversham widow £20.00. To my niece Sampson £20.00. To my cousin John Bix of Bapchild Esq £10.00 and to William his son and to Katherine his daughter £10.00 a piece. To my cousin Nicholas Ady £20. To my cousin Elizabeth Adye alias Smith, sister to said Nicholas £40.00. To my cousin George Hicks £10.00. To my cousin Adye Hicks £10.00. To my cousin Elizabeth Frinde £10.00. To my cousin Ann Bradley alias Brockwell £20.00. To my cousin Elizabeth Bradley alias Upton £10.00. To my cousin William Bradley £20.00. To my cousin William Allen of Morston £10.00. To my cousin Allen of Sittingborne, tailor, £5.00. To my cousin Edward Tomlyn of

91

Sittingborne £10.00 To my cousin Thomas Currall of Rochester, boatswain £20.00. To Robert Currall and Thomas Currall sons of said Thomas £10 a piece. To Elizabeth Currall daughter of said Thomas Currall £20.00. To John Pawson of Sittingborne £30.00. To my servant Elizabeth Midler £20.00. To Henry Lawrence £10.00. To Solomon Bowell £10.00. To my cousin William Catlett of Fong £20. To my cousin Richard Catlett, son of said William £20.00. To my cousin Susan Allen alias Lambert £10.00. To John Lambert of Blackwale, husband of said Susan 40/–. To my cousin George Catlett of Blackwale £20.00. To John Clench of Starfield £5.00. To Jane Burges alias Sharpe £5.00.

Nuncipat Codicil made about 12 o'clock at night after Tuesday 19 October 1647.

Being put to mind by Samuel Packer on that very night attended on him of some about him that had done him service and that he did not or had not remembered them they would condemn him. Testator said he had done so and given something to poor but not much. Asked who should be executor he answered his cousin John Bix of Bapchild Esq.

Witness. Samuel Packer and John Pawson both of Sittingborne.

Probatum 23 October 1647 by said witnesses and John Bix executor.

It is, of course, necessary to know the date or approximate date and place of death in order to start looking for a will. For pre-registration dates, parish registers may give this information. From the date of compulsory registration, with diligent searching the date of death can be found in the death indexes in St Catherine's House. Census records can also give a clue. If an elderly person in the family 'disappears' in the ten years between one Census return and the next while all the other members of the family can be found, a reasonable assumption is that they have died. This is not always the case, but you could narrow your first search to that period of ten years. Newspaper announcements can also give information relating to deaths and burials. Personal columns sometimes carry entries of anniversaries of deaths paid for by a surviving spouse or son or daughter whose names and relationships are also given.

Pre-Registration Wills before 1858

Many wills were never proved or lodged for registration anywhere, either because it was not necessary to do so, or the estate was not large enough to warrant the expense. Even when registration became compulsory there was and still is no requirement to prove or register a will or letters of administration with a value below a certain amount. Where there were family disputes there might be several years' delay between the date of death and the proving of a will or letters of administration. Original early wills can be found in many places. Before January 1858 when wills and letters of administration came under the jurisdiction of the Principal Probate Registry, wills could be proved in ecclesiastical or church courts, the main courts being the Prerogative Court of Canterbury (P.C.C.) and the Prerogative Court of York (P.C.Y.). Records of wills for the P.C.C. are held in the Public Record Office and those for the P.C.Y. at the Borthwick Institute in York. It is possible, where a testator left property in more than one parish, that their wills came under the jurisdictions of both courts. Searching for early wills is difficult even if they were proved, since it is necessary to decide in which court the will might have been proved. Start by a process of elimination, searching all the indexes of all the courts known to cover a particular parish where the testator died. If no wills appear in either the P.C.C. or P.C.Y. records, they could appear in the records of the lower courts, many of which are held in local County Record Offices. Bundles of wills deposited by churches and solicitors are also held by County Record Offices and local archives. The Society of Genealogists also hold many documents deposited with them by private persons. Other sources of pre-registration wills are detailed in the leaflet relating to wills and probate available from the Public Record Office. Pre-registration wills for Wales are held in the National Library of Wales, those for Scotland at the Scottish Record Office. Those that survive in Ireland are held in the Public Record Office of Ireland in Dublin.

Principal Probate Registry

Wills from January 1858 onwards are much easier to find. All wills and letters of administration proved in England and Wales are held at the Principal Probate Registry, Somerset House in London. The wills are indexed chronologically with surnames in alphabetical order for each year. Base your search of the index on the date of death obtained from the death certificate, remembering that it could be some years after the date of death that a will or letters of administration are proved. The indexes also give such information as the value of the estate, the address of the testator and the names of the executors. There is no fee charged for a search of the indexes. You can inspect copy wills after paying a fee and submitting an application form – there is a notice in the index room telling you how to apply. You will be able to take notes from the wills (using pencil), and remember to make a careful record of the source of your information, with any references, in case you wish to return for further research. A photocopying service is also available on payment of a fee per page copied, either to be collected personally or mailed to you. You may like to have copies of the original wills, showing your ancestors' signatures, and these can also be ordered, for a fee. Your order form should clearly state that a copy of the original will is required.

Scotland

From 1823 onwards wills for Scotland were proved in the local Sheriff's Court where they may still be held. Otherwise, they are all deposited at the Scottish Record Office.

Ireland

Irish wills are once again difficult to trace since many were destroyed in 1922. Indexes, even of those destroyed, do exist and are held in the Public Record Office, Dublin. Many wills are also held in the Registry of Deeds in Dublin.

Isle of Man

All the early wills from 1631 are held on microfilm in the Manx Museum. There are also original wills held in the archives which have not yet been indexed. Wills commencing in 1916 are held in the General Registry Office and the originals can be inspected. There is a search fee payable at the Registry.

The Channel Islands

Wills and Probate records for the Channel Islands are held by the Registrar General in Jersey for Jersey and the Registrar General in Guernsey for Guernsey and the other Channel Islands. Postal enquiries in the first instance are recommended.

When searching any indexes for wills it is sensible to take time to search each year for all wills under the family surname which you are currently researching. You may come across a will which looks as though it belongs to you, the address of the deceased or the names of the executors pointing to an association with a known member of your family. You need only request a sight of the originals of those that seem markedly of interest.

When you have found your will or letters of administration, extract as much information as you can to enter in your notebook and transfer to your index cards. Make a note of where the will is kept, the date you saw it and reference number ascribed to the document in case you should need to refer to it again at a later date. Important facts to look for are the following:

1. Name of testator/testatrix.
2. Occupation of the testator.
3. Date of will, date of death and date of grant of probate, which could all be different.
4. Address of the testator when the will was made.
5. Names and addresses of executors and relationship to the testator if given.
6. Names and addresses of all beneficiaries with relationships to testator and to each other (wife, children, brothers, sisters etc.).
7. Names of people excluded by definition and relationship to testator.
8. Names, addresses and occupations of the witnesses to the signature of the testator. Witnesses are not allowed to be

beneficiaries under a will and possibly will be neighbours, solicitors or their clerks or members of the clergy, not necessarily related to the family. A full note should be taken, if only for the purposes of elimination.

9. Any burial instructions given.
10. Any special bequests, particularly land or houses, that might prove a point of interest for your family history write-up.

If you find some pages of particular interest, such as those with the signatures, names and relationships of beneficiaries or unusual bequests, ask for a photocopy for your documents books.

Cemeteries and Monumental Inscriptions

Your researches amongst parish registers, wills and newspapers should enable you to find the burial places of some of your ancestors. Death certificates may also give you a clue. Give yourself the pleasure on a bright summer's day of a visit to a churchyard or cemetery. If the parish registers you are seeking are still held by the local church you could combine the register research with a visit to the churchyard.

Unfortunately inscriptions on old tombstones, which can suffer from pollution, vandalism, weathering and general neglect, are fast becoming unreadable. Churchyards are also being cleared and 'tidied up'. If you find evidence of a burial, make a visit to the churchyard or cemetery a priority amongst your researches before destruction takes place. Take a camera with you. You may be able to obtain pictures of gravestones with monumental inscriptions (usually referred to by family historians and genealogists as M.I.s) for your documents books before they are gone for ever. Many local Family History Societies are recording M.I.s and have recorded some that have now disappeared. Contact your local society to enquire whether they have any records relating to the churchyard in which you are interested. It should be borne in mind that not all burials had tombstones and tombstones were sometimes erected in memory of people who died abroad, particularly members of the forces killed in action. M.I.s can also appear on public war memorials, inside churches on pews which have been dedicated by a family and in stained glass church windows. Local war memorials in particular should not be overlooked since they could give a clue to a missing person whose death you have been unable to establish.

Due to the rapid increase in population, churchyards became overcrowded particularly in cities. By 1820 the overcrowding of churchyards in London reached epidemic proportions and private graveyards or cemeteries began to appear. They were not subject to the same controls as churchyards and their upkeep was generally in the hands of private individuals. Many have since disappeared or been incorporated into public gardens. Local authorities were empowered to establish cemeteries and other cemeteries, such as the famous Highgate Cemetery in London, were set up by companies who sold burial plots on a profit-making basis. Some churchyards, local authority cemeteries and the private company cemeteries kept plans, numbering each grave and entering the names of the persons buried. Highgate Cemetery which closed in 1975 has records from 1839 showing how burial plots passed from one member of a family to another, the size of the plots and the cost, including descriptions of the memorial stones erected. These records are very helpful if they can be found. Often they will show members of one family buried near to each other, with in-laws, and connecting families all buried in the same churchyard or cemetery.

The information on a tombstone can be the bare facts such as 'John Henry Smith 1820–1888', which is not particularly helpful, but many families purchased plots and several members of one family may be buried together, their tombstone providing names, dates and relationships, added as each person died, such as:

John Henry Smith
born in this parish 1820
died of a chill 29 January 1888
beloved husband of Mary Ann
also
Mary Ann Smith
born in the parish of Asprey 1825
daughter of George and Katherine Howes
beloved mother of Henry Smith and Alice Green
who died June 10 1898 aged 73 years
also
Alice Green
daughter of John Henry and Mary Anne Smith
wife of Daniel Green
died April 21 1900 aged 55 years.

An M.I. with this amount of information can be of great help to a family historian, possibly giving details of members of the family not previously identified, or confirming information previously uncertain.

10

The Public Record Office

The Public Record Office (P.R.O.) is a vast repository of records, deeds and documents, being one of the finest archives in Europe. The documentation is housed in two separate buildings, one in Chancery Lane in London which holds the medieval and early modern records, and one in Ruskin Avenue, Kew, which holds modern departmental records. The Census Returns Office, also at Chancery Lane, about which I have already written in Chapter 7 is the third part of the Public Record Office.

Although many famous documents are on view in the Museum of the P.R.O., such as the Domesday Book, Shakespeare's will and the log book of HMS *Victory*, those most likely to be of interest to you are the ones that record events in the lives of ordinary people, such as divorces, Army, Navy, Air Force and Merchant Seamen records. Additional documentation relates to court cases, government department records including maps and plans, Home, Foreign and War Office, and special groups of people such as Civil Servants, bankrupts, clergymen, criminals, emigrants and many more.

It is necessary to obtain a reader's ticket if you wish to engage in research at the Chancery Lane and Kew departments of the P.R.O., either at the Enquiry Office at Chancery Lane or at the Reception Desk at Kew. Existing but expired tickets can also be renewed at those desks. No charge is made for the reader's ticket which will be issued to you on production of formal proof of your identity, such as a driver's licence, passport or bankers card or a letter of recommendation from a suitable professional person (doctor, lawyer, teacher etc.). The same ticket can be used at either branch. The times of opening are shown in the

Appendix, but it is always worth a telephone call to ensure that no changes have been made and also to enquire whether the records you wish to see are at Chancery Lane or Kew. The P.R.O. usually closes for two weeks at the beginning of October for stocktaking, making a telephone call at that time of the year most essential.

The rule of using only a pencil applies in all areas of the P.R.O. Readers are requested to take care of any fragile documents entrusted to them and not to put their notebooks on top of the documents nor to trace from them. Readers are allowed to request up to three documents at a time and there is no limit set on the time you may keep the documents. A request in advance for documents to be available on a certain day can be made by telephone the day before or by written request. This is particularly helpful if you know what documents you will require as it saves waiting time, which can be up to thirty minutes. A photocopying service is available at all branches of the P.R.O. and a leaflet giving their fees and charges is available at the enquiry desks.

Kew

Allow a whole day for your visit to the Kew department of the P.R.O., which is a short distance from both the Underground and British Rail stations, has ample parking space and is also served by several bus routes. In most cases you will find your one day will extend to many others. The main reading room is on the first floor with a smaller room for maps and large documents on the second floor. The Enquiry Desk, your first port of call, is in the Reference Room which also houses indexes, lists and reference books. There is a self service restaurant and drink vending machines on the premises of the P.R.O. No food or drink may be consumed in the reading rooms.

Documents at Kew are ordered by computer in the Reference Room and it is necessary to have a seat number. When you have obtained your reader's ticket apply in the Search Room for a bleeper which will also give you a seat number. Search the indexes for the reference numbers of the documents you require and enter the documents and reference numbers together with your seat number on one of the computer terminals. If you have never met a computer before or feel a little bewildered, seek assistance from an attendant. You will soon find out how things work once they are explained to you, and if you make notes, you

100

can practise on your own. Remember you can request up to three documents at a time. When your documents are ready for collection from the desk, your bleeper will bleep.

Chancery Lane

The Chancery Lane branch of the P.R.O. has two reading rooms on the ground floor. There is a reference room on the first floor, together with the Probate reading room and the reading room for large documents and maps. The reading rooms are known as either the Round Room or the Long Room. It is not necessary to obtain a seat number at Chancery Lane. The ordering of documents is again by computer, but instead of a seat number you quote 'Round' or 'Long' according to which room you use for your research. Hopefully by the time you get to the desk in the room you have chosen, the documents will be ready for you. If not, use your waiting time to investigate the books on the open shelves. There are drink vending machines but no restaurant; however readers may eat their own food in the public waiting room. Chancery Lane is in an area surrounded by the law courts, newspaper offices and commercial offices. There are many self service restaurants, expensive executive restaurants, sandwich bars and 'pub lunches' available.

The P.R.O. publish many leaflets giving details of the records they hold, including a general Information Leaflet and their staff are helpful. They will advise what records are available, how the coded reference system works and how to obtain documents for research. They cannot, however, assist with personal research. It is not possible in this book to give an indication of all the records available. There is a published guide available in several volumes from H.M.S.O. (Her Majesty's Stationery Office). It is possible that your local reference library or County Record Office will keep copies of this Guide. The following are some of the records available at the P.R.O. which may be of most interest to the family historian.

Divorces

Up to date Divorce records, like Census returns are not available to the public. A rule exists restricting the availability of files for 75 years from the date of the divorce. The indexes nevertheless are available for inspection. Application to see recent papers can be made to the Family Division of the Registry in some cases. Divorce records open for research date from 1858.

Soldiers, Sailors and Airmen

Almost everyone has somebody in the family who became a member of the armed forces, whether a Cavalier or Roundhead in the civil war of 1642–1649, a regular soldier serving in the South African war or Royal Marine serving in the Second World War.

The War Office records held in the P.R.O. are by no means complete, but they are extensive. There was no regular army in England before the civil war. Earls, Barons and Kings raised armies as their needs dictated and no formal records were kept. Any records that were kept were in the hands of the regiments raised which were usually named after their colonels. There are some records relating to the armies of the civil war with regiments listed together with their officers.

More and better service records were maintained after 1660 and many are available for research at the P.R.O., Kew, both for officers and other ranks. Applications for pensions by army widows may give full names, addresses, dates of birth and marriage and names of children. Birthplaces of soldiers can also be found in Casualty Returns, Description Books and Pension Lists. Details of marriages and children are to be seen in Muster Rolls, Discharge Certificates and Regimental Pay Lists. If you are looking for an ancestor who served in any regiment, search the indexes of available material, or tell an attendant what you are looking for. They will be able to direct you to the correct documents.

The Admiralty and Navy Board records are equally detailed and extensive. They relate to Commissioned Officers, Warrant Officers, Ratings and Coastguards, covering all aspects of their service. Various documents giving names, places of birth, ages, and family details are available, such as Continuous Service Engagement Books for the years 1853–1872, Ships' Pay Books, Bounty Papers and Records of Officers' Services. Here again the P.R.O. staff will be able to advise you of the reference numbers and where to look if you are able to give them some information such as dates, or names of ships.

In addition to naval records there are separate records for the Royal Marines covering service records of officers and other ranks. There are records of the Marine Pay Office, Letter and Description Books, all giving details of interest to the family historian.

Air Ministry records relating to personnel are not so extensive, relating mostly to operational records which do sometimes refer to specific men and women in the service. There is some information available about R.A.F. prisoners of war and casualties.

Wills and Probate

Such records as exist relating to Wills and Probate prior to 1858 are held at the P.R.O., Chancery Lane. Few wills are available but information can be seen in the records of the Probate Courts where wills were proved by the executors in order that they could legally act in accordance with the instructions given in the will. Most wills prior to 1858 were dealt with by ecclesiastical or church courts, mainly the Prerogative Court of Canterbury (P.C.C.) or the Prerogative Court of York (P.C.Y.). Where each will was dealt with depended upon the place of death and the size of the estate of the deceased. After 1769 a Legacy Duty became payable on a grant of probate and the Legacy Duty Registers are held in the P.R.O. These Registers which are unfortunately closed to the public for 125 years from the date the duty was entered in the Register state in which court the probate was granted. There are also records of litigation relating to wills and inventories of goods listed in wills. A preliminary search of the indexes relating to Wills and Probate will give some idea of the material available.

Emigrants and Immigrants

There is no complete index of the names of foreigners entering England for the purpose of immigration, but there are many records in the P.R.O. There are documents relating to alien clergymen, strangers in London, and documents from German, Swiss, French and Dutch churches. There are also Treasury records, Certificates of Aliens, Lists of Immigrants made by Ships' Masters, and Registers of Passenger Lists.

Those leaving England to emigrate are also well represented in the records of the Colonial Office, the Home Office, the Board of Trade and the Treasury. There are lists of criminals deported to America, army pensioners who emigrated to Australia and New Zealand. If your researches lead you to think that one of your ancestors emigrated, it may take you a long time, but you could find him or her somewhere in the records at the P.R.O.

Unclaimed Money

You may have heard stories from your relatives of money due to the family but lost because of lack of evidence, or because

'Uncle George married again and we never found out what happened to the money'. The stories are various and inventive. There is a department of the Chancery Court that since 1876 has dealt with money deposited by solicitors who were unable to trace the next of kin or beneficiaries of an estate. If you can provide evidence of beneficial interest, the details of such accounts can be inspected free of charge. There are also lists published by the London Gazette which can be seen at the P.R.O. It may be worth a try if you think your family story is founded on facts which you have substantiated by your researches.

The Police
Certain documentation relating to the Metropolitan Police is available at the P.R.O., such as certificates of service from 1889–1900 and registers giving names of those who joined the police and those who left between 1829–1947. If you have a family tradition of fathers and sons joining the police force, you may be able to trace several generations using these records.

There are many other categories of records in the P.R.O. available to you, to help you trace your ancestors, including Change of Name deeds, Shipping records, Private Conveyances or sales of land, Manorial Court Rolls and maps, Apprenticeship Records, Railway Companies before nationalisation to name but a few. They are all there waiting for you. All you need is time, patience and perseverance.

Pay a short visit to the branch of the P.R.O. which is nearest to you to collect as much literature as is available giving details of all the records and familiarise yourself with the layout of the building. At the same time you can obtain a reader's ticket and possibly spend a little time finding out how to use the computer ordering system. When you have sifted through information in the leaflets, make a list of any of the records that you think might assist you and then spend a full day, using all your time there to best advantage by preparing thoroughly for your visit before you go.

The P.R.O. are slowly moving all their documents to the Kew repository which is being enlarged. They do give notice where possible, but some of the documents you require may not be available while in transit. During the time of transition it is always wise to telephone in advance of a proposed visit to check that the documents you require are available.

11

More Sources for Research

Now that you are beginning to build a picture of your family history where else can you look to help you? There are many other sources of information available to you to assist in your search for your living relatives and your ancestors. Even the most experienced family historian or genealogist can get lost and does not always know where to look. Always be ready to listen and take advice. Family historians can be helpful to each other. When you do find a new source, keep a note of the address and telephone number in your Information Book with an indication of what records are available, the times of opening and any fees charged. Make a note of the name of someone who has been particularly helpful. Keep your Information Book up to date when you learn of any changes. You may be able to help someone else with that information.

Telephone Directories
Have you tried telephone directories? You have probably at some time seen your surname in telephone directories and wondered whether there is any relationship to yourself. If you have an uncommon name, once again you are lucky, there will not be so many to choose from. When you have found some addresses from the certificates you have obtained, look through the telephone directories of those areas. Your local library may have a collection of telephone directories in its reference department, either for the present day relating to other areas or old directories relating to your own area. If they do not, they may be able to tell you where you can see them. A telephone call to your local telephone sales department or

public relations department might give you the answer.

You may be surprised to find that someone with the same family name is still living at the address given in your certificates. If they are, try phoning them, they can only say no, but they may say yes and another door will open. It would have to be quite a coincidence if they were not a branch of the same family. Alternatively, write to people with the same surname telling them you are working on your family history. Give them a few details of your family and ask if they are a branch of your family. Send a stamped addressed envelope for their reply. Be careful in your approach by letter and telephone. Make sure that you establish a definite relationship, by discussing other relatives, before you make any form of personal contact.

Information Available on Computers

A great deal of information is available on computers, particularly on the system of CD-ROM (Compact Disk – Read Only Memory). CD-ROM drives are available to add to your own home computers. The I.G.I. (see page 110) is being updated onto CD-ROM and many libraries and information centres are putting their available information onto CD-ROM. A CD-ROM disk can carry a great deal more information than a floppy disk or a microfilm. The I.G.I. is being up-dated using this new system and now covers 80,000,000 names.

In addition, if you have access to Compuserv on Internet there is a Genealogical Forum where a vast amount of worldwide family history information is exchanged. There may be someone in the Forum who is researching your family name with whom you can exchange information. If you need to know where to find books or research sources it is all there on the Genealogical Forum, for the cost of a phone call.

Television and Radio Programmes

Watch out for factual television and radio programmes, particularly those in your local region, relating in detail historical incidents or events concerning the lives of famous people and places. There have been very interesting and informative programmes about the building of railways, war episodes, village life, church buildings, financial institutions, famous hospitals, children in Victorian times, statesmen, soldiers, and many other subjects. These programmes are often well researched and factually correct. They may throw some light on a subject of interest to you as a family historian, giving you some ideas for sources of research that you had not previously considered. Those about places directly of interest to your family can be very helpful, even if they relate to today. Interviews with local characters on regional programmes can provide odd items of interest, opening up more areas for research.

Early black and white films especially those made in England can show places and buildings long demolished but about which somewhere there must be some written information.

Directories

Street and trade directories can give invaluable assistance in tracing members of your family. These can also be found in local reference libraries and County Record Offices. If you are searching to establish an address in the City of London or a London Borough, the Guildhall Reference Library in the City of London has an extensive collection of street and trade directories commencing as early as the middle of the 18th century. Their collection also extends beyond the London area, covering many parts of the country. The Guildhall has much to offer the family history researcher and genealogist which I will refer to specifically in a later chapter. Most areas, rural and urban, published directories, and families, particularly those in business or tradespeople, can be traced through many years in those directories. Directories are also useful if you wish to trace roads or streets. If you find a reference to a family name at a given address in an early directory, you can check that address in the Census returns. If your family appears, you will once again have a grouping and not just one person. Approaching the problem the other way, if a Census return has given the occupation of a member of the family, there may be a trade directory relating to their trade or occupation where their name appears with details of what they did. Anyone connected with a bank or merchant house would probably appear in the Bankers Almanac, another kind of trade directory. Well known directories covering a wider area are Kelly's, Whites and the Post Office directories. Some commence as early as 1750 and continue through to the 1950s. Local directories often give a short history of the surrounding area, mentioning places of special interest, churches, schools, inns, public houses, institutions, working men's clubs, hospitals and workhouses. People mentioned by name will be local gentry, publicans, schoolmasters, town officials and clergymen. Trade and street directories are a rich source of information.

Newspapers and Magazines

Newspaper, periodical and magazine archives are another area for research which should not be overlooked, containing, as they do, news and stories relating to family life. Newspapers were first published early in the 17th century and offer much to the family historian in the way of historical happenings, including names of people and places and pictures. Even the advertisements can tell you something. There are many collections of newspapers both local and national. Some are held on microfilm, others hold the original newspapers bound into volumes. Ask at your local library where you can see newspaper archives. Try your local newspaper, if you have one. They will probably have copies of their own publications. Early newspapers may be available at your local reference library or County Record Office. The Guildhall in the City of London has a complete collection of *The Times* newspaper on microfilm. It also has copies of the London Gazette. As well as local Record Offices and libraries there is a vast library of national, provincial and overseas newspapers and periodicals held in the British Museum Newspaper Library in Colindale, London. The British Museum Library in Great Russell Street, London also has a collection of newspapers, as does the Bodleian Library in Oxford. Readers' tickets should be obtained for both the British Museum Library and the Bodleian Library.

How can newspapers help you? Announcements of births, marriages, divorces and deaths appear in the personal columns. If you have a birth or death certificate search the personal columns near the dates. A birth will give the names of the parents and possibly an address. A death notice often gives the names of several members of the family together with information concerning the burial which might lead you to the churchyard and a memorial stone. A death notice may give an indication of an inquest which could be followed up. Engagement and marriage announcements can also be informative, giving the names of the parents of the intended bride and groom. If one of the parents is a widow or widower the marriage announcement usually gives that information. Photographs of weddings often appear in local newspapers accompanied by descriptions of the occasion, giving names of those present at the reception. On their deaths obituaries of local gentry and other prominent people appear. Details of fatal accidents appear which might finally dispel the family story of how 'great uncle George died'. Details of Court cases are given and reports of many local happenings which may have affected members of your family. Strikes, house fires, floods, murders, all are chronicled somewhere in newspapers. Look through the notes you have made from the information given to you by members of your family. If there is a particular item of interest with a 'near enough' date, look for it in the newspapers around that date. You may find full details and a photograph. Not all the stories you read in the newspapers will be completely factual, but they may be able to confirm in more detail some family stories that you have already obtained. We have to remember that they were written for the reader from a journalistic point of view with the aim of selling as many copies as possible. Headlines in particular can be very misleading. In many cases it will be possible to obtain photocopies of the items you are seeking which you can add to your supporting documentation. Advertisements can also be a source of information: notices of auctions, houses for sale, etc., often give the name of the vendor, shopkeepers, and tradesmen offering services. From about 1840 shipping companies offered sailings to Australia and America, giving details of the names of ships, dates of sailings and the cost. Theatrical productions are also advertised giving the names of the performers. If one of your forebears was a travelling player you might follow his progress through newspaper advertisements – 'Direct from the Palace Theatre London' or 'Next week at Scarborough'.

If you do not find any reference to your family in early newspapers, it is still worthwhile looking through them for the places where they lived. It will help you to form a general picture of their lives, the clothes they wore, the houses they lived in, the work they did, their leisure pursuits, the illnesses and disasters they suffered as seen through the contemporary reports.

County Record Offices

Many counties in England and Wales have a Record Office, created in an effort to preserve and gather together local records and documents. There are also Record Offices in some of the London Boroughs and one in Edinburgh. They house original parish records, wills, court records, civil records, family archives, manorial documents and many other documents relating to local affairs which have been deposited with them. Some counties have several Record Offices, some only one. Each Record Office has its own rules and regulations, days of closing, and hours of opening. Some of the documents may be available on microfilm only. Before making your journey to the Record Office, make a telephone call to enquire whether you need to reserve a microfilm machine or make an appointment and the hours they are open. This will save time for both you and the archivist. In most Record Offices the rules about not eating or drinking while carrying out research on original documents and the use of pencils only for making notes apply. Make a list of what you are looking for. This will also save time and will assist the archivist who will help you by providing the films or documentation you are seeking. If he is told of your particular interest in a simple manner he will know where to look for the documents which will be most useful to you. The staff in the Record Offices have expert knowledge of the documents in their care and are usually very helpful. You may have to wait a little time while those documents are being found but there will be open library shelves with directories, street maps and books of local interest which may offer sources for research while you wait. There may be a limit to the number of documents you can have for your use at one time, so return a document as soon as you have made your notes and finished with it. Photocopies and copy certificates are obtainable on payment of fixed fees. Take enough money with you to cover these charges, particularly small change since you may need it if you are able to make your own photocopies by putting coins in a machine.

The International Genealogical Index
The Genealogical Society of the Church of the Latter Day Saints in Salt Lake City, Utah, USA, is compiling on microfiche an index of worldwide baptisms and marriages, known as the I.G.I. The reason for this dedicated undertaking, which by its very nature can never be finished, is that according to Mormon beliefs they can baptise their ancestors into their faith. Whatever their reasons, their work is greatly appreciated by family historians and genealogists. The I.G.I. is a vast area for research, believed to record over 80 million entries and growing all the time. It is based on the computer records held in Utah. The records are taken from pre-civil registration vital records and

church records and relate to persons no longer living, the earliest entry being for the year 1538. The microfiche are purchased by many outlets such as Record Offices, The Society of Genealogists, libraries and Family History Societies. The use of microfiche is a method of recording a large amount of data on a small area of film. A microfiche is about the size of a large postcard and is read by inserting the film, flat, into a special machine so that the contents are thrown up onto a screen, similar to those on a microfilm machine. The microfiche is moved about, forwards and backwards, to the right or the left, in order to bring into focus the names you are seeking. The microfiche machines are very simple to use.

The index is chronological and alphabetical by surname with the first names also given in alphabetical order, county by county and parish by parish within each county for England and Scotland. Wales and Ireland are each shown as a single unit without counties. It is not a complete record of each county, some counties having better coverage than others. On each microfiche is a list of its contents which should be consulted first to check that you have the correct film and to find out whether the parish you require has been recorded. It is also possible to obtain these lists in printed form from a London research agency, the Mormon Church having given permission for the reprint. The series is not published in order of counties as on the microfiche, but in volumes of geographical areas. These listings also have a very good introduction and explanation of how best to use the I.G.I. indexes.

The information given in the I.G.I. in relation to a baptism is the name of the person, the date, the names of the parents and the parish where the baptism took place. Marriages show the names of both parties, which are cross referenced, the date and the parish. Not all the information is gathered from parish records. There is a column headed 'Type' which shows which event is recorded or where the information was obtained. Initial letters are used as follows:

A = Adult christening   M = Marriage
B = Birth   N = Census
C = Christening   S = Miscellaneous
D = Death or Burial   W = Will or Probate
F = Birth or christening of first known child

The I.G.I. in total can be seen at the Society of Genealogists in

London. The microfiche of the British Isles are available at the P.R.O., Chancery Lane, and the Guildhall Library in London as well as Record Offices and reference libraries in other parts of England. The I.G.I. for Scotland is available at the National Library of Scotland in Edinburgh, that for Northern Ireland at the Mormon Branch Library in Belfast, and that for Wales at the Mid-Glamorgan County Library at Bridgend. Many local Record Offices hold the I.G.I. for their own counties as do local Family History Societies. If you wish to carry out research, when you have decided where it is available nearest to you, telephone or write in advance in order to reserve the use of a microfiche reading machine. Instruction on how to read, interpret and evaluate the information contained in the I.G.I., both positive and negative, is deserving of a chapter of its own. The I.G.I. contains an immense amount of data. However, it must be emphasised that the I.G.I. is only an aid to your research, it does have many errors and omissions and any information gained must be checked against the original records.

12

Libraries and Research Centres

Most librarians and archivists are helpful people, willing to devote their time and interest if you approach them in a sensible and friendly manner. Their time is precious and many people seek their assistance. Polite requests for help and an indication that you are willing to wait will usually achieve better results than demands for instant attention. Make your requests as short as possible, but give as much information as you have. They do not usually have time to hear the whole history of one of your ancestors, leading up to a simple question, much as they may wish to. If you know dates or places, write them down and give them to the librarian so that he can take the information with him when looking for documents for you. There are many places where you can carry out your own research once you have obtained a little help and a nudge in the right direction from an expert.

The Society of Genealogists
The Society of Genealogists was founded in London in 1911 and was granted a Coat of Arms in 1986 to mark the 75th anniversary of its foundation. Its members, numbering about 13,000, are professional genealogists, amateur family historians and anyone interested in family history research. Its head-quarters were in Harrington Gardens but due to expansion of their ever growing library they moved to Charterhouse Build-ings in the City of London, which was once a silk warehouse, making access easier and their proximity to the other major research centres an advantage for their members. The Society is a non profit making registered charity whose objects are to

promote and encourage the study of genealogy. Anyone interested in genealogy and family history research can apply to become a member. Members pay a yearly subscription, those living outside London or overseas paying less than those living in London. There are also concessions for retired persons, students and married couples. Non members may use the library facilities of the Society on payment of search fees, by the hour, half daily or by the day.

The Society issues a quarterly magazine free to its members, holds meetings and runs classes on many subjects that fall within the realm of genealogy. Introductory Saturday mornings are run for new members, giving an extensive tour of the library with instruction on how to use the facilities.

The Society of Genealogists claim that its library is unique in England and that no other library can offer such extensive research facilities for the family historian. Almost all the books are on open shelves, giving researchers immediate access so that time is not wasted waiting for books to be brought by attendants. In addition, borrowing facilities are available to members by mail, upon payment by the member of the mailing charges. The books on the shelves are arranged alphabetically by county with a separate section for countries and relate to all aspects of family history. There are local history books, poll books, directories, county records, genealogical periodicals and magazines. Details of the Monumental Inscriptions that have been copied and indexed are available filed under each county, as are books and information relating to minority religions. Most of the material held relates to the period before registration (1837) which makes it all the more useful.

In addition to printed books the Society holds a large collection of manuscripts and typescripts deposited with them by private persons, including family histories. These are available in boxes on open shelves, arranged alphabetically by family names and places. The Society holds a large collection of parish register copies, the largest in the country, in printed, typescript and manuscript form, dating from as early as 1538 through to 1812 and some through to 1837. All are listed in the library catalogue. If you are unable to find the one you wish to see, ask the library attendants, since some of the unbound copies are not on the open shelves. Boyd's Marriage Index, a collection of over 500 volumes indexing marriages between 1538 and 1837 is held by the Society. It covers many counties of England (not Wales or Scotland) and some counties have separate indexes for males and females. Boyd's gives information relating to dates and places of marriages indicating the parish register in which more detailed information can be traced.

Indexes of early marriage licences, wills and apprenticeship records are available. These are particularly useful since you can search them while on a visit to the Society and decide whether a visit to other repositories such as the P.R.O. or County Record Offices to inspect the original documents would prove useful.

The I.G.I. on microfiche is available at the Society covering the whole of the British Isles and all of the world. If you wish to search the I.G.I. it is not necessary to telephone or write in advance to reserve the use of a microfiche machine. A copying service is available on payment of a small fee per page.

Many trade directories are on the library shelves, filed alphabetically under the counties. There are London directories starting as early as 1677 and a collection of Dublin directories covering ninety years from 1761.

Other subjects covered are schools and universities with an extensive collection of registers. Directories and registries of professions including law lists of solicitors and barristers, clergymen, doctors and surgeons, judges, architects, musicians and many more.

As you will appreciate, there is a wealth of information to be gained from a visit to the Society of Genealogists. By using the library, in one day you might possibly save yourself several separate visits to more distant research repositories or could at least form some idea of whether a visit would prove fruitful. The library, which is closed on Mondays, is open on other days for as many as 8 hours giving you the advantage of a good long day for research. In order to make the best use of the Society's library, make a list of all the names or subjects you wish to research and follow it closely. You may be tempted, but unless you have a spare day on which to indulge yourself, do not dip into books that attract your attention or you will be side-tracked and not look for all you are seeking, as I know to my cost. The Society's library is an Aladdin's Cave of genealogical and historical data.

The library is arranged on three floors. Researchers are requested not to take bags and briefcases into the reading rooms and a cloakroom with lockers is provided on the ground floor.

The ground floor is the Lower Library which holds miscellaneous card indexes, the I.G.I. and microfilm collection, together with the microfilm and microfiche machines, catalogues for the films and the microfiche. There is also what is known as 'The Great Card Index' which contains several million cards filed alphabetically by surname, giving any miscellaneous data that has been collected by the Society – a good place to start on your first visit.

On the first floor is the Middle Library where you will find an enquiry desk and all books on open shelves filed by county. There is also a separate section for the volumes of 'Boyd's Citizens of London'. There is a photocopying machine in the Middle Library. A small fee is charged for each photocopy. There is a card index catalogue of all the available material but if you require advice or something that is not on the shelves, the librarian at the desk will help. There are tables and chairs in all the rooms for the use of members.

On the floor above is the Upper Library where there are the special document collections and family histories together with reference books relating to education, the armed forces, heraldry, overseas and 'Boyd's Marriage Index'. The document collection is on the left as you enter and consists of six sets of shelves reaching almost to the ceiling (ladder provided) full of boxes containing manuscript and typescript documents filed in envelopes under surnames in alphabetical order; another interesting area for research for a first time visitor. There is a typed list of all the names on a table near the shelves. It is thought to contain about 11,000 names.

In the basement, in addition to the toilets there is a lecture room and a comfortable rest room where your own food may be consumed. Coffee and tea making facilities are provided for a small fee. There are also toilets on the other library floors and a book stall on the ground floor near the main entrance.

Guildhall Library

The Guildhall Library in London has a department devoted to genealogy, covering in detail the City of London, London Boroughs and the Greater London area together with information relating to other counties. There are no search fees, all that is required is a signature in the visitors' book at the enquiry desk in the manuscript room. There is usually an attendant on duty just inside the entrance to the library who will direct you to the manuscript room which is up a small flight of stairs to the left through the map room. To the right is the reference library. The manuscript room and library have a plentiful supply of desks and comfortable chairs for the use of readers.

The manuscript room, which has both microfilm and microfiche machines, has a collection on microfilm of the parish registers of the City of London, the London Boroughs, parts of Greater London and the County of Middlesex. They also have the microfiche of the I.G.I. covering the same areas. The microfiche for the British Isles are held in the library where there are several microfiche and microfilm machines available for use and it is not necessary to make an appointment. There are also copies of Census Records in the reference library. This is particularly helpful since you do not have to wait for the films to be brought to you, but can help yourself, and view them on the microfilm machines in the library room. Copying facilities are also available (again small change necessary).

There are extensive records relating to the City of London, including City institutions such as the famous Goldsmiths and Silversmiths, together with other less well known Guilds and Livery Companies with apprenticeship records, such as the Clock and Watchmakers and the Fishmongers. If you have an ancestor who was a tradesman or craftsman in the City of London these records are very helpful. There are Law Lists from 1797, records of the Royal College of Surgeons of England from 1518. There are records relating to the House of Commons, Old Bailey trials, naturalisation papers and Change of Name deeds.

Books on the shelves of the reference library cover a wide range. One of the largest collections of trade and street directories in the country is held by this library. Some on open shelves, some locked behind glass fronted shelves and others kept elsewhere on the premises. If you do not see the directories you require, ask at the desk where there are several archivists and librarians available to assist you. Tell them the number of the table where you are sitting and complete an application form and the books will be brought to you. There is a large card index of all the books and manuscripts available and if anything you wish to see is not readily available, ask at the desk. The archivists and librarians are very knowledgeable about the books on their shelves and very willing to help with problems. If they do not have the information on their own shelves, they will probably be able to direct you to another library or repository where you can find the information you are seeking.

In addition the reference library holds on microfilm a complete run of *The Times* newspaper.

City of London Corporation

The Record Office of the City of London Corporation is also in the Guildhall. This record office holds additional records relating specifically to the City of London.

Federation of Family History Societies

There are many Family History Societies throughout the country which come under the umbrella of the Federation. Most local societies concentrate on family history research within their own county and produce a regular journal relating to their work. If your research takes you outside the county in which you now live, write to the secretary of the society in the county you wish to research, giving the surname or place names in which you are interested. The local society may have someone amongst them who has been researching that name or can tell you about the place. If you join your own local society, they will exchange information through the Federation with other societies. The Federation also publish many useful booklets relating to different aspects of family history research. There is also a Guild of One Name Studies affiliated to the Federation, specialising in the study of one name only. If there is a society for your name, or any of the family names that you are researching, their research and publications may be of interest to you although they may not necessarily have any information relating to your particular family even if the name is the same.

Borthwick Institute of Historical Research, York

The Borthwick Institute in St Anthony's Hall, York is a research institute of York University, and holds many original manuscripts which could help those in the north, who do not have the time and money to make protracted journeys to London. They specialise in the study of church history, particularly in relation to administration and law in the northern province. The Institute is mainly for the use of research students, but it is open to the public. It is necessary to make an appointment in advance if you wish to carry out research on their archives. There is a room where readers can consume their own food and facilities for making tea and coffee supplied for a small charge. There is also a copying service available for some classes of documents.

The library known as the Gurney Library holds approximately 14,000 books on its shelves, relating to all aspects of historic research including local societies and most record offices. Copy parish registers, probate records and Bishops' transcripts are held, as are original manuscripts and typescripts deposited by private families and individuals relating to Yorkshire and Nottinghamshire. Estate records, Charity papers, school records, and wills are also available. It is advisable to enquire whether they hold the documentation you are seeking before embarking on an appointment to carry out research. The Institute publish a helpful guide giving details of their genealogical sources which may be of assistance to family historians. The Institute specialise in document conservation and restoration and if you can take a tour of their work and conservation rooms I would urge you to do so. You will be privileged to see many famous early documents and manuscripts and the meticulous loving care and scientific research carried on by the 'backroom boys' at the Institute.

The Newspaper Library

The Newspaper Library at Colindale is a branch of the British Library where you can research amongst nearly 600,000 volumes, and 220,000 microfilms housed on about 18 miles of shelving. Their stock is increased each year with up to date newspapers, but it is the past that will interest you more. It is easy to reach, being almost opposite the Colindale underground station which is on the Northern line. There is also a small car park.

Admission to the library is free. It is restricted to those over 21 years of age and it is necessary to obtain a reader's ticket by producing proof of your identity. The library suggest that you telephone before you visit them, in order to ascertain that they hold the information you require and what proof of your identity you will be asked to supply. There are over 100 seats for readers including more than 30 with microfilm machines. There is a catalogue of all the newspapers in a card index and in loose leaf folders together with indexes to *The Times* and the *New York Times*. The library offers copying facilities and will also supply copies by post if you can give them an exact reference of the piece you are seeking. There is a refreshment room with drinks and food vending machines where you can also eat your own food.

The newspaper collections dating from 1800 are daily and weekly papers and periodicals including London newspapers. Provincial, Welsh, Scottish and Irish newspapers are held dating from 1700 as well as foreign newspapers. There is also a collection of printed books relating to the newspaper industry, journalism and the history of the press.

India Office Library

Many of us have ancestors who were connected with India, either through work or through the armed forces. Young men set out for India to make their fortunes by working for the British East India Company or joined regiments of the army which were based in India. There they married, had families and often died. Some fell in love with the country and on discharge from the army remained there to work on the railway. All those lives were well documented and the records are today held in the India Office Library which is at 197 Blackfriars Road, London.

The library which is on the fourth floor consists of a catalogue room, and a readers' room. Admission, which is free, is by a reader's day pass which is obtained by signing the visitors' book on the ground floor. Bags and briefcases may not be taken into the library, but there is a cloakroom inside the entrance to the catalogue room and an attendant will give you a numbered disc in exchange for your bags and coat. An enquiry desk in the catalogue room is manned by very helpful librarians and archivists. There are a number of tables in the reading room and it is necessary to obtain a seat with a number so that you can give the number of the seat when you order a book or document which will be brought to you, normally very quickly. Reference numbers of documents and books can be obtained from the indexes in the catalogue room and entered on printed forms together with your seat number which are then handed to the desk. The use of pencils only rule is strictly enforced and if you should forget your 'travel pack' this is one of the libraries where you can purchase pencils. All materials should be returned to the desk after use. The library offers copying facilities and a printed leaflet gives details of costs and procedures. There is a refreshment room on the 11th floor where there are drink vending machines and you may eat your own food.

The library publish a number of free guides giving details of the collections they hold and how to gain access to them. There is also a guide to the library which is in the catalogue room.

The extensive records which are of most interest to the family historian are the ecclesiastical and army records giving details of births, marriages and deaths, service records both civil and military, wills, probate and pension funds. They cover The East India Company from 1600 to 1858, the Board of Control from 1784 to 1858, The India Office from 1858 to 1947 and the Burma Office from 1937 to 1948. The records cover much written material, that which was sent to India from England and that sent to England from India. They cover not only India, but parts of Burma, Indonesia, Malaysia, St Helena, China and Japan. An interesting item amongst the records of St Helena is the death certificate of Napoleon Bonaparte. Unfortunately in 1858 many records were disposed of as 'waste paper' and were sold to a dealer. Fortunately the dealer realised how important the 'waste paper' was and spent the next fifty years selling the records back to the India Office so all was not lost.

Trade Museums and Libraries

There are very many museums and libraries devoted to one subject, tucked away in back streets, not necessarily in London but all over the country. If by tradition your family or ancestors specialised in a particular trade or interest, passing down their knowledge from father to son over the ages, there is probably a museum for you somewhere, where you might find specific reference to your family name. You may even find photographs amongst their archives. Most of the Guilds and Livery Halls in the City of London have museums. If your ancestors were stonemasons, or train drivers, worked in the potteries, were butchers, glass blowers, doctors, carpenters, or opera singers, there are collections of records looked after by devoted archivists somewhere waiting for you. It is well worth making enquiries. Your local library should have a copy of the 'Museum Year Book' which gives all the museums in the British Isles with addresses, telephone numbers and hours of opening.

There is a Mining Museum in Stoke on Trent, a Bagpipe Museum in Morpeth, a Museum for Chartered Insurance in London and a Historical Exhibition of the British Red Cross in Guildford in Surrey. Principal museums in cities and large towns mount special exhibitions from time to time. Watch out for announcements and articles in the local or national press. The subjects are varied, some local and some based on international events, but many are of interest to the family historian.

St Paul's Cathedral in London had an exhibition of Jewish records in the crypt, showing many early photographs. The Print Library in a small back street near St Bride's in London has a permanent collection related to all aspects of the paper trade, including the manufacture and printing of paper and books. I was directed to that particular library by a librarian at the Guildhall Library when I was researching someone connected with the paper trade. The archivist was very helpful and eventually found a collection of house magazines for the company where the person concerned had been an apprentice. In one of those little booklets I found a detailed written history giving his full name and date of birth, his father's name, their address at the signing of the indentures together with a history of his rise in the company's employment and details of his marriage and his children. A really wonderful find!

There is also an excellent series of books divided into geographical areas, published by H.M.S.O., giving full details of most museums.

13

Book One of Your Family History

One of the pleasures of tracing your family history is the fact that you can take a rest whenever you wish and return to it at any time. Some of those 'bitten by the bug' spend most of their leisure time working at their family history, often using their weekends and annual holidays to visit archives, record offices and registries or the places where their forebears originated. For those living in England whose forebears originated elsewhere, a visit to Ireland, Wales, Scotland or even further can combine a very pleasant holiday with an opportunity to continue the research. The Society of Genealogists and the Federation of Family History Societies offer interesting and valuable evening classes, weekend and week long seminars and conferences. A few days spent in the company of dedicated family historians and genealogists gives renewed energy and determination to continue. And what a lot you can learn in those few days! If you have become a member of the Society of Genealogists you will receive information of all lectures, seminars and conferences. If not, write at the beginning of the year to ask them for their programme so that you can plan any trips you wish to make.

Once you have found addresses where your forebears lived and the locations of some of their burials, visit the places if you can, taking your camera or persuade a photographer friend to accompany you. Some of the houses and buildings mentioned in your documentation may have disappeared by now. In towns and cities whole streets of houses have been demolished to make way for modern redevelopment and country areas are now crisscrossed by motorways. You may be lucky, however and find the house where a great great grandparent was born. I found one such house in a small town in Scotland. The male members of the family had been stonemasons through the ages and there was a carving over the front door of the house showing stonemasons' tools with the date 1720. I could picture George Thompson carefully carving that stone, little knowing how delighted one of his ancestors would be to find it 260 years later. A photograph of the house and the carving now form part of my documentation. I was also able to purchase a booklet, in a small local museum, giving the history of the area. All these things give depth and perspective to a family history. Visiting houses, towns and villages brings you closer to the people you are researching and makes you aware of the pleasures and difficulties of their lives.

Visiting churchyards and cemeteries can also bring pleasure as well as sadness. Branches of families die out or move away leaving gravestones neglected. The weather and time are very destructive, but a tranquil picture of a churchyard, a memorial stone standing under a tree and a close-up of that stone will add greatly to the narrative of a family history.

If you should get a little bored ploughing your way through the indexes, take a rest and turn to other things. You have your records to keep up to date, a good task to undertake in the winter months when the nights are longer and travelling is not so easy. Your family chart should be revised and updated as you delve further into the past. You also have the task of bringing all the information together on paper.

Not all of you will wish to write a book, but page by page your manuscript will grow. Once you have sufficient information start to write your family history, which will eventually combine with your family tree, photographs, original and copy documents. Use a loose leaf ring binder adding separate pages as you write. You can also keep them in chronological order, inserting them in the correct place without difficulty.

Although you are writing the story for yourself in order to bring together the results of your researches, it will undoubtedly be read by others. Members of your family will wish to read it and you may care to deposit a copy with the Society of Genealogists to assist the generations to come. Make it as interesting as you can. If you have the necessary information, describe what people looked like, the colour of their hair and eyes, how tall they were, together with a reference to any outstanding features. You will find that members of your family will sometimes be surprised by descriptions of their distant kinsmen and recognise in those descriptions likenesses to today's descendants.

Start by making notes of one person on the first sheet of paper. Try using yourself as the first person. What do you know? Your name – put that at the top of the page. On this page which is a guide for yourself on which to base the final manuscript, add your reference numbers so that you can refer to your records. The final manuscript does not need to show the reference numbers since they will become a distraction to anyone reading the family history. On each line underneath, add another piece of information, date of birth, place of birth, parents' names, schools attended, examinations passed, degrees won, interests and unusual hobbies, residences occupied with the dates of the moves. If you are married, the date and place of your marriage, the name of your spouse, the names and dates of birth of any children, present address. In the case of yourself, all these things will be known to you from memory, but you should support them with as much documentation as possible. When you write up the pages relating to your parents, grandparents and great grandparents, most of your information will come from the results of your researches, and will also include the date and place of death. The longer they lived, the more information you should have. These notes will form the bare branches on which the leaves will grow.

The following is a copy of the first notes made relating to a member of my family whom I knew and who was able personally to give me many details on which to base my researches. It is therefore recent history:

Fanny Rayner (A1)
Born: 7 May 1896, Bilgoraj, Poland
Parents: Maurice Rayner (A3), Esther? (M36)
Schools: Hackney Primary, Green's Grammar School, Stepney.
Residence: 306 Wick Road, Hackney
Occupation: hairdresser
Married: 18 October 1926 Hackney Registry Office
Alfred Gennings (S4) – Occupation: Engineer
Present: Rebecca Gosman and William Edward Gennings (S7) (Groom's brother)
Female child born 3 October 1928 Elizabeth Esther (S12)
Residences: 1926–1929 21 Greenwood Road, Hackney

1930–1940 91 Farley Road, Stoke Newington
1941–1949 9 Wellington Road, Leyton
1950–1965 33 Naverino Road, Hackney
1966–1979 18 Kirkstead Court, Hackney
Died: 21 November 1979

All the necessary facts are there, but how bleak and uninteresting. The following page is the beginning of the rounded history of Fanny Rayner:

'Fanny Rayner, the daughter of Maurice and Esther, was born in Bilgoraj, Poland, on 7 May 1896. The maiden name of Esther is not known since no birth certificate is known to exist for Fanny but an Affidavit sworn by her father in January 1956 gives the details of her birth. Maurice and Esther, with Fanny, emigrated to England in 1900.

The family lived at 306 Wick Road in a prosperous part of the London Borough of Hackney over the hairdresser's establishment opened by Maurice where he catered for the local population, both men and women. The shop was well situated between a public house and a grocer's store, close to Victoria Park, in an area comprising both shopping and residential accommodation. Fanny attended the local primary school and gained a scholarship to Sir George Green's Grammar School in Stepney. She remained at the school until the age of 16 and then joined her father in his shop as an apprentice hairdresser. Fanny was 5ft 2in tall, had dark hair and brown eyes. At the age of 28 years on 18 October 1926, Fanny married Alfred Gennings, an engineer, of 9 Etropol Road, Hackney. The witnesses to the marriage were Rebecca Gosman, a friend of Fanny, and William Edward Gennings, Alfred's younger brother. Fanny ceased her occupation as a hairdresser and took up residence with her husband Alfred in rented accommodation at 21 Greenwood Road, Hackney where they were living when her only child, a daughter, Elizabeth Esther was born at the Mother's Hospital in Hackney on 3 October 1928. Elizabeth Esther weighing only 4½ lb at birth was born prematurely and Fanny was unable to have any more children.

Fanny remained at home looking after her family while Alfred continued to work as an engineer. They moved house in 1930 to 91 Farley Road, Stoke Newington, once again in rented accommodation. Fanny became a voluntary school assistant in 1935 at Upton House School, Hackney and a School Governor in 1937. In 1939 she assisted with the evacuation of the children of Upton House School to Thetford in Norfolk, where she remained for a year acting as a liaison between the children, their parents and the local population. Later she returned to London to work in a munitions factory . . .' and so the story continues until her death in 1979.

The story is Fanny's with references to her father, mother, daughter and brother-in-law. Her parents Maurice and Esther each have their own page and story, as do her husband Alfred and her daughter Elizabeth Esther. Elizabeth Esther's children and grandchildren also make an appearance further on in the saga. Fanny's story is by no means complete. You will have noticed that there is a gap between her age at 16 and at 28. Other parts of her early life are only sketched in with the information at present known. There is a need for much more research. So it always will be with family history and genealogy – a never ending journey.

The documents supporting this part of the family history are the original Affidavit of her father, three school reports, a photograph of Fanny standing on the doorstep of her father's shop. Her original marriage certificate, letters written from Thetford in Norfolk, a photograph of a group of factory munition workers, and her death certificate.

You may notice that Fanny's date of birth of May 1896 does not agree with her age at her marriage. Perhaps her father was mistaken about her date of birth or the incorrect age was entered on her marriage certificate. This is just one example of the inconsistencies that you may find as you research your family history.

The following are brief extracts from manuscripts written by a family historian in 1850 which were given to me as part of the family documentation of a family for whom I prepared a family history. The style of writing is very different from that used today and very little detail is given, but the writer conveys to the reader his sensitivity and the tender feelings he still held for his deceased wife. The first and second refer to one of his relations and the third although apparently written from a distance, to his own wife.

'Angus Bantry son of Jonathan Bantry a yeoman of Eden End Northamptonshire and grandson of Samuel Bantry was sent to Highcroft school with the idea of being a farmer, but not liking it, and farming being bad, he came to Manchester as a boy of fifteen with ten shillings in his pocket and obtained a post in a bank and became rich.'

The second by Angus himself refers to a letter he received from a clergyman.

'This letter from Rev Mr. Tree the clergyman then residing at Eden End was written about the 12th January 1808 and the half guinea enclosed to me was all my capital for starting life. Before my good father left me in Manchester he gave me a five pound note because at that time I had no salary from the Banking House and to the best of my recollection I never received further assistance from him or any one else.'

The third written by Daniel Bantry.

'Alice the beloved wife of Daniel Bantry was the eldest daughter of Thomas and Nancy Harding and was born at their house in Manchester on March 22nd 1793. She was married on April 9th 1817 and soon afterwards attended at Chapel and was with her husband baptised June 30th 1821. Eighteen years before her decease her growing afflictions prevented her from regular attendance on the means of grace and for the last ten years of her life she was almost entirely confined to her habitation. She suffered most patiently from what was supposed to be a heart disease and died on November 3rd 1850. She was buried in Oldham cemetery in a family grave which is indicated by a neat marble monument.'

These pages including the one from my own Family History give an idea of how to begin writing your own Family History. Develop your own style and add to your manuscripts as your research progresses.

Having conveyed to you the enjoyment and pleasure that can be derived from the pursuit of family history, I wish you success and leave you to draw up your own tree. There are many elements of family history research that I have not dealt with and some that have been mentioned only in passing. Inevitably you will have many questions you would like to ask. There is more detailed information relating to the I.G.I., museums and the P.R.O. and I am conscious of the fact that I have not dealt with how to find your ancestors if they were originally immigrants or if they emigrated. I am sure, however, that I have given you more than enough to whet your appetite and keep you occupied, and your own researches will lead you to many answers.

One more thing before we part company. I realise I have made the point many times, but record offices, museums and repositories do change their hours of opening and sometimes have to close for stocktaking, conservation or redecoration. Please do telephone in advance to check times and availability of records so as to avoid a wasted journey.

Part 2

Where Does Your Surname Come From?

14

The Rise of Surnames

Perhaps surprisingly, surnames are a relatively recent phenomenon. Most experts believe that they came into common use in the eleventh century, so they've yet to be around for a thousand years.

Surnames were needed for a variety of reasons. The growth of cities was certainly one of these. A man could be known as just plain John in a small village but the designation simply wasn't specific enough in a city. So he became 'John the Baker', 'John at the Water', and so on. Three other events helped surnames to spread.

The first, taxes, were hardly new in the year 1000. However, about then they did become better organised and the record-keeping which resulted required an accurate designation of those on the rolls.

Secondly, man was becoming a far more communal animal. In virtually all cases this coming together involved a contractual, though often unwritten, exchange of loyalties. Families owed their allegiance to and expected protection from others. In turn, others were allied to and protected by them. Over the course of time these relationships became codified and in the process gave rise to a large number of surnames, as we shall see in the chapters which follow.

Finally, as Christianity spread, baptism and (often) subsequent confirmation came to be common.

All the above normally involved written records and, per-force, the ability to designate accurately one person as opposed to another. Thus surnames became an absolute necessity. The story of how our names came about and how they've changed takes up much of each of the chapters that follow.

Roots and Foreign Branches

Seventy-six major surnames are examined here, together with over one thousand other names which share part or all of the same background. Where a name comes from, how it grew and when it first appeared are all covered. With rare exceptions the precise roots for any given surname are ambiguous; this is notably true of the British Isles. Over the centuries Britain has received a vast host of (sometimes unwanted) foreign visitors. So the roots of British surnames have many branches. As a result a Cornishman and a Scot may share a common surname, but for entirely different reasons.

This book does not attempt to identify *all* sources and roots for all the names covered. There are two good reasons for this. Many origins are lost in the mists of time, and to list all those which are known would result in a daunting, academic work of thousands of pages. Instead, the book profiles the most common sources for the names involved.

At the same time it gives a selection of the many other surnames which have much in common with the name under discussion. Sometimes, as in Roberts and Robertson, the connection is obvious, while in others – the connection between Richards and Dixon, for instance – the relationship may be surprising.

Surname Sleight-of-Hand

One of the many charms of the study of surnames is the surprises they yield. Some become extended by the addition of letters up front – the Welsh 'ap', the Irish 'O' and the Scottish 'Mac' are classic examples; while others have their extensions tacked on at the end – 'son' and 'ton' are two common examples.

Some names take on pretensions via hyphens and the like, while others shed letters, and indeed syllables.

Yet another group of names is positively acrobatic in its ability to do about-turns, while still others have a perverse quality of meaning the exact opposite of what you would expect (many Kings, for instance, do not come from royal roots).

Oddities

A 'miscellany' follows each history. As its name implies, this section provides a selection of interesting facts. You'll find murderers and millionaires, explorers and eccentrics, saints and sinners, nicknames and all sorts of fascinating information.

Each section ends with a listing of places around the world which are similarly named, giving cities, towns, rivers, lakes, mountain ranges and islands which are namesakes.

15

The Origins of Surnames

With rare exceptions, virtually all British surnames are based on or have grown from one (or very occasionally more) of fourteen starting points. Where our ancestors lived and what they looked like, their work and their hobbies all played a part in forming the surnames which surround us today.

Sometimes the association is direct, as in Baker or Fisher, though even here one encounters amusing subtleties. For example, most villages had one baker, one smith, one cooper, so these names can accurately describe what an ancestor did. Fisher is a totally different matter. Those who lived by the sea were never called Fisher for a good reason: because so many men in the area earned their living in this manner hopeless confusion would have resulted if the name had been in general use. Only when a fisherman moved inland was he so designated in honour of the curiosity value of his former profession.

Here then are the fourteen different areas which have given rise to our British names:

The Origins

Names derived from first names or patronymics
This category accounts for by far the largest number of modern names. Common examples here are: Jones, Nixon, Fitzhugh, McDonald, Johnson, Jackson, Wilson, Robinson, Tomlinson, Simpson, Dixon, Dickinson.

Names derived from other relations
Examples here are Eames, which means son of an uncle; Neave,

the medieval word for nephew; Cousins, Godson, Kinderson.

Names derived from physical characteristics
Some of the most obvious examples here are Beard, Whitehead, Brown, Redd and Reed, Long, Short, Small, Longfellow, Dark, Goodbody, Dunn (meaning 'dark').

Names derived from traits
Not only were some of our forebears named for their appearance, others bore labels describing their personalities or actions. Among these names one finds, for instance, Giddy, Swift, Hardy, Goodpastor (note the profession hiding there), Fox (as in 'smart as a —'), Smart, Worthy, Harty, Goodfellow, Gray, Moody (meaning brave), Wise, Keen, Bright, Pratt (meaning 'cunning').

Names derived from metaphor and ritual
Many of our ancestors took their names either from the way others regarded them or from roles they played in village pageants. Popular examples of these are King, Pope, Abbott, Lord, Duke, Priest.

Names derived from literature, myth and fable
The Bible is the all-time name generator here. Some examples are Aaron, Simons, Peters, Johns, Matthews, Joseph, Luke, Jude and Thomas.

Names derived from occupations
Smith is the champion in this category, but the world is full of those whose names tell us what their forefathers worked at. For example, Gardener, Skinner, Carter, Clark, Taylor, Fuller (one who 'fulled' cloth to clean it), Parson, Potter, Wright (including derivations such as Cartwright, Wheelwright and so forth), Archer, Miller, Weaver, Mason, Cooper, Glover, Goldsmith, Butcher, Chandler, Spicer, Sawyer, Draper, Waller, Slater, Spooner, Collier, Fisher, Brewer, Saddler, Carpenter, Baker (and Baxter), Farmer, Barber, Cook, Day (meaning 'dairyman'), Fowler.

Names derived from sayings
Once, England was full of hawkers proclaiming their wares, as exemplified by the street cries of London. Often the cry became

the surname. Two examples of this type are Goodall – from 'Good Ale' – and Pardie – 'Per Deum' (for God).

Names derived from actions and events
Things which happened to our ancestors, or events in which they took part, can be reflected in the names we live with. Among names of this type are Drum, Shakespeare (a spearbearer), Voyager, Conquest.

Names associated with animals and plants
Some families took their name from the everyday animals and plants with which they came in contact such as Salmon, Apple, Rose, Vine, Bull.

Names which indicate nationality
Long before passports, many of us bore names which stated where we came from. Among these are English, French, Norman, Saxon, Fleming, Dennis (meaning Danish).

Names associated with a man-made landmark
In the absence of a numbered street address, it was often handy to have a name which helped direct people to you, especially in larger towns. Examples of this kind of name includes Bridges, Bell, Castle, Hall, Street, Towers.

Names associated with natural landmarks
In rural areas nature itself gave rise to an enormous number of names like, for instance, Banks, Ford, Rivers, Holloway, Westbrook, Grove, Brooks, Downs, Field, Moore.

Names which are status-oriented
Names of this type are largely medieval and derive from positions in the feudal hierarchy. Among the more frequent examples of this type are Squire, Sargeant, Bailey, Butler, Chamberlain, Ward (and Warden, Warder), Knight, Page, Marshall.

16

The Surnames

Related Names
Other surnames which are related as to root, derivation or usage include:

Alain	Allain	Alleyn	FitzAllan
Alan	Allanson	Alleyne	FitzAllen
Alano	Allenby	FitzAlan	Van Allen
Aleyn	Allens		

The surname Allen also occurs as Allan, Alleyne, Allain and derives from the popular first name Alan which also gives rise to FitzAlan. The origins of the name remain uncertain. It is possible that it derives from 'the Alan', meaning a member of the nomadic Scythian tribe which emerged from Central Asia in the centuries before the birth of Christ. The first references to the name are found in early Breton ballads. Here the name occurs in the form 'Alamn'. The name soon standardised to Alan in Old Breton and Alain in Old French, though it remained a Breton name. Its popularity increased as a result of one Alan, Bishop of Quimper, a Welsh-Breton, whose holy life led him to become the first St Alan. It is perhaps from the example of St Alan that it was said in those days that the name Alan meant 'harmony', though this remains unconfirmed from etymological sources.

The name Alan first came to England with the Norman

Conquest. Amongst William the Conqueror's companies in arms were several Alans (and Alains), notably Alain le Roux (Alan the Red). After the Conquest, along with several other Breton first names, the first name Alan became widespread in England. Several remain popular as surnames to this day. Examples include Brett, Jewell, Brian, Justin and Wymark.

Curiously, the first name Alan became most popular in England in its Old French form of Alain, rather than the Old Breton form of Alan. In the centuries after the Conquest this name was found most frequently in Lincolnshire, where many of William the Conqueror's Breton soldiers settled as farmers. The first recorded English mention of the surname dates from the earliest records of the Domesday Book which record a certain Alanus in Suffolk in 1086. This is the Latinised form of the name; the additional '–us' may well have been little more than a clerical formalisation (Latin being the prevalent written language of the time). The name also appears in this form in the Domesday records for Lincolnshire in 1150.

The name Allen as a surname, and as a first name (with various spellings in both cases), is also popular in Scotland, though there is no question of Breton links in these cases as this part of Britain was not subject to Norman conquest. Here the name derives from the Gaelic personal name Ailin, from 'ail' – 'stone'. It may thus be originally a place name – for a man who lived by, or under a large, prominent stone or rock; or in some cases it may have been a nickname, attributing stoniness – either of strength, or character, or brain – to its owner. These early nicknames were often the result of local wit – and were often ironic – the local Alan (or stone) could therefore frequently have been not the village Sampson, but rather the village simpleton or weakling.

As Allan (the most frequent Scottish form) this name is often found in Northumberland. Here some of the derivations are doubtless from the Breton, though the large majority are of Scottish (Gaelic) origin.

An Allen Miscellany

Allens can take pride in two of Ireland's most notable geographic features – the Bog of Allen, over 378 square miles of peat bogs in East Central Eire; and Lough Allen, on the Shannon, which is 8 miles long and up to 3 miles wide.

☆

Allen's rule is the zoological principle that cold-climate animals have shorter smaller appendages and thus keep body heat loss down. It is named after US zoologist, Joel Asaph Allen.

☆

The Van Allen radiation belts, 600 miles from the earth, have a major effect on our planet's atmosphere and rotation. They're named after their American discoverer, physicist James Alfred Van Allen.

☆

The British Field Marshal, Viscount Allenby, Edmund Henry Hynman (1861–1936), is best remembered today for his invasion of Palestine during World War I, when he captured Jerusalem. This led to the fall of Damascus, and ultimately Turkey itself. The Allenby Bridge, which today links Israel and Jordan across the Jordan River, is named after him.

☆

There are 5 towns in the United Kingdom which contain either Allan or Allen in their names. These range from Allanaquoich to Allensmore. The United States has 5 towns named Allen, along with another 8 towns which have Allen contained in their names. Both Syria and the United Kingdom have Allan Rivers, while New Zealand and the United States have Mount Allens.

✳✳✳✳✳✳✳✳✳✳✳✳✳✳✳✳✳✳✳✳✳✳✳✳✳✳✳✳✳✳✳✳
✳　　　　　　　　**ANDERSON**　　　　　　　✳
✳✳✳✳✳✳✳✳✳✳✳✳✳✳✳✳✳✳✳✳✳✳✳✳✳✳✳✳✳✳✳✳

Related Names
Other surnames which are related as to root, derivation or usage include:

Anders	Andison	Andrew	Andris
Andersen	André	Andrews	Andrisoune
Andersons	Andrea	Andrewson	Androson
Andersson	Andreas	Andrey	Endherson
Anderton	Andress		

Anderson is a modified form of Andrewson, meaning son of Andrew. Similar modifications and variations are fairly common amongst popular surnames, other widespread examples being Benson from Bennettson, Henderson from Henryson and,

141

in certain cases, Alison from Allanson. Andrewson certainly passed through many forms before it finally became formulated as Anderson – this can be seen from the several 'in-between' derivatives which remain to this day (especially in Scotland). These include Andison (almost certainly derived from the shortened form of Andrew, Andy), Androson, Andrisoune, and even Endherson (though not Henderson which, as mentioned previously, comes from Henryson).

The first name Andrew comes from the Ancient Greek, where it means 'manly'. It has thus been in use for well over 2,000 years. The most famous Andrew is certainly one of the earliest recorded – St Andrew was Christ's first disciple. Legend has it that the remains of St Andrew were brought to Scotland in the fourth century by St Regulus. True or not, St Andrew is now firmly established as the patron saint and knightly champion of Scotland, his diagonal white cross featuring on the Scottish flag. Naturally enough, the name Andrew has long been popular in Scotland, its popularity first coming to the fore in the twelfth century. Thereafter, the name Anderson became prominent. Though the Scots haven't had it all their own way; the most concentrated populations of Andrews are found in the West Country, in Cornwall and Devon, while concentrations of Andersons are found slightly further east in Dorset and Hampshire.

The earliest British mention of any name connected with Andrew or Anderson is in the Domesday Book, where a certain Andreas is mentioned in 1086. It is nearly 200 years later before the first Andersons begin to make their recorded appearance. In the early-fifteenth-century Scottish records there are several Andrewsons and Androsouns, while in England, in the venerable-sounding *Register of the Guild of the Corpus Christi of the City of York*, one Androson appears in 1455 and an Androwson in 1482.

Owing to its popularity in Scotland, the name Anderson has proliferated wherever Scots have emigrated. This accounts for the large number of Andersons in New Zealand, Canada, and the United States. However, many of the American Andersons are of Swedish origin (Anderson is the most prevalent name in the Stockholm telephone directory.)

To a lesser degree, Andersons are indigenous all over Europe. The origin of the name is the same, and its pan-European popularity undoubtedly stems from St Andrew (who was also patron saint of Russia). The name Andrew has many European forms – ranging from the French André to the German Andreas. Curiously, despite the name's popularity, there have been no major European kings called Andrew. Neither Scotland nor England has had a King Andrew, though the Queen's second son is so named. Also, there have been no popes named Andrew.

An Anderson Miscellany

Andersons have been involved in a number of record-breaking crimes. George 'Dutch' Anderson pulled off a 1921 mail van stick-up which yielded over £500,000; Charlie Anderson took part in the first Wild West train robbery (1866); and 'Boston Pete' Anderson successfully talked a reclusive miser out of £850,000 in 1866 and sensibly retired.

☆

The Anderson Shelter, invented by one-time British Chancellor of the Exchequer John Anderson, was a simple affair which could easily be installed (as over 3 million were) in a back garden. It saved countless lives during World War II air raids.

☆

Andersen's disease is one of five types of hereditary glycogen-storage diseases. Metabolic problems affect the liver, spleen, muscles and lymph nodes, the liver ultimately deteriorates and the patient dies.

☆

Andersonville Prison in Sumter County, Georgia, was notorious during America's Civil War. In the two years of its existence (1864–5) this log stockade of at most 26 acres housed over 32,000 Northern prisoners, half of whom died.

☆

Andersons have long figured prominently in the arts. Hans Christian Andersen (1805–75) created some of the world's best-loved fairy tales, while America's Sherwood Anderson (1876–1941) and Maxwell Anderson (1888–1959) were prize-winning poets and novelists.

☆

There are towns called Anderson in the United Kingdom, Argentina and the United States, rivers of this name in Canada and the United States, and islands so named in Canada and Australia.

```
************************************
*               BAILEY              *
************************************
```

Related Names

Other surnames which are related as to root, derivation or usage include:

Baile	Baillie	Bayle	Baylis
Baileff	Bailly	Bayless	Bayliss
Bailie	Baily	Bayley	Baylot
Bailiff	Bally	Baylies	Bayly

Over half a dozen variations of the name remain in common use. These range from Baillie and Bayly to Baylis and Bayless.

Bailey is an occupational name deriving from the Old French words 'abillif' and 'baillis'. In medieval times a bailiff was anything from a Crown official to a King's officer in a town or county, a keeper of a Royal household, or simply a Sheriff's deputy. On feudal estates he was often a manorial official of some importance. For instance, the medieval records for the Manor of Droxford show the bailiff as receiving no less than the sum of £6 per annum – whereas the ploughman received only 8 shillings: a mere 1/15th of the bailiff's wage (the poor shepherds received only 4 shillings). What's more, the bailiff lived in the manor house at his lord's expense. For this princely wage, he acted as a kind of agricultural supervisor-cum-foreman for his lord's estate. His task was to make sure that the lands were properly and efficiently farmed, and to allot tasks to the workers. If a feudal lord was lazy or away at the Crusades, the bailiff virtually ran the estate. Thus he was a key man in its financial success or failure.

The name Bailey came across to England with William the Conqueror – probably in its original form of Bailiff. The origins of this name remain obscure, though it is possible that it derives from the Ancient Roman word for a burden – bajalus. Thus, a bailiff would be a person who bore a burden, or responsibility. The first English mention of the name Bailey appears in the thirteenth century. It is mentioned in the *Friar's Tale* by Chaucer (' "Artow then a bayley?" "Ye", quod, he.'); Harry Bailey was the name of the Host in Chaucer's *Canterbury Tales*. The name also appears in the Hundred Rolls of 1273, where a certain Alvered Ballivus (the Latinised form) appears in the records for Lincolnshire.

The name Bailey is also common in Scotland, where a Scots alderman is still referred to as a bailie. The earliest Scottish mention comes in the 1311–13 records for Lothian, where one William de Baillie appears as a juror. The 'de' means this name almost certainly refers to a place, probably a keep or castle. In Lancashire also the surname Bailey appears as de Baylegh (1246), from the place Bailey (near Stonyhurst), a name meaning 'glade where berries grow'.

During this time, and in subsequent centuries, there was some confusion about the name Bailey (or Baillie and so on) in Scotland. According to popular Clydeside myth all Baileys had originally been called Balliol, but changed their names because of the two unpopular Scottish kings of that name. In most instances this was not the case.

A Bailey Miscellany
In medieval times a bailey was a fort surrounded by a deep ditch and protected on the inside by a wooden palisade.

☆

The Old Bailey, London's Central Criminal Court, is named for the street in which it stands, whose name in turn derives from the days when a medieval fort stood on the location which was just outside the City's walls.

☆

The Bailey Bridge invented by Sir Donald Bailey was first used in 1942–3. Made of uniform prefabricated girders, it was easy to transport and erect, yet strong enough to bear tanks or trains.

☆

The Baily Cup (1920 onwards) is the top prize in British Amateur Real Tennis doubles.

☆

Baily's beads, named for their discoverer Francis Baily (1774–1844), are seen during an eclipse of the sun. Just before total eclipse, the narrow crescent of the sun's rays is broken by the moon's mountains and valleys. Seen from the earth, this gives a bead-like effect.

☆

Since 'baile' means town in Gaelic, Ireland abounds in the name and in the corruption 'Bally', such as Ballycastle and Ballyshannon. Baile Atha Cliath (town at the ford of the hurdles) is Dublin's official Gaelic name.

145

The only town to bear a version of this surname in the United Kingdom is Bailleston. However, there are two Baileys in the United States and South Africa also has a town so named.

```
*********************************
*              BAKER            *
*********************************
```

Related Names
Other surnames which are related as to root, derivation or usage include:

Bachuss	Backus	Bullinger	Pistor
Backhouse	Bakker	Pestor	Pullinger
Backster	Baxter	Pillinger	

Like many other widespread English names, Baker is an occupational name, Brewer and Taylor being two other common examples. The name Baker derives from the Old English word 'baecere', for the man who worked in the 'baechus' (bakehouse).

Throughout history the baker has played an important part in community life. According to feudal law, peasants (or serfs) were allowed to grind corn only at their lord's mill. Likewise, they were allowed to bake only at their lord's oven. Thus the village oven became a vital part of the community, and its overseer was a personage of some importance. Soon the name 'baecere' acquired many variations. The fourteenth-century Midlands poet, Langland (author of *Piers Plowman*), mentions 'bakesteres' and 'brewesteres'. This form contains the female suffix – ester as in spinster (compare spinner), a more recognisable modern form. Later, this feminine form became standardised as Baxter or Backster – two names which remain widespread to this day.

Names related to the original 'baechus' include Backhouse, Bachuss and Backus. (Contrary to popular myth, these last two names have nothing whatsoever to do with the Greek god Bacchus or any nickname stemming from associated bibulous characteristics.)

Other names which are synonymous with Baker include Bullinger, Pullinger and Pillinger, from the Old French 'boulenger' which means 'baker', and Pistor and Pestor, Latin translations which were felt to have snob appeal.

As the centuries passed, the public baker became an integral part of medieval urban life. As with many other trades, bakers would often congregate on one street. This sometimes accounts for the occurrence in towns of street names like Baker Street and Baxter Street.

One of the first mentions of this name comes in the Norfolk Pipe Rolls of 1177, where one William le Bakere is listed. By the time of the Hundred Rolls of 1273, the name was being listed all over the country – from Walter le Baker in Devon to Alan le Baker in Sussex. This year also saw the first listing of the feminine form; in the Rolls for Norfolk one John le Bakestere is listed.

A Baker Miscellany

London's Baker Street is named after the manager of the Portmans' Marylebone Estates, William Baker. He leased fields for building.

☆

221B Baker Street was Sherlock Holmes's address, according to Sir Arthur Conan Doyle. The number doesn't actually exist but a building society which has the nearest real address receives thousands of letters sent to Holmes each year.

☆

London's Bakerloo Underground line is so named because originally it ran from Baker Street to Waterloo.

☆

'The Baker' was the derisory nickname given to Louis XVI after he and Marie Antoinette (known as 'the Baker's Wife' ever after, which wasn't long) dispensed bread to the rioting mobs at Versailles in 1789.

☆

Robert Baker was a seventeenth-century London tailor whose collar borders were called pickadillies, the origin of Piccadilly. The land he willed to his two sons, John and James, is also commemorated today as Upper and Lower John and James Streets.

☆

The 'Baker Flying' is a red flag used by the US Navy to warn those in the vicinity to stay well clear when a dangerous operation such as loading ammunition is under way.

☆

A Baker's Dozen is 13 rolls for the price of 12, as well as being a nickname for the 13th Hussars.

☆

The London livery company, the Worshipful Company of Bakers, dates from 1486.

☆

Bakers are geographically well represented. The UK has towns called Baker's End and Baker Street. No fewer than 8 US states have towns called Baker, and there are 3 Bakers-fields as well. The United States also oversees an uninhabitable South Pacific Baker Island which was once British. Canada, Australia and the United States have Baker Lakes, while Chile has a Baker Canal.

❋❋❋❋❋❋❋❋❋❋❋❋❋❋❋❋❋❋❋❋❋❋❋❋❋❋❋❋❋❋❋❋❋❋❋❋
❋   **BENNETT**   ❋
❋❋❋❋❋❋❋❋❋❋❋❋❋❋❋❋❋❋❋❋❋❋❋❋❋❋❋❋❋❋❋❋❋❋❋❋

Related Names
Other surnames which are related as to root, derivation or usage include:

Ben	Bennet	Bennitt	Benoit
Bence	Bennetts	Bennitts	Bense
Benedict	Bennie	Benns	Benson
Benét	Benniman	Benny	Benyson
Benn	Bennison		

The name Bennett comes from the first name Benedict. This name originates from the Latin word 'benedictus' which means 'blessed' – a popular Christian name in late Roman times. It was also the name of the fifth-century founder of the Benedictine Order. Since that time, no fewer than fifteen popes have taken the name Benedict.

With the decay of Latin, the popular name Benedict was adapted into many languages. In Italian it became Benedetto, in French Benoit. The French form came to England with the Norman Conquest, then gradually evolved to Bennett. In the process many variations arose, some of which remain in common use today. Bennetts, for instance, means 'dependant of Bennett'; Benson means 'son of Bennett', if it is not the alternative surname derived from the place in Oxfordshire. The surname Benn also derives from the old source (and, so far as we can tell, not from *Ben*jamin). The variation Bennett is usually found in the north of the country.

The records of Furness Abbey, which was run by the Benedictine Order, indicate a great number of baptisms with the names of Bennet and Benson. Indeed, these names (the two most popular forms) are found to be particularly prevalent in areas where the Benedictine monks flourished. Other variations found in Benedictine baptismal records include the names Bennison, Benns, Bence, Bense, Bennie and Benny.

The earliest reference to a Bennett is in the 1193 records for Oseney Abbey. Here the name appears as Beneit, which is a variation of the Old French form. The earliest Bensons appear in the 1326 Rolls of Wakefield Manor, where John Benneson and Adam Bensome are listed. A rare variation of the name appears in Shakespeare. In *Much Ado About Nothing* one of the characters is called Benedick.

Bennett remained for many years a popular first name, but it is now rare. Likewise, the *first* name Ben is nowadays usually short for Benjamin, rather than for Benedict. Thus Bennett curiously remains a popular surname which derives from an original first name now almost unused.

A Bennett Miscellany
Bennettitales is an alternative name for an extinct species of palm-like plants which constituted a major portion of the earth's vegetation during the middle Mezozoic period some 150 million years ago.

☆

Bennett's Fracture is a fracture of the base of the thumb, named in honour of Edward Hallaron Bennett, the eminent Irish physician who was an expert on breaks and dislocations.

☆

The geographical term 'ben' comes from the Gaelic word for peak (beann). Thus parts of Britain – especially Scotland and Ireland – abound in mountains incorporating the word: Ben Nevis, for instance, and Ben More.

☆

There are no United Kingdom towns incorporating the name Bennett. Australia and the United States have Bennett mountains while New Zealand has a Cape Bennett.

149

```
*********************************
*              BROWN            *
*********************************
```

Related Names

Other surnames which are related as to root, derivation or usage
include:

Broun	Browning	Brownson	Brunet
Broune	Brownjohn	Brownutt	Brunsen
Browne	Brownsmith	Bruin	Brunson
Brownett			

The name Brown is an old colour-name which is a form of
nickname. Colour-names usually referred to the complexion or
hair of the owner. There are several common names which
began life as colour-names. Thus the name Reed, Reid (or Read)
derives from the Old English word 'read' which means 'red'.
Similarly, Blake is thought in most cases to derive from the Old
English word 'blac' which means 'black'; and Blunt derives
from the Middle English word 'blund', meaning 'white' or
'fair-haired'.

The name Brown derives from the Old English word 'brun',
meaning 'brown', though in some cases it may derive from a
foreign version of the same word. The name Brown, in the form
Brun, was certainly prevalent throughout the country before the
Norman Conquest. However, a number of Bruns came across
the Channel with William the Conqueror so, in some cases, the
name Brown derives from the French root (the modern French
word for brown is 'brun').

In the 1066 records of the Domesday Book we find reference
to one Brun, and the Latinised form Brunus. These were personal names. However, by 1273 we find the surname form with
Hugh le Brun in Suffolk and Robert le Brun in Buckinghamshire.

Naturally enough, such a simple and widespread name soon
acquired many variations, several of which remain in use to this
day. Brownett and Brunet are diminutives of the Old French
Brun. Browning represents Old English Bruning from the Old
English Brun – in the same way as Dunning or Downing from
Dunn, 'the dark, swarthy or dun-coloured one'. Brownutt comes
from a medieval nickname describing its owner as 'brown as a
nut'. Brownsmith comes from the Old English 'brun' and

'smith', meaning 'a worker in copper or brass'. The names Brownson and Brunson simply mean 'son of Brown'. And Brownjohn derives from an old medieval nickname meaning 'John with the brown hair (or face)'.

For many years Brown has been Scotland's third most numerous surname – after Smith and McDonald. However, some Scottish Browns may derive their name from a different source from their English counterparts. In England the name usually comes from the Old English, or sometimes from the Old French, but in Scotland and parts of the north of England, the name may sometimes come from the Old Scandinavian 'Brúnn' – a subtle distinction, but it spreads the origins of the Browns from Norway to Brittany.

A Brown Miscellany
Brown vs Board of Education of Topeka, Kansas (1954) was a landmark decision of the United States Supreme Court which marked the beginning of the end of segregation. The Court ruled that 'separate but equal' educational facilities for people of different races were inherently unequal, and thus violated the US Constitution's 14th Amendment, which guarantees all citizens equal protection under the law.

☆

The cross-the-chest military fashion called the Sam Browne belt is named after General Sir Samuel Browne (1824–1901) who made it popular.

☆

Brownies have long been fairies in Scotland and Eire, while around the English-speaking world they are the descriptive term for the youngest group of Girl Guides. Their name derives from their uniform.

☆

Browns have been exceptionally inventive on both sides of the Atlantic. Inventions include all sorts of precision instruments (Joseph Rogers Brown – USA, 1810–76), armour plate (Sir John Brown – UK, 1816–96), hoisting and conveying machines (Alexander Ephraim Brown – USA, 1852–1911), the Browning submachine gun and numerous other firearms (John Moses Brown – USA, 1855–1926), and the gyroscopic compass and aeroplane speed indicator (Sydney George Brown – UK, 1873–1948).

☆

Brownian Motion, the common term for the rapid oscillating movement of particles suspended in liquid or gas which, when viewed through a microscope, is evidence of molecular motion, is named after the Scots-born botanist, Robert Brown (1773-1858).

☆

Browns have been notable warriors in exotic places. Admiral William Brown (1777–1857) led the Argentinian fleet to two famous victories over the Brazilians. George Browne served the Czars, was enslaved in Turkey, escaped with state secrets, commanded the Russian Armies during the Danish War and retired to become the much revered Governor of Livonia in the Baltic for over 30 years.

☆

As a colour-related name, towns and geographic features which contain the name Brown are frequent. The United Kingdom alone has 7 towns ranging from Brown Candover to Brownston while the United States has no fewer than 27 towns which contain the name. Australia has mountains called Browne and Brown, a peak named Brown Hills and a Brown Point.

****
*   **BYRNE**   *
****

Related Names
Other surnames which are related as to root, derivation or usage include:

Björn	Byrnes	MacBrannan	O'Boirne
Braniff	Byrns	MacBrinn	O'Brani
Brann	Byrom	O'Biorain	O'Broin
Brannan	Byron	O'Birn	O'Byrne
Byram	MacBrann		

The surname Byrne almost certainly has two derivations, while it has also spawned many variations.

The first derivation is from the Irish O'Birn. This means 'a descendant of Biorn', a name which came to Ireland with the Norse invaders. In Old Norse this name is written Björn, and it remains unchanged in modern Scandinavia, as in Björn Borg. Björn originally meant 'bear' and was probably a descriptive

152

nickname pertaining either to the appearance or to the fighting qualities of its holder.

The other derivation of Byrne is from the Irish O'Broin, which means 'a descendant of Bran'. In Old Irish 'bran' meant 'raven'. Thus originally this was probably a descriptive name or nickname, alluding either to the appearance or to some hoped-for quality of its holder. So, it is probable that many original Brans had very dark hair.

Through the centuries Byrne has been a major family name in East Leinster, and Byrnes have traditionally played a major role in resistance to English rule in Ireland.

Apart from the surname Byrne, there are many variations derived from the original Irish word 'bran'. These include such names as MacBrinn (son of Brinn) and MacBrann (found mostly in County Clare). Braniff and O'Brani derive from the Irish Brandinbh, which is made up of the Irish words 'bran' (raven) and 'dubh' (black). This name is found mainly in County Down. The name Brann occurs in East Ulster. Another variation is MacBrannan, or Brannan, which is distinct from the more common name Brennan, whose roots are entirely different.

In rare cases Byrne has a purely English derivation. Byrne and Byron are variants for the place names Byram (a township in the parish of Brotherton in Yorkshire) and Byrom (a small settlement near Winwick in Lancashire). This rare derivation of the name Byrne goes back many centuries, the first mention of it occurring in the Feet of Fines for Yorkshire (1240), where one Roger de Birum is listed. It is reported by Woulfe that Byram and Byron were sometimes used as English substitutes for Irish O'Byrne, etc, but most of the Byrams and Byrons are in fact derived from the Yorkshire and Lancashire place names.

A Byrne Miscellany

The colourful Irish adventurer Miles Byrne (1780–1862) had one of the most unusual military careers of the nineteenth century. After joining the unsuccessful Irish rising which was defeated at the Battle of Vinegar Hill, he fled into hiding in the Wicklow Mountains. Here he met the great Irish leader Robert Emmet, who sent him to Paris to raise support. Napoleon gave Byrne a commission, and he then served with distinction in several of Bonaparte's famous campaigns. Byrne was eventually made Chef de Bataillon and given the Legion of Honour.

Today a monument marks his tomb in Montmartre cemetery.

☆

Contrary to popular misconception, Scotland's national poet 'Rabbie' Burns (1759–86), author of 'Auld Lang Syne', is not a Byrne. His name comes from Burness. The emphasis in this name is on the first syllable and 'Rabbie's' family shortened it to Burns.

☆

The most celebrated of Romantic poets was Lord Byron (1788–1824). His long autobiographical poem, *Childe Harold's Pilgrimage*, brought him fame and fortune. His subsequent notorious behaviour led him to live in self-imposed exile, in Switzerland and in Italy, where he met Shelley and Keats, and where he wrote his great satiric epic, *Don Juan*. He finally died while on an expedition to Greece to fight against the Turks for Greek independence.

☆

Byrness in north-east England is the only town containing the word Byrne.

✳✳✳✳✳✳✳✳✳✳✳✳✳✳✳✳✳✳✳✳✳✳✳✳✳✳✳✳✳✳✳✳✳✳✳
✳　　　　　　　　　CAMPBELL　　　　　　　　✳
✳✳✳✳✳✳✳✳✳✳✳✳✳✳✳✳✳✳✳✳✳✳✳✳✳✳✳✳✳✳✳✳✳✳✳

Related Names
Other surnames which are related as to root, derivation or usage include:

Camble	Camel	Cammel

The Campbells are Scotland's largest clan, though historically speaking they remain under something of a cloud for their notorious part in the Glencoe Massacre of the MacDonalds.

The surname Campbell originated as a nickname. The word Campbell comes from the Scots Gaelic 'caimbeul', which means 'wry (or crooked) mouth'. This is much the same as the origin of the name Cameron, which comes from the Scots Gaelic for 'wry (or crooked) nose'. These nicknames almost certainly referred to an element of character rather than just appearance.

According to the tradition of the Clan Campbell, the Campbells were originally known as 'Clann Duibhne' or 'O'Duine' and were descended from one Diarmed O'Duine of Lochow.

Diarmed, in his turn, was said to be a direct descendant of the great Diarmed, 'the Fingalean hero who slew the wild boar'. Curiously, the father of this Diarmed was known as Fergus Cerr-beoil or Fergus the Wry-mouth, and it is just possible that the name Campbell originates from this. There is no Gaelic equivalent for the Clan Campbell, it still being referred to as Clann O'Duibhne, after Diarmed O'Duine.

Apart from these meagre facts, origins of the Clan Campbell are lost in mythology. The name appears in many ancient ballads and manuscripts, all of doubtful veracity. In one of these the Campbells are said to be descended from King Arthur, while another maintains that they are descended from Adam, no less.

The earliest mention of a Campbell comes in the Exchange Rolls for 1263, where one Gillespie Campbell is listed. However, even as late as 1447, we find in the manuscript *History of Craignish* a man called Duncan le Campbell, where the name is used as a mere nickname. (Here the 'le' is not French, but denotes that what follows is vernacular. Loosely translated, the word means 'known as'.)

Despite the vague origins of the name Campbell, there is one popular myth which can be dismissed. Contrary to the legend, the Campbells are not of French origin, and the word Campbell is not derived from the Norman French 'de campobello' meaning 'of the beautiful plain'. If this were the case, the earliest listings of the name Campbell would be preceded by a 'de', as in the origins of such Norman French names as Beauchamp (now usually Beecham) meaning 'beautiful field'. There is no mention of any 'de Campbell'.

Campbell has few variations. The only notable ones are Camble, Camel, and Cammel. The last two forms are also in some cases descended from nicknames. A 'Camel' would be a large strong fellow capable of carrying great weights for a long distance, as we see in Shakespeare, who refers to 'a Dray-man, a Porter, and a very Camell'. There is also an etymological oddity attached to the name Camel. In the north-east of Scotland a pig was often known as a 'sandy camel', and this name passed to Holland, where it became 'kumpel'.

A Campbell Miscellany

In the great age of world speed records, the Campbell family was the greatest of them all. Sir Malcolm Campbell (1885–1949) broke the world land-speed record nine times between

155

1924 and 1935, and later broke the water-speed record 3 times. His son Donald Campbell (1921–67) also broke both land and sea speed records several times and his tragic death while attempting a new water-speed record ended an era.

☆

The girl nicknamed 'Highland Mary', who inspired many of Robbie Burns' greatest love lyrics, was almost certainly one Mary Campbell. There are now several statues to 'Highland Mary' in the Burns country around Greenock and Dunoon.

☆

'The Campbells are coming' goes the famous refrain in the song – and one Campbell at least lived up to his name. One Robert Campbell, a fur trader, travelled over 3,000 miles from the Yukon to Montreal on snow shoes – an unparalleled feat. The Campbells can also sing. The queen of Britain's jazz singers, Cleo Laine (b.1928), the wife of bandleader Johnnie Dankworth, is in fact a Campbell. Her real name is Clementina Campbell.

☆

The United Kingdom has a Campbelltown, a Campbelton and a Campbeltown. No fewer than 5 American states have towns named Campbell; so do Australia, South Africa and New Guinea.

```
**********************************
*                 CARTER                 *
**********************************
```

CARTER

Related Names
Other surnames which are related as to root, derivation or usage include:

Carters   Cartier   Cartwright   Charter

The surname Carter was originally an occupational name, for a person who drove or made carts. ('Cart' is a diminutive from the same root as the word 'car', which originally meant 'convey-ance'.) In early times carts were virtually the only form of overland transport of both goods and people; thus many original carters would have been as vital to everyday life as modern-day drivers of anything from lorries to taxis.

The origins of the word 'carter' are various depending on the basic form of the word for a cart in the derivation – Latin 'carettum', 'carettarius'; Old French 'charette', 'carette', etc. A related word, 'craet', was in use in England well before the Norman Conquest and there was also an Old Norse equivalent, 'kartr'. From these could well come English Carter. After the Norman Conquest, a French version was introduced – the Old French 'charetier', which originally meant 'chariot-driver'. (The well-known French name Cartier derives from a similar source.) This last derivation is probably responsible for the variant surname Charter, though most of the original French forms have been absorbed without trace into plain Carter. Another widespread derivative of cart is Cartwright (see Wright), which means 'a maker of carts'.

The earliest reference to the name Carter appears in the Latinised form. In the 1177 Pipe Rolls for Cambridgeshire one Fulco Carettarius is listed.

The French form of Carter, Cartier, could be confused with another series of French surnames, Cartier, Carteret, etc. ultimately from 'quartier' ('a quarter' – a measure for land and goods). Also the name Charter could be confused with Charters, Charteris or Chatteris, derived from Chartres in France or Chatteris in Cambridgeshire.

A Carter Miscellany

Jewellers and gem merchants, Cartier, have, at one time or another, appraised the Topkapi collection, sold the Hope Diamond, the Romanov crown, a necklace given to Empress Marie-Louise by Napoleon, and the 69.4 carat pear-shaped Taylor–Burton diamond.

☆

Tutankhamen's fourteenth-century BC royal tomb was discovered by British archaeologist Howard Carter (1873–1939). Probably the world's pre-eminent archaeological find, its treasures attracted unprecedented crowds when exhibited in Britain and America.

☆

Jacques Cartier (1491–1557) was a famous French explorer who discovered Canada's St Lawrence River while looking for the fabled Northwest Passage to the Pacific. Believing he might have discovered it, he sailed down the river to the present site of Quebec, claiming the land for France as he went. As a result he might justifiably be identified as the source of Canada's separatist problems.

☆

The United Kingdom has towns called Carter's Clay and Carterton. This latter name is also a town in New Zealand, while Australia has a Carter Mountain.

****
* **CLARK** *
****

Related Names
Other surnames which are related as to root, derivation or usage include:

Clarke	Clarson	Clerk	Clerke
Clarkson			

Clark is an occupational name, coming from the Old English 'clerec' or 'clerc' and the Old French 'clerc', both of which originate from the Latin 'clericus'.

The earliest Clarks were often clerics, i.e. clergymen or others in religious orders. In the Middle Ages literacy was largely confined to those in the Church, so most writing and secretarial work (including recording deaths, births, taxes and wills) was done by clerics or clergy.

As literacy grew and names became hereditary, the surname came to mean a scribe or administrative assistant who could draw up required papers. Thus did both the professional name 'clerk' and the surname Clarke catch on and endure.

Besides the obvious Clarkson (and the related Clarson) save in minor spelling alterations there are few variations of the name. The 'er' version, as in Clerke, is the more original version of the name. The 'er' often changed to 'ar'. A modern example is the way we pronounce Berkshire, Hertfordshire and Derbyshire. This change was fairly common. Other examples: 'varmint' (from the original 'vermin') and 'varsity' (from university).

The earliest mention of the name Clark is found in the Domesday Book for Hampshire. Here the records for 1086 mention one Richard Clericus.

A Clark Miscellany
One of the most notorious royal mistresses of all time was Mary Anne Clarke (1776–1852). She became mistress to Frederick, Duke of York, George III's second son. Frederick was

Commander-in-Chief of the Army, and Mary Anne used her position to secure promotion for several friends, accepting large bribes for her services.

The 'Trumpet Voluntary' is often mistakenly attributed to Purcell. In fact, it was composed by Jeremiah Clarke (1674–1707).

The only man to have won all 25 Grand Prix in the World Motor Racing Championship is James (Jim) Clark (1936–68). This he accomplished in 1965, breaking Fangio's record of 24. Clark died tragically in an accident at the Hockenheim circuit in Germany.

During 1940 Colonel William Fredman and Harry Lawrence Clark managed to break the Japanese secret code. The code-breaker they created was nicknamed 'Magic' and it intercepted messages showing that the Japanese were planning to attack. Unfortunately, they were unable to discover the exact location of the attack – Pearl Harbor.

The first overland trip across the continent of North America set off in 1804 and was led by Captain Meriwether Lewis (1774–1809) and Lt William Clark (1770–1838), who acted as map-maker and artist.

Clarkston is the only United Kingdom town with this name. However, throughout the Commonwealth the name Clark and variations on it are common both as town names and as names of geographic features. Clark's Harbour in Nova Scotia and Clark's Town in Jamaica are two examples. Some 21 towns and cities in the US are Clark-related.

****
* **CONNOR** *
****

Related Names
Other surnames which are related as to root, derivation or usage include:

Connors   O'Connor

Connor (or O'Connor) is an Irish surname. It derives from the

Irish Gaelic 'Conchobhar'. Thus, O'Connor means 'the descendant of Conchobhar' (the descendant of 'high-will'). This refers to a quality in its possessor, just as the similar O'Connell refers to 'the descendant of Conale', or the descendant of 'high-powerful'.

Connor was the name of six entirely distinct leading families in Ireland and was found all over the country, though it was rare in Kerry.

Perhaps the most renowned of the six Connor families, or clans, originated in Connacht. This clan was called O'Connor or O'Connor Don. The last High King of Ireland came from this clan, which has many branches. Other O'Connor families include O'Connor Roe and O'Connor Sligo (from Sligo) and O'Connor Faly (from Offaly), as well as branches in Kerry and North Clare. All members of these branches can properly claim to be descended from kings.

The name Connor is sometimes confused with the completely English occupational name of Conner, which stems from the Old English word meaning 'inspector' or 'examiner'. Likewise, Connor (or O'Connor) has nothing to do with the similar but distinct Irish name of Connery (or O'Connery), which originated in Munster, mainly in and around Cork and Limerick.

A Connor Miscellany

At the 1906 Athens Olympics Irish Peter O'Connor won a gold medal for the Hop, Step and Jump. When the Union Jack was raised during the presentation of his medal, this so incensed O'Connor that, ignoring the ceremony in his honour, he descended the awards podium, climbed the flagpole and replaced the English flag with Ireland's own.

☆

Ireland's best known short-story writer of the twentieth century was Michael O'Donovan (1901–66), who wrote under the name of Frank O'Connor. Called by Yeats 'the Irish Chekhov', he is best remembered for his stories about life in his native Cork, notably the collection *Crab Apple Jelly* (1944).

☆

Rory O'Connor (1116–98), also known as Roderic, who was Turlough's son and the last High King of Ireland, failed to defeat the Anglo-Norman invasion which led to English rule. He retired to a monastery where he died.

Connor has few towns and geographic features named in its honour, but Australia does have a Mount Connor and a Connors Range.

****
*   **COOK**   *
****

Related Names
Other surnames which are related as to root, derivation or usage include:

Coke	Cookes	Cooks	Cuckson
Cooke	Cookman	Cookson	Cuxon

Cook is an occupation surname from the Old English word 'coc'. Originally a cook might have been anything from a cook as we know it to a cooked-meat seller or even the keeper of an eating-house.

There are many variations on this surname from the obvious Cookson (which gives us Cuckson and Cuxon) to Cookes, Coke, and the more popular Cooke. Many commentators consider the final 'e' in Cooke as snobbish and affected. However, this is the spelling which is found in the fourteenth century from *Piers Plowman*, which refers to 'Brewester, Batess, Bochers and Cookes'.

After the Norman Conquest a French variation appeared. This is Lequeux, which despite its exotic appearance means simply 'cook'. It comes from the Old French word 'queu', meaning a 'cook', a 'seller of cooked meats', or an 'eating-house keeper'. (The strikingly similar English word 'queue' does not, however, come from this source. It comes from the Old French word for a tail – le queue – which may have been the origin of Kew Gardens. Alternatively, the name Kew sometimes derives from a place name, a (now vanished) town near Boulogne.)

Naturally, this good old English name for a vital activity abounds in ancient records. The earliest mention of the name comes over a century before the Domesday Book, in an Anglo-Saxon will dating from approximately 950, where one Aelfsige Se Coc is mentioned.

A Cook Miscellany

The explorations of Captain James Cook have left the name Cook all over the Pacific Ocean. The two most notable geographical features named after this famous navigator are the Cook Islands in the South Pacific and Cook Strait, New Zealand. Many other places are named after members of his crew, or even the days on which they were discovered (Christmas Island, for instance).

☆

To be given a 'Cook's Tour' of somewhere is to be shown round it, usually by a guide, and comes from the first great travel firm, Thomas Cook & Co, started in 1841.

☆

The hat we today call a 'bowler' was introduced by one William Coke, a Norfolk huntsman, in 1850. Mr Coke asked his hatter, Mr Beaulieu of Nelson Square, London, to design him headgear more suitable than the then fashionable tall riding hat. The new hat became known as a bowler after the anglicisation of the designer's name, though at the beginning it was also often referred to as a 'Coke'.

☆

The United Kingdom has 10 Cook-related towns – these range from Cookbury to Cookstown. Predictably the Pacific Ocean and Australia are full of Cooks including Cook Island, Mount Cooke, the Cook District of Canberra and a major reef in New Caledonia.

```
***********************************
*              COOPER             *
***********************************
```

Related Names

Other surnames which are related as to root, derivation or usage include:

Cooperman	Copper	Cowper	Cupper
Coopper	Couper	Cupere	

The surname Cooper is an occupational name. It stems from the Middle English word 'coupere', meaning 'a maker or repairer of wooden casks, buckets or tubs'. The Middle English word derives from a Latin word, 'cuparius'.

In medieval times the occupation of cooper played a vital part in commercial and community life, for in those days all liquids were conveyed in tubs and barrels. The craft of coopering is still practised today to produce wooden barrels for real ale, whisky and port (and any other liquid to be 'matured in wood').

As to be expected of such a widespread profession, the name Cooper is relatively evenly distributed all over the country, with the unaccountable exception of parts of the North. For this reason, there are many spelling variations. These include Couper, Cowper and even Cupper. Another variation is Copper, though in some cases this means 'worker in copper' (as in the variation Coppersmith). Another variation of Cooper is spelt Coopper, though it is now rare.

The earliest mention of this name occurs in the Pipe Rolls for Surrey of 1176–7. Here one Robert (le) Cupere is mentioned. The Pipe Rolls for Norfolk of 1181–2 also mention two le Cuperes. The French 'le' is strictly Norman, becoming widespread in England after the Conquest. It was particularly prevalent in occupation names – thus Robert the Cooper, Charles the Baker, and so on.

A Cooper Miscellany

The Worshipful Company of Coopers in the City of London was founded in 1501. This Livery Company maintained the standards of the trade, also supervising apprenticeships. Originally it was a guild which consisted of makers of all kinds of wooden casks and buckets, as well as barrels.

☆

The Cooper was a famous British racing car. The first version was built in 1946 by John Cooper and his father, Charles. By 1955 the Cooper was a world-beater and, with Jack Brabham driving, won the Australian Grand Prix. From 1959 through the early 1960s the Cooper (now with a Coventry-Climax engine) dominated the Grand Prix field and won the World Championship.

☆

The surname has long dominated the world's stages and cinemas. Notable thespians include Dame Gladys Cooper (1888–1971), Gary Cooper (1901–61), Lady Diana Cooper (b.1892) and Jackie Cooper (b.1921).

☆

The United Kingdom has a Coopersdale Common and a town called Coopernook. The United States has 7 Cooper-related

163

towns including Cooperstown, well known in America for its Baseball Hall of Fame. New Zealand has a Cooper Island while Canada and Australia have Cooper mountains.

```
***********************************
*           DAVIS    DAVIES            *
***********************************
```

Related Names

Other surnames which are related as to root, derivation or usage include:

Dakins	Davideson	Davisson	Dawe
Davage	Davidge	Davitt	Dawes
Daves	Davidson	Davson	Daweson
Daveson	Davie	Davy	Dawkins
Davey	Davison	Davys	Daws
Daveys	Daviss	Daw	Dawson
David			

The surname Davis (or Davies) stems from the first name David, usually by way of the nickname Davy which was also the French popular form, much in use after the Norman Conquest. Davis means 'son of Davy' or, more formally, 'son of David'.

The first name David is found in the Bible and is of Hebrew origin. The original meaning of the name was 'darling', often used in lullabies or as a term of endearment to a child. Later, the word came to be used to mean 'friend'.

The popularity of the name David stems from Biblical times, largely as a result of the exploits of King David. Its popularity in the British Isles has been reinforced by the fact that the patron saint of Wales is St David, and two Scottish kings (in the eleventh and thirteenth centuries) bore the name. The Welsh patron saint was Archbishop of Menevia in the sixth century. His popularity accounts for the frequency of David as a Welsh first name, with its attendant nicknames Dai and Taffy. The latter is the colloquial name for a Welshman, used only by outsiders and generally with slightly derogatory connotations – as in the case of Paddy, or Limey, or Yank.

It is thus no surprise to find that the derivative surname Davies is common in Wales. (Traditionally, Davies is the Welsh version, Davis the English.) The name is found most frequently in South Wales, as well as among the farming communities. A recent survey showed that one in twenty Welsh farming families was named Davies.

Though Davies is the most popular form of 'David's son', there are other variations. The most obvious, Davidson, while widespread, is found most frequently in Scotland and the border counties. Other variations include Davison and Davidge. Related names include Davey, Davy and Davitt (usually found in Ireland). These last, strictly speaking, are variations on the original David, also a popular surname in South Wales.

Daw, Daws and Dawson are all medieval short forms of the name Davy which it is thought was then pronounced as though spelled Dawy; while Dawkins is an affectionate pet name for the first name David.

The first name David and the surname Davies (and related names) have been widespread in England from the twelfth century, and in Scotland and Wales since even earlier times. There are references to the first name David and the surname Davy in the twelfth-century records, but the first more recognisable references are to Richard Davi of Suffolk and William Davy of Oxford, both in the Hundred Rolls of 1273.

A Davis Miscellany

Those belonging to the family of Davis have the rare distinction of having a number of ingenious devices named in their honour: a double quadrant, Davis' Quadrant, invented by John Davis (Davys) (1550–1605); the Davy lamp, the first safe lamp for miners because it used gauze to separate the flame from potentially explosive gases, invented by Sir Humphry Davy (1778–1829); and the Davis Escape Apparatus, which lets submariners do just that, invented by Sir Robert Henry Davis (1870–1965).

☆

The Davis Cup is the International Lawn Tennis Challenge Trophy and is competed for annually by all tennis-playing countries (rather than by individuals). It was donated in 1900 by Dwight Davis (1879–1945) who won the US doubles championship three years running – in 1899, 1900 and 1901.

☆

There are no Davis-derived towns or cities in the United Kingdom and few elsewhere in the world. Canada has one town called Davis, so do 5 American states. There is a Davis Sea in the Antarctic and a Davis Island in Burma.

Related Names

Other surnames which are related as to root, derivation or usage include:

Daugherty	Doherty	Dougharty	O'Docherty
Docharty	Dorrit	Dougherty	O'Doherty
Dockerty	Dorrity		

Docherty (or O'Docherty) is a popular Irish name which comes from the Gaelic O'Dochartargh (the prefix 'O' means 'descendant of'). O'Dochartargh is derived from the Gaelic first name Dochartach, which was originally a nickname meaning variously 'stern', 'obstructive', or 'hurtful'.

As with virtually all names transliterated from the Gaelic – where the letters are often not equivalent in sound to the corresponding letters in English – there are many variations of Docherty. The most frequent are Dougharty, Dougherty, Doherty, Docharty and Daugherty. All originate mainly from Ulster and Donegal (part of the ancient Ulster, but not of the modern province so named, being now part of the Republic), and are still found there in profusion. The name also occurs, though rarely, on the Isle of Man.

Furthermore, the form Doherty (or O'Doherty) is corruptly derived from the name O'Doorty, a Tipperary name which derives from the Gaelic O'Dubhartargh. The root here is utterly different from Dochartach and its actual meaning remains obscure, apart from the prefix 'Dubh-' which means 'black'.

Dorrity is a corrupt variation of Doherty found in Oriel. Contrary to some opinions, the name Doggett is not related. It is an Old English name whose origins are obscure – possibly deriving from an Old English diminutive for dog.

A Docherty Miscellany

Two brothers, Reginald and Laurence Doherty, dominated English lawn tennis in the late 1800s and early 1900s. Reginald, known as 'Big Do', was All-England Singles Champion at Wimbledon from 1897 to 1900 and was followed, from 1902 to 1906, by Laurence ('Little Do'). They were also doubles champions from 1897 to 1905, while Laurence became American national champion in 1903, the year in which the brothers jointly wrote the sports classic, *On Lawn Tennis*. Between them, the pair won 19 championships in 10 years.

Dora Jean Dougherty, US aviation psychologist and pilot, set two world records in 1961 for women helicopter pilots. She flew a Bell 47G-3 helicopter to an altitude of 19,406 feet. Two days later she climbed back into her machine and made a 404-mile hop in only 4 hours 26 minutes, beating the existing record by nearly 60 miles. She also claimed a third record for the point-to-point speed of the flight. All world records for women helicopter pilots had previously been held by Russians.

The surname (and its variations) is uncommonly used as the name of towns and geographic features. There is a Dochart River in central Scotland and a small town in the United States (Georgia) called Dougherty Plain.

DOYLE

Related Names
Other surnames which are related as to root, derivation or usage include:

Doole	D'Oyley	Doylie	O'Doyle
Dougal	Doyley	MacDowell	

There are two entirely separate Doyles, that which occurs more frequently being of Irish origin. Here Doyle (or O'Doyle) stems from the Irish Gaelic O'Dubhgail, which in turn comes from the first name Dubhgail. In Irish Gaelic 'Dubh' means 'black' and 'gail' means 'foreigner'. Thus Dubhgail should originally have been the name given to any dark foreigner. However, with a typically Irish twist, Dubhgail, 'dark stranger', was the name which the Irish chose to give to their blond Scandinavian invaders during Viking times. Thus many Irish Doyles were originally Vikings, of Norse origin.

The Vikings aside, this name was well established in Ireland long before the Anglo-Norman invasion. Three other well-known Irish names stem from the same non-Nordic root as Doyle. These are Dougal, Doole and MacDowell.

Doyle, Dougal, Doole and MacDowell all originate from the Gaelic word Dubhgail, yet their occurrences and history appear to be quite distinct. Doyle is one of the most popular names in Leinster, whereas Dougal is found in both Scotland and Ireland. MacDowell, on the other hand, is the Irish form of a Scottish family name which originates in the Hebrides. The MacDowells probably came to Ireland as servants of the Norse settlers. The name MacDowell is now wide-spread in Ulster, but in large part this is due to immigration from Scotland since Cromwellian times. These MacDowells were originally Scottish, though the origin of the name is the same.

The English name is quite distinct from the Irish name and its Celtic variations. This Doyle is a place name, stemming from the Old French de Oilgi or de Ouilli, and came to England with William the Conqueror. The variation Doyley clearly indicates the French connection. There are no fewer than five villages called Ouilly in the Calvados region of Normandy (the place name means 'Olius's place' and contains a late Latin personal name). The English Doyles are thought to have originated from the village of Ouilli-le-Bassett in the canton of Falaise.

Several Doyle, D'Oyley variations appear in the Domesday Book for 1086. These range from de Oilgi to de Olgi and even de Oilleio.

A Doyle Miscellany

The doily takes its name from a seventeenth-century shopkeeper in the Strand by the name of Doyle. He sold a popular light woollen fabric much favoured for summer wear which, by the eighteenth century, had moved to the table.

☆

America has had a number of notable criminal Doyles, including Little Patsy Doyle, vicious leader of New York's nineteenth-century Hudson Dusters Club; Jess Doyle, a member of the notorious Ma Barker gang of bank robbers and kidnappers whose criminal forays, executed with military precision, netted over £1.5 million; and Dorsey Doyle, a kingpin in the Whyos Gang, whose members didn't exactly enjoy good health: over a hundred murders took place in their club house.

☆

Sir Arthur Conan Doyle's Sherlock Holmes is perhaps the most enduring detective in all of fiction. Part of that fame, however, is built on sand: in none of the stories does Holmes say, 'Elementary, my dear Watson'.

☆

Famed caricaturist Richard Doyle (1824–83) designed *Punch*'s original cover, which remained unchanged until the 1950s.

☆

Just 5 towns in the world bear this name. New Zealand has a Doyleston while the United States has 2 Doyles, a Doylestown and a Doylesville. No significant geographic feature relates to Doyle.

✳✳✳✳✳✳✳✳✳✳✳✳✳✳✳✳✳✳✳✳✳✳✳✳✳✳✳✳✳✳✳✳✳✳
✳   EDWARDS   ✳
✳✳✳✳✳✳✳✳✳✳✳✳✳✳✳✳✳✳✳✳✳✳✳✳✳✳✳✳✳✳✳✳✳✳

Related Names
Other surnames which are related as to root, derivation or usage include:

Beddard	Edkins	Edwardes	Edwardson
Bedward	Edward		

The name Edwards means 'dependant of Edward', as in the rarer, more specific form Edwardson. The surname and the modern first name both derive from the Old English name Eadweard, which means 'guardian of prosperity or happiness'. This name is closely related to, but quite distinct from, those other Old English names Edwin (meaning 'prosperity-friend' or 'rich friend') and Edmund (meaning 'prosperity-protector').

The first name Edward was popular in England long before the Norman Conquest, and has remained so ever since. No fewer than eight Kings of England since the Norman Conquest have been called Edward (equalled only by the Henrys). Prior to the Conquest, Edward was the name of several other English kings. Alfred the Great was succeeded by his son Edward (899–925), Edward the Martyr reigned from 975 to 979, and the last Saxon king before the unfortunate Harold was Edward the Confessor (1042–66). This last Edward also became a saint, and as such became patron saint of England until the adoption of the foreign St George.

Edward is one of the few purely English first names to have spread to the Continent, where it retains a certain popularity to this day. (Here it is usually adapted slightly, as in the French Edouard, the Scandinavian Edvard, and the Spanish Eduardo.) Edward has several popular English variations as well. Some of these have become permanently associated with other fields. Ned has been a widespread variant of Edward since the fourteenth century, and Neddy is now the popular name for a donkey. Ted and Teddy are also well known. Ed and Eddie are more modern variants, sometimes deriving from Edmund or Edwin, though the surname Eddy is quite distinct from the surname Edwards. It derives from the Old English Eadwig meaning 'prosperity war'. Bedward and Beddard are Welsh variants from 'ab Edward', 'son of Edward'.

There are numerous references to Edwards in the 1066 Domesday Book – in the form of Eaduuardus, Aeduuardus, Eduuard(us). (These variations show that the letter 'w' in Edward literally originated as a 'double u' – neatly illuminating the origins of that letter.) However, by 1219 we can see the name used in its present spelling – when one William Edward appears in the Curia Regis Rolls for Suffolk.

An Edwards Miscellany
The most Noble Order of the Garter was founded by Edward III in 1348. Members of the Order have included the Duke of Wellington and Winston Churchill.

☆

The American clergyman Jonathan Edwards (1703–58) was renowned for his gift as a preacher. Unfortunately, such was the powerful effect of his oratory, that when he led a religious revival in 1734 he drove many of his converts to suicide. After this, he became president of the college which later became Princeton University.

☆

The United Kingdom has one related-name town, Edwardstone, while Australia has an Edwardstown and New Zealand an Edwardson. The United States has 7 Edwards-related towns.

170

Related Names

Other surnames which are related as to root, derivation or usage include:

Beavan	Bevens	Evanston	Heavens
Beavon	Evan	Evens	Hevens
Beevens	Evance	Evins	Jones *(see*
Bevan	Evanson	Heaven	*also)*
Bevans			

The surname Evans derives from the first name Evan, or Ewan. The suffix '-s' means 'dependant of'; so Evans means 'son or dependant of Evan'. Evan, or Ewan, is the Welsh name for John and was originally Ioan, which is now more common in Wales in the form of Iean (pronounced Yian, to rhyme with 'iron'). Ewan is now more common as a Scots first name, deriving from the original John by way of Scots Gaelic.

It is also possible that some examples of the widespread and historic Welsh name Owen could be derived from variants of this source (it usually represents a quite separate tradition). Indisputably certain is the fact that the Welsh name Jones (i.e. 'son of John – Johnson – Jones') is equivalent to Evans. Thus two of the most common Welsh names, Jones and Evans, originate from the name John.

The first name John originates from the Hebrew Jochanaan, which means 'God is gracious'. The Latin form of this name was Johannes, and in this form it was brought back to Central Europe by the Crusaders. Here it became popular in many countries, each forming their own variation. Thus John is Johan or Hans in Germany, and Jean in France. The name was largely popular because of its Biblical use – with John the Baptist, and St John the Divine, author of the Book of Revelations.

In rare instances the surname Evan(s) represents a substitute for Owen(s) derived from the Latin first name Eugenius (now found in the form Eugene). Eugenius originally meant 'high-born'.

There are many variations of the surname Evans – the most common being Evens, Evins, Heaven, Heavens, Evance and Evanson.

The earliest references in the records to the name Evans came in the 1568 Subsidy Rolls. Here the Rolls for Suffolk list one John Evans. This reference is late compared with most other popular names, because the name Evans only evolved as such about the year 1500.

An Evans Miscellany
The Welsh archaeologist, Sir Arthur Evans (1851–1941), is famed for his excavations at Knossos on Crete which uncovered the Minoan civilisation. This provided the vital missing link between Ancient Egypt and the rise of Ancient Greece.

☆

The Evans Cup is the name of the Major Public Schools squash competition.

☆

There are towns called Evanton and Evans Mead in the United Kingdom. Australia and New Zealand have Evansdales while Canada has an Evansburg and an Evansville. This latter town name is common in the United States where there are 6 out of a total of 13 Evans-related towns and cities. Bermuda and New Zealand have Evans Bays.

✳✳✳✳✳✳✳✳✳✳✳✳✳✳✳✳✳✳✳✳✳✳✳✳✳✳✳✳✳✳✳✳✳
✳   **GALLAGHER**   ✳
✳✳✳✳✳✳✳✳✳✳✳✳✳✳✳✳✳✳✳✳✳✳✳✳✳✳✳✳✳✳✳✳✳

Related Names
Other surnames which are related as to root, derivation or usage include:

Galbraith	Gallaher	Galsworthy	Gaw
Gall	Galle	Gaul	O'Gallagher
Gallacher			

The surname Gallagher is of Irish origin. The Irish Gaelic form of Gallagher (or O'Gallagher) is O'Gallichobhair, and derives from the Gaelic word 'gallchobhar', which means 'foreign help'. This has a similar root to the Scots name Galbraith, which comes from the Scots Gaelic meaning 'foreign Briton' (which usually refers to early Welsh settlers in Scotland), and to the English name Gall (or Gaul) which is of Breton Gaelic origin and means simply 'foreigner'.

    The name Gallagher came mainly from Donegal and the

eastern Ulster borderlands, where it was often one of the main family clans.

The name is highly popular in Ireland and is also amongst the top sixty names in Scotland. The Scottish popularity is due entirely to Irish immigration and does not stem from any native Gaelic derivation.

The name has been popular and widespread in Ireland since the fifteenth century. However, there are no references to this name in any early English records or rolls. The presumed reason for this is because the name did not appear in England in large numbers, or with its holder having sufficient status, until the major immigrations during the nineteenth century.

Because Gaelic and English do not run parallel in a strictly literal sense, the transliteration of the original O'Gallichobhair into English has resulted in a wide variety of different spellings. This is frequently the case with Gaelic names, though the twenty-three variants of Gallagher would seem to be exceptional. The main variations in the anglicised Gallagher are Gallacher and Gallaher, though some variations begin with 'Gol-'.

A Gallagher Miscellany

Saint Gall (c.550–645) and twelve disciples established a monastery at the source of the Steinach from which the famous monastery, present Swiss town and canton all take their names.

☆

'Gallagher's Frolics' is a traditional Irish jig.

☆

The cooperative retail movement in Ireland was founded by one Patrick Gallagher (1873–1964).

☆

There are no towns, cities or major geographic features which are Gallagher-related.

✳✳✳✳✳✳✳✳✳✳✳✳✳✳✳✳✳✳✳✳✳✳✳✳✳✳✳✳✳✳✳✳✳
✳   **GREEN**   ✳
✳✳✳✳✳✳✳✳✳✳✳✳✳✳✳✳✳✳✳✳✳✳✳✳✳✳✳✳✳✳✳✳✳

Related Names

Other surnames which are related as to root, derivation or usage include:

Greenacre   Greenall   Greenaway   Greenbank

Greenberry	Greenham	Greenlees	Greenwood
Greenburgh	Greenhead	Greenley	Grene
Greenbury	Greenhill	Greenman	Grenfell
Greene	Greenhoff	Greenough	Grenville
Greener	Greenhouse	Greenshields	Grindlay
Greenfield	Greenhow	Greenslade	Grindley
Greenford	Greenhowe	Greensmith	Grinham
Greengrass	Greenidge	Greensted	Grinley
Greenhalf	Greening	Greenstreet	Grinnell
Greenhalgh	Greenist	Greenway	Grinstead
Greenhall	Greenleaf	Greenwell	Grinsted

The name Green stems from the Old English word 'grene', which means village green. Originally this was part of the common land where the villagers all had certain free grazing rights. Green is one of the oldest names in England, for obvious reasons in a country which was once such a 'green and pleasant land'. In this short form the name meant 'one who lives near the village green'.

There is, however, another derivation of Green. Since very early times the word green has meant young, fresh, immature or callow. Often a villager would be called 'green' because of something he had done in his youth; the nickname would stick and in time it would become the family name. Despite this, Green has long been a popular English name. In 1853 Green was the seventeenth most popular name in England. Now it has crept up to sixteenth.

Some of today's Greens (or Greenes or Grenes) are shortened versions of 'attegreen' – at the green. The word green enters into many place names which have given rise to surnames, and these each have their own different meanings, many not so obvious as they would appear.

Most Greenfields, for instance, derive not from 'green fields', but from Grenville, a place name in France and the name of several Anglo-Norman families. Many Jews who fled from the pogroms of Eastern Europe during the final decades of the nineteenth century decided to take English names when they reached the safety of these shores. Some simply chose any English name which took their fancy. Others adopted the name of the place where they had landed in England; there are, for instance, several Jewish families called Hastings. (As Michael Hastings, the Jewish writer, remarked, he was lucky his family didn't arrive at Dungeness or Wapping.) Other Jews anglicised their original names so that, for example, German-Jewish Grunwalds might become Greenwoods.

Some Greenfields derive from an earlier anglicisation. Several of William the Conqueror's men who crossed to fight at the Battle of Hastings came from the tiny Normandy village of Grainville-la-Teinturiere (which is now in the Seine-Maritime department). When they settled in England their name was quickly corrupted to Grenville (or even Grenfell), and later became Greenfield. These, and other, apparently far-fetched changes are easier to understand when you realise that in those times there was no standardised spelling in English. People even spelt their own name in several different ways. As late as the sixteenth century we find as many as thirteen different variations in the spelling of the name Shakespeare, many deriving from Shakespeare's own casual usage.

Another related surname is Greenford. This literally means 'ford at a green', but where the name is concerned it derives from a particular place, the small town just west of London in Middlesex. Greenhalgh, another common name, means 'green place' (especially the Lancashire examples), and Greenacre means 'green field' (not necessarily a strict acre). This latter name is thought to have originated from Norfolk.

Greenham sometimes meant 'green river meadow', while this name also originates from the places of the same name in Berkshire and Somerset, though the Greenham in Somerset may be a corruption of 'grind', describing a millstream. Greenhowe and Greenhoff mean 'green mount or hill' and mainly originated (with many variations of spelling) in north and west Yorkshire.

Greensmiths, on the other hand, were originally coppersmiths. The reason they were called 'green' was because the flames of their fires would turn green as they worked their copper, or, according to some, because copper acquires a green patina as it is worked.

The earliest Green in the records is Geoffrey de Grene, who appears in the 1188 Pipe Rolls for Kent.

A Green Miscellany
A Green was making aviation history before the Wright brothers were born. Balloonist extraordinary Charles Green (1793–1841) astonished the world by flying from Vauxhall Gardens,

London, to Weilberg, Germany (480 miles), in just under 18 hours (1836). In all, he made 527 ascents, including one which exceeded 27,000 feet in height.

☆

The popular English melody 'Greensleeves' is of Elizabethan origin (published 1581) and is mentioned in Shakespeare. It was initially described as 'a new courtly sonnet of the Lady Greensleeves'.

☆

George Green (1793–1841) is widely regarded as the father of modern physics in Great Britain. He was the first to attempt to apply mathematical formulae to electricity and magnetism. 'Green's Theorem' is named after his work.

☆

Baron William Wyndham Grenville (1759–1834), as Prime Minister, abolished Britain's overseas slave trade on his last day in office.

☆

A man bearing a Green-related surname caused the American Revolution: politician George Grenville (1712–70) initiated the tax acts which caused the colonies to revolt.

☆

The 'Green Man' is now a common name for a pub. The origins of the name go back to pre-Christian times and are thought to be connected with fertility cults. The image of the Green Man is found on some thirteenth- to fifteenth-century churches in connection with the Easter resurrection.

☆

David Green (1886–1973) is better known by his pseudonym, David Ben-Gurion, Israeli statesman and first Premier of his country.

☆

One Edward W. Green committed the first bank robbery in American history, in 1863. He was caught within 24 hours.

☆

Richard Grenville (1542–91) is one of Britain's greatest naval heroes. Separated from his own fleet, his ship *The Revenge* took on 15 Spanish men-of-war and fought them for over 12 hours. Finally Grenville was captured and died of his wounds. His exploit is celebrated in Tennyson's poem 'The Revenge' and in Charles Kingsley's novel *Westward Ho!*

☆

A total of 109 towns and cities contain the word green. The United Kingdom alone accounts for 42 of these, ranging from Green Bank to Greenthorpe. This includes no fewer than 5 Greenfields. The United States has 9 towns and cities with this latter name, as well as 6 Greensboros and 5 Greensburgs.

Given its descriptive nature, countless rivers, lakes, mountains and islands bear the name; so does a country – Greenland.

✳✳✳✳✳✳✳✳✳✳✳✳✳✳✳✳✳✳✳✳✳✳✳✳✳✳✳✳✳✳✳✳
✳ **GRIFFITHS** ✳
✳✳✳✳✳✳✳✳✳✳✳✳✳✳✳✳✳✳✳✳✳✳✳✳✳✳✳✳✳✳✳✳

Related Names
Other surnames which are related as to root, derivation or usage include:

Griffen   Griffin   Griffis   Griffith

The surname Griffith (whence Griffiths) derives from the Old Welsh Griphiud. The suffix '-iud' means 'lord', though the meaning of the stem remains debatable. One plausible explanation is that it derives from the common Latin appellation Rufus, which means 'red-haired', though there is no proof as to this root.

Griffin is a pet-name form of Griffith which is popular in Wales; this was the name given to many early Welsh princes. Griffin is also the name given to a Welsh heraldic dragon seen on the Welsh national flag, as well as on many Welsh pub signs. The pub-sign griffin is normally green, though on the flag it is red on a half-green, half-white horizontal background.

However, the name Griffin is not always Welsh (whereas the name Griffith is). It originates from two distinct areas – the Welsh border country and the eastern counties of England. The eastern Griffins are of Breton origin, coming to England after the Battle of Hastings.

The earliest reference to the name Griffin is in the Calendarium Genealogicum during the reign of Edward I, where one Tuder fil Griffini is mentioned. (The 'fil' is short for the Latin filius, meaning 'son of', the consequent name being Latinised from the doubtless spoken form of Griffin to Griffinus.)

The earliest reference to the name Griffiths is found in the Wills at Chester for the year 1585. Here one John Ap-Griffith is recorded. ('Ap' or 'ab' is Welsh for 'son of' – as in John ab Evan, which became corrupted to the name Bevan.) The root name Griffith gave rise to the variants Griffiths and Griffis. Both of these mean 'dependant of Griffith', the suffix '-s' meaning 'dependant of' or 'son of' (compare the name Bennett, which gives Bennettson and Bennetts).

A Griffiths Miscellany

In Elizabethan times Sir Henry Griffith's daughter, Ann, devoted all her love and energies to their Yorkshire mansion, Burton Agnes Hall. One evening, while returning from a visit, she was set upon by robbers and savagely beaten. Before she died she begged her family to let her head remain within the walls of her beloved house. She threatened to make the house unliveable if they failed to honour her wish, and promptly proceeded to do so when the family, believing her injuries had deranged her mind, buried her in the family vault. Moans, loud crashing noises and the sound of slammed doors filled the house and strange personal disasters befell the inhabitants until the skull was disinterred and brought inside. Today it is firmly ensconced behind a massive screen in the central hall.

☆

In March 1925, one of America's most violent tornados hit Griffin, Indiana. It destroyed 196 out of the 200 buildings in the town and left 50 dead in its wake.

☆

The first of the great clipper ships such as the *Cutty Sark* was the *Rainbow*, designed by the American naval architect, John Willis Griffiths (1809–82).

☆

D.W. Griffith (1874–1948) is regarded by many as the father of the film industry. In search of sun he moved his studio to a sleepy town called Hollywood.

☆

This name is relatively rarely incorporated in towns and geographic features. In the United Kingdom there are towns called Griff and Griffithstown, the United States has a Griffithville and a Griffin while Australia has a Griffith, which is also the name of a Canadian island.

Related Names

Other surnames which are related as to root, derivation or usage include:

Alstead	Hallé	Halline	Halman
Hailey	Haller	Hallman	Halsted
Hallam	Halley	Halls	Halston
Halle	Hallfield	Hallstead	Halstone

The surname Hall is a local name from the Old English Hall or Heall, meaning 'a hall or large house'. The name Hall was originally given to someone who lived in or by (or was employed at) the hall or manor. Field, Castle and Stone are other common examples of local names of this type.

However, not all Halls derive from this source. This name frequently occurs in the north-east of England, and it seems that here the name Hall is a local name deriving from the Old Norse for a 'boulder or slope' and was given to someone who lived on, near, or under some prominent boulder or hillside. (As such, it would mean much the same as the name Stone.)

A variation of this latter derivation is the name Hallam, which is found mainly in nearby West Yorkshire. Here, Hallam is a local name deriving from the Old Norse for 'at the stone or slope'. However, in some cases the name Hallam was given to a native of Hallam in the old parish of Sheffield.

The surname Hall goes back to early feudal times. One Warin de Halla is mentioned in the 1178 Pipe Rolls for Essex, and two examples of the name appear in the Hundred Rolls of 1273. Here one Roger de la Halle is recorded in the Cambridgeshire records, while a Walter de la Halle appears in the records for Salop. (The Norman French 'de la' would suggest that in these cases they were probably employed at the hall or manor.)

A Hall Miscellany

Halley's Comet, named for Edmond Halley (1656–1742) and first observed by him in 1682, is probably the brightest and most spectacular known to us. Its brilliant passage across the heavens has long been thought to presage great historical events. It was seen in 1066 at the time of the Norman Conquest

☆

Big Ben, actually the name of the bell, not the clock, was named either after the rotund parliamentarian Sir Benjamin Hall (1802–67), who was Minister of Works when the bell was cast for St Stephen's Tower, or after a famous prize-fighter of the time.

☆

Aluminium was made practicable by the invention of the electrolysis process by the American chemist, Charles Martin Hall (1863–1914).

☆

The United Kingdom has 21 Hall-related towns and cities. These range from Halland to Hall Thwaites. Canada has 4 towns with Hall-related names while the United States has 14. Related town names are prevalent throughout Europe, there being 32 in all. These range from Austria's Hall to Denmark's Hallundback. Hall is unusually common as a geographic name ranging from the United Kingdom's Halley Bay to Hall Table Mountain in Mozambique.

HARRIS   HARRISON

Related Names
Other surnames which are related as to root, derivation or usage include:

Harison	Harriott	Henderson	Heriot
Harrey	Harriss	Hendry	Herriot
Harrie	Harrisson	Henrieson	Herry
Harries	Harry	Henry	Herryson
Harriot			

The name Harris is an English derivative of the colloquial pronunciations of the name Henry (Herry and Harry). All the English kings we now call Henry were known in their time as King Harry. The first King Henry (or Harry) was the first Norman king to be born on English soil. This fact encouraged his popularity, and in turn made the name itself popular. Between the eleventh and sixteenth centuries there were eight English kings so named – a number equalled only by the

180

Edwards. Amongst these were three of England's greatest kings: King Henry V who won the Battle of Agincourt and is now immortalised in Shakespeare's play; King Henry VIII with his six wives and decisive ways with matrimonial disputes; and the less spectacular Henry VII whose long and prosperous reign laid the foundations for the glories of Henry VIII and then the Elizabethan age. Before Henry I there were just five Henrys listed as tenants in the Domesday Book, but after his reign the name quickly grew in popularity, becoming amongst the dozen most popular English first names.

The origins of the name Henry go back to Old German. Here the name Heimirick first appeared. This was a compound of the word, 'haimi', meaning 'house' or 'home', and 'ric', meaning 'ruler'. With the coming of the Romans, the name Haimiric became Latinised to Henricus. Post-Roman migration spread the name which evolved into Italian, French, Spanish, and so on. Thus there are now forms of the name Henry in almost all European languages. In German it is Heinrich, Heinz or Heine. It is Hendrik in Dutch, Henri in French, Enrico in Italian and Enrique in Spanish.

In England the name Harris spawned a further set of names. The best known of these are Harrison, Henderson and Hendry. The rarer name Harrissmith is not derived from Harris, but is almost certainly a corruption of Arrowsmith, a maker of arrowheads.

Of the many surnames derived from the original Henry (or Harry), Harris and Harrison are by far the most popular, both names appearing all over England and Wales. However, each has its prevalent areas. In the south of England, below a line drawn between Lincoln and Chester, you are more likely to come across the name Harris. It is most frequent in Gwent and South Wales as well as in the South Midlands, especially Worcestershire, Warwickshire, Oxford and Northampton. It is also fairly popular down in Devon and Cornwall. Inexplicably, it is less frequent in the eastern part of England.

Harrisons, on the other hand, are mostly found in the north, appearing most frequently in Cumbria, Lancashire and Yorkshire. Recent evidence seems to suggest that the Harrisons are on the march south and large numbers have been noted in Derbyshire and Nottinghamshire, with concentrated outposts as far south as the English Channel coast. Indeed, if present trends continue in the war between Harris and Harrison, the outcome is inevitable: Harrison domination throughout the land.

Harris was also a very popular name with the Jews who fled to England in the last decades of the nineteenth century to escape Russian and Polish pogroms. Their Eastern European names were often unpronounceable to the English and made their owners feel socially conspicuous. Consequently, they often adopted solid English names; many chose Harris.

A great many of these immigrants were in the garment trade, but the famous Scottish Harris tweed has nothing to do with either the Jewish Harrises or the English ones. This tweed cloth is named after the Hebridean Island of Harris where the cloth is woven.

One of the earliest references to the name is to one John Herryson mentioned in a charter dating from 1376.

A Harris Miscellany

The Harrison Cup is one of the main events in the polo calendar and takes place at Cowdray Park each July.

☆

There have been two Presidents of the United States called Harrison (the 9th and the 23rd), a distinction shared only by the Johnsons and the Roosevelts.

☆

The Harris Movement takes its name from the founding prophet, William Wade Harris (1858–1929). It is the largest mass movement for conversion to Christianity in West Africa, while another major movement is also Harris-connected. Chicago lawyer Paul Harris (1868–1947) founded the worldwide Rotary Club in 1905.

☆

The first true English encyclopaedia, the *Dictionary of Arts and Sciences* (1704), was edited by John Harris (c. 1666–1719).

☆

Britain's most successful arsonist, Leopold Harris (b.1894) caused the Great Arson Scandal of 1933 which revealed that insurance-company employees and members of the Fire Brigade had helped to defraud the insurers of hundreds of thousands of pounds annually for years.

☆

The entertainment world abounds with stars with the surname: Kathleen Harrison (b. 1898), Julie Harris (b. 1925), Rosemary

182

Harris (b. 1930), Phil Harris (b. 1906), Rex Harrison (b. 1908), Richard Harris (b. 1932) and Rolf Harris (b. 1930).

☆

The United Kingdom has towns named Harris and Harrishead. There are also Harristowns in Canada and the US which has 2 out of a total of 23 Harris-related cities and towns. Mountains, lakes, rivers and islands around the world bear the name as does a forest in the United Kingdom.

✳✳✳✳✳✳✳✳✳✳✳✳✳✳✳✳✳✳✳✳✳✳✳✳✳✳✳✳✳✳✳✳
✳   **HILL**   ✳
✳✳✳✳✳✳✳✳✳✳✳✳✳✳✳✳✳✳✳✳✳✳✳✳✳✳✳✳✳✳✳✳

Related Names
Other surnames which are related as to root, derivation or usage include:

Greenhill	Hille	Hillings	Hills
Hellman	Hillers	Hillis	Hilman
Hilhouse	Hillhouse	Hillman	Hilton
Hillas	Hilling		

The surname Hill is a local name derived from what is believed to be the Old English word 'hyll'. The name originally meant 'he who dwells at, by, or on the hill'. The reasons for its popularity are self-evident, in much the same way as other local names from medieval village life – such as Green, Hall and Ford.

There are, however, two other rare derivations of Hill. In one case it is a pet name derived from the first names of German origin beginning with Hild- (as in Hildegard), where the prefix 'Hild-' means 'battle'. In very rare cases Hill is an abbreviation of the first name Hilary, which came from the Latin and means 'cheerful'. (We get the word 'hilarious' from the same root.) In former times, Hilary was more popular as a male first name.

The name Hill is mentioned in records as far back as the 1191 Pipe Rolls for Norfolk, where one Gilbert del Hill is mentioned. 'Del' here is not Spanish or Italian, but a corruption of the Norman French 'de la', meaning 'of the', as in Walter de la Hille whose name occurs in the 1273 Hundred Rolls.

As usual, there are a number of variations on this simple local name. Hillhouse (which corrupts to Hillis and Hillers and Hillas) means 'dweller at the house on the hill'. Hilling seems to represent an Old English word 'hylling', 'hilldweller', though Hillman can derive from two sources. It can either mean the obvious 'dweller by the slope', or it can mean 'servant of Hild' (who would originally have been 'Hild's man'). The widespread Hellman is also a corruption of this last name.

Several other names which seem to contain Hill are not derived from it. The most widespread of these are Hilliar (a form of Helliar, an occupational name, which derives from the Old English for a slater or tiler), and Hilliard (a form of Hildyard, from the Old German personal name Hildigard).

A Hill Miscellany
The green belts which surround most major British cities are the direct descendants of the 'open spaces' created by pioneering social and housing reformer, Octavia Hill (1838–1912), who was convinced that escape from overcrowding reduced crime and poverty.

☆

Hills have been notable Grand Prix drivers. Phil Hill (b. 1927) was the first American to win the World Championship (1961). Graham Hill (1929–75), who took the Indianapolis 500 in his first attempt (1961), won Le Mans in 1962 as well as the Grand Prix Championship; he won the latter again in 1968. Shortly after retiring he died in a plane crash. His son, Damon, later followed him onto the motor racing circuit.

☆

Sir Rowland Hill (1795–1879) reorganised the postal system and introduced the penny post (1840), the precursor of all modern postal systems. His first stamp, the famous 'Penny Black' with its 'bun' outline of Queen Victoria's head, is now a collectors' item. These stamps established a precedent still in force: Britain's name never appears on her stamps. Later, as Chairman of the London and Brighton Railway, Sir Rowland pioneered both express train service and special excursion fares.

☆

Henry Hill (1809–81), one of Britain's all-time great punters, also owned an exceptionally successful stable. He won the Derby in 1846, the Two Thousand Guineas in 1850 and the Goodwood Cup in 1856 – all races he had bet on heavily: he needed the winnings to offset his heavy losses on the Stock

Exchange (£40,000 in one year alone).

☆

Hill's Equation in physiology is a mathematical formula for the shortening of skeletal muscle when load is increased.

☆

The first Hillman car, then called Hillman-Coatelen, was built in 1907.

☆

Americans Patty and Mildred Hill wrote one of the world's most popular songs, 'Happy Birthday to You' (1896). Not wishing to capitalise on this happy tune, it was not copyrighted until 1936. All royalties go to charity.

☆

Sir Rowland Hill was Lord Mayor of London in 1549.

☆

Largely due to its descriptive nature, Hill is remarkably prevalent both as the name of towns and cities and as a geographical name. The United Kingdom has 38 towns and cities whose names are related, including 4 Hillheads and 3 Hillsides. The number of related towns and cities elsewhere include 7 in Canada, 3 in Australia, 2 in New Zealand, 3 in South Africa and 42 in the United States (including an impressive 14 Hillsboros).

****
HUGHES
****

Related Names
Other surnames which are related as to root, derivation or usage include:

FitzHugh	Hewson	Hudsmith	Hughson
FitzHughes	Hooson	Hudson	Huglin
Haw	Hoosun	Hue	Hugo
Hew	How	Huetson	Hugon
Hewe	Howe	Huett	Hullot
Hewes	Howes	Huggell	Huson
Hewett	Howkins	Huggett	Huws
Hewitt	Howlett	Huggins	MacHugh
Hewlett	Hows	Huggon	Pugh
Hewlin	Huckin	Huggons	Pughes
Hews	Hudd	Hugh	

The surname Hughes derives from the first name Hugh and means 'dependant of Hugh'.

The first name Hugh is of Old German origin and comes originally from the first name Hugo, which means 'heart or mind'. The same Hugo also appears in Latin (almost certainly from the same source) where it became corrupted to Hewe and Howe. Both of these names, as well as Hugo, now appear as variant surnames.

The variants Hew, Hewes, Hews and Hewson often come from a different root – the Middle English word 'hewe' meaning 'maidservant'.

The surname Hughes is found all over England, Scotland, Wales and Ireland, though it appears in its greatest concentrations in North Wales. Here it may well have Gaelic origins as does the name when it occurs in those parts of Scotland and Ireland that have remained relatively free from English influence. In these cases, Hughes is descended from the Irish Gaelic first name Aodh and the Scottish Gaelic names Eoghann (in Argyllshire) and Uisdeann (in the remote north-west). In Ireland the names Hugh and MacHugh (son of Hugh) are the equivalent of the Scottish name MacKay. In Wales the name Hughes has sometimes become Pugh, Hew, or Haw.

All in all, there are nearly one hundred variations of the surname Hughes in present use. These include the first syllable varying from 'Hew-' to 'Huw-' to 'Hu-', and suffixes ranging from '-son', '-kin' and '-man' through to '-in', '-on', '-et' and '-ot'. Many of these variations stem from the widespread popularity of the first name Hugo after the Norman Conquest. As such, the name appears in the 1066 Domesday Book records for Huntingdonshire and Suffolk, though by 1084 in the Geld Roll (part of the Domesday Book) the name appeared more recognisably as Willelmus filius Hugonis. The name achieved further popularity through St Hugh of Avalon, who was Prior of Witham and Bishop of Lincoln at the turn of the thirteenth century.

The common pet form of Hugh was Hud, hence the surnames Hudd, Hudson and Hudsmith (from Hudsmough, 'Hugh's brother-in-law').

A Hughes Miscellany
British showman Edwin Hughes (1813–67) originated the

word 'circus' in its entertainment sense, with 'Hughes' Great Mammoth Equestrian Circus' which pioneered the use of wild animals, such as elephants, in harness.

☆

'John Hughes won't save you' was a derisory World War I expression applied to prospective British draftees. Hughes, a greengrocer, was tried and convicted for concocting a scheme to save men from serving in the army.

☆

Tom Brown's School Days was written by Thomas Hughes (1822–96) as an affectionate tribute to his own Rugby school days.

☆

All those who wear hearing aids are indebted to British professor David Edward Hughes (1831–1900) whose experiments in the transmission properties of carbon fibres were critical to the development of the hearing aid as well as to that of microphones. He also invented the earliest telegraphic teleprinter. His very substantial fortune was bequeathed to London hospitals.

☆

American Peter Cooper Hewitt (1861–1921) invented the mercury vapour lamp and a remarkable early version of the helicopter (1918).

☆

Noted English navigator and explorer Henry Hudson (d. 1611) reached America on his third attempt to find the legendary Northwest Passage to the Orient. After cruising off Newfoundland he explored the coast of what is now New England, then proceeded as far south as Delaware Bay. Along the way he discovered the New York river that now bears his name. A fourth voyage took him to what is now Hudson's Bay where his ship was frozen in, the crew rebelled and he was set adrift. It is probable he perished in his namesake.

☆

There are no name-related towns or major geographic features in the United Kingdom. Australia has a town called Hughes, and there are 2 such towns in the United States as well as a Hughes Springs and a Hughesville. Canada has a Hughes river in Manitoba.

```
*********************************
*            JACKSON            *
*********************************
```

Related Names

Other surnames which are related as to root, derivation or usage include:

Jack	Jacking	Jacson	Jagger
Jackalin	Jacklin	Jager	Jaggs
Jackaman	Jackling	Jagg	Jakeman
Jackard	Jackman	Jaggar	Jakes
Jackett	Jacks	Jaggard	Jaxon
Jacketts	Jacot		

The surname Jackson, meaning 'son of Jack', stems from the first name Jack, but it is difficult to know whether Jack is a derivative of John or of Jacques (French for James). Certainly most of the diminutive forms, Jacklin, Jackett, Jaggard and so on, are from James (which see).

There are many early references to Jack and its diminutives. One Andreas filius Jake appears in the 1195–97 Pipe Rolls for Cornwall, while a Jakelinus is recorded in Yorkshire in the Book of Fees dated 1219. The earliest reference to the name Jackson itself appears in the 1327 Subsidy Rolls for Suffolk, where one Adam Jackessone is listed.

A Jackson Miscellany

Jacksons seem to be born fighters. John 'Gentleman' Jackson (1769–1845) was a famous barefisted pugilist who held the English championship for eight years, then retired in 1803 to coach Lord Byron, amongst others. Peter Jackson (1861–1901), the first great black boxer, won both the Australian heavyweight title (1886) and the British Empire title (1892) while Henry Jackson is the real name of Henry Armstrong (b. 1912), who held three world boxing championships simultaneously: featherweight (1937), welterweight (1938) and lightweight (1938).

☆

The renowned English test cricketer, Sir Stanley Jackson (1870–1947), played against Australia in the famous 1893 series, then went on to become Governor of Bengal as well as Chairman of the Conservative Party.

☆

The 1901 Jacksonville, Florida fire destroyed a total of over 1700 buildings.

American President Andrew Jackson (1767–1845) originated the ubiquitous American slang expression 'OK'. Jackson's grammar and spelling were as rough as his frontier origins. Therefore he approved presidential papers with the notation 'OK', his way of abbreviating 'Oll Korrect'.

☆

The 'Major Mite', whose real name was William E. Jackson (1864–1900), was one of the world's shortest dwarfs. He was only 27 in (70 cm) tall. On the other hand, another Jackson, Baby Flo (Mrs Flora Mae Jackson), weighed over 60 stone just before her death in 1965.

☆

There are no Jackson-related towns or major geographic features in the United Kingdom. Canada's Newfoundland has a town called Jackson's Arm, New Zealand has a Jackson Head (as well as a town called Jacksons) and South Africa has a Jackson's Drift. Australia has a town called simply Jackson, as do no fewer than 16 states of America where 30 towns and cities are name related, including the well-known Jacksonville, Florida (one of 9 Jacksonvilles). Mountains in Western Australia and the United States are called Jackson, as are bays in Canada and New Zealand.

```
***********************************
*                 JAMES                 *
***********************************
```

Related Names
Other surnames which are related as to root, derivation or usage include:

Gemmes	Jacques	Jameson	Jayme
Jacob	Jago	Jamie	Jeames
Jacobs	Jagoe	Jamieson	Jem
Jacobson	Jakes	Jamison	Jemme
Jacoby			

The surname James derived directly from the first name. This in its turn is a form of the original Hebrew name Jacob, and first became popular through the two Apostles. The Hebrew Jacob comes from the word 'aqob' which means 'supplanter' or 'usurper' (all too appropriate in the case of Jacob, the son of Isaac – one of the earliest Jacobs – who deprived his brother Esau of his birthright).

The original Jacob became Latinised to Jacobus, and from this we get the French first name Jacques, as well as the identical Welsh and Spanish form Iago. The Latinised form later became Jacomus, and it is from this root that we get our name James. It is also the source of the Spanish form Jayme (Jaime), the Italian Giacomo, and the Irish version Seamus (pronounced Shaymus).

The name, in all its varied forms, began to gain popularity all over Europe during the twelfth and thirteenth centuries. It has been suggested that the name came to prominence around this time as a result of its having been brought back by the Crusaders, and this may have been a contributory factor.

The surname James has several variations, the most widespread being Jameson, Jamison, and Jamieson (which almost certainly derives from the Scottish abbreviation 'Jamie').

References to the name James start occurring in the English records around the turn of the twelfth century. One of the earliest of these is a certain Jam de Sancto Hylario who appears in the Early Charters for Northamptonshire for 1173–6.

The surname James is popular all over England (despite the closely related Jamisons being found almost exclusively in the Scottish lowland region). The greatest concentrations of James are now found in the West Country.

A James Miscellany

The 'King James Version' is another name given to the Authorised Version of the Bible which was ordered by King James I. The resonant style of this classic translation remains one of the finest examples of our language.

☆

Jakes was a popular Elizabethan slang word for a lavatory – which accounts for the word's frequent sly appearances in Shakespeare's comedies. The word survives in our language today as 'the Jacks', a slang expression with the same meaning.

☆

'BBC English' was created by the British phonetician, Arthur Lloyd James (1884–1943), who was the arbiter on all matters of pronunciation during the Corporation's formative years.

☆

Jesse James (1847–82) and his brother Frank were legendary Wild West desperadoes and bank robbers. Together they gunned down at least ten men.

☆

Jameson's Raid (29 December 1895) was Doctor Leander Starr Jameson's ill-fated attempt to overthrow the Transvaal Republic by fomenting an uprising in Johannesburg. Mounted with Cecil Rhodes' backing, Jameson and his fellow soldiers of fortune were surrounded and surrendered abjectly before they ever reached the city.

☆

The United Kingdom has a Jameston and 3 Jamestowns. Canada and South Africa also have Jamestowns while 10 states of America have towns and cities bearing this name. In all, 18 US locations are name related. The name is geographically common around the world, including South Africa's Jameson Park.

JOHNSON

Related Names
Other surnames which are related as to root, derivation or usage include:

Fitzjohn	Jan	Jenkin	Johncook
Hancock	Janet	Jenkins	Johnes
Hanken	Janks	Jenkinson	Johns
Hankin	Jann	Jenks	Johnsen
Hann	Janson	Jennings	Johnston
Henkin	Jaynes	Jinkin	Johnstone
Jack	Jeakins	Johan	Johnys
Jackson	Jean	John	Joinsen
(which see)	Jehan	Johncock	Joynson

The surname Johnson has two main subdivisions – one with, and one without, the intrusive 't' (as in Johnstone). Both of these subdivisions have a wide variety of different spellings. The former often means 'son of John', while those variations with the 't' often refer to places – 'tons' named after John, notably in Scotland. In practice (and often in spelling) it is easy to see how the 't' got lost in pronouncing the name.

The first name John derives from the Ancient Hebrew name Jochanaan, meaning 'God is gracious'. In its Latin form the name Johannes came west with the returning Crusaders, and during the twelfth and thirteenth centuries it spread all over Europe. Doubtless it was assisted by the popularity of St John the Baptist and St John the Divine (author of the Book of Revelations).

As the name Johannes crossed national and linguistic borders, it became changed into many local variants. In Germany it became Hans, in Holland Jan, in France Jean, in Ireland Sean (pronounced Shawn), and in Scotland Jock.

Early reference to Johnsons began appearing in the English records around the thirteenth century. One John Jonessone appears in the Ancient Deeds for Surrey in 1287. Variations with the intrusive middle 't' appeared early on to denote 'John from the place ('ton' or 'tun')'. One Alan de Johannestun appears in the Assize Rolls for Staffordshire in 1227. The variations with the intrusive 't' are more common in the north of England and in Scotland.

In some rare cases the name Johnstone may be a local name deriving from places in Staffordshire and Dumfriesshire (the second syllable in this case being Old English). It is also just possible that this name is a local name for a man from Perth which used to be called St Johnstone (as its football team still is).

The name Johnson is related to the surname Evans (which also means, literally, 'the dependant of John' – see Evans) and also in this way to many widely differing names – from Jackson to Jones. Jack, like Jenkin, Hankin and Hancock, was a common pet form of John.

A Johnson Miscellany

Andrew Johnson (1808–75) was the seventeenth President of the United States. He purchased Alaska from the Russians for just $7,200,000 in 1867.

☆

The three founders of the firm of Rolls-Royce were the Hon. C.S. Rolls, Mr F. Henry Royce and Mr Claude Johnson. Having at first contemplated calling the car the Rolls-Royce-Johnson, they decided that it somehow lacked zip and the name Johnson was dropped.

☆

The 1889 flood in Johnstown, Pennsylvania, ranks among the world's all-time disasters. When the South Fork Dam broke after excessive rain, the 450-acre lake vanished in under 40 minutes as a 70-foot-high wall of water roared through the town at over 15 miles per hour. One in 10 of the citizens (well over 2,000 people) was killed and the town was virtually levelled. Johnstown was rebuilt, but in 1977 a freak storm deposited 9 inches of rain in 8 hours and the Laurel Run dam broke, releasing over 100 million gallons of water with the resultant deaths of 77 people; it totally destroyed over 500 houses and caused over $200 million in damage.

☆

Famed aviatrix Amy Johnson (1903–41) captured the imagination of the nation with her record-breaking solo flight to Australia in 1930 – so much so that the song 'Wonderful Amy, How Can You Blame Me for Loving You?' was the smash hit of the year.

☆

Samuel Johnson (1709–84) took a mere eight years (1747–55) to write his famous dictionary of the English language.

☆

The United Kingdom has towns named Johnston, Johnstone and Johnstone Bridge, Canada has a Johnsen's Crossing and a Johnstown, New Zealand has a Johnsonville, and there are also Johnstowns in the United States (4) and Ireland (2). There is a Johnson Island off the coast of Chile, a Johnson's Point in Antigua, and a Johnson mountain range as well as a group of lakes in Australia.

```
************************************
*                JONES             *
************************************
```

Related Names

Other surnames which are related as to root, derivation or usage include:

Fitzjones	Joanes	Joynes
Joan	John	*see also* Johnson

The surname Jones literally means 'dependant of John', and Jone was a common form of the Christian name in England. In Wales, John had the characteristic form Evan (see Evans), but the Welsh Authorised Bible popularised a more latinate form

Ioan, which gave rise to the patronymic Jones in Wales, where it is exceptionally common.

The first name John is Hebrew in origin and means 'God is gracious' (for further details see Johnson).

Jones has many related variants, which range from John to Joan, Joynes to Fitzjones (son of Jones). Like Jones, most of these variants have particularly strong Welsh connections.

References to the surname Jones appear in many of the early records, but more often than not the earliest references are to its related names. Thus one Alanus filius Jene appears in the 1275 annals of Lincolnshire, and there are several Johannes in the same records. However, in 1279 the more recognisable name of Walterus filius Jone appears in the annals for Huntingdonshire, and from then on the name Jones becomes a regular feature in our records, proliferating all over the country – though still retaining its highest concentrations in South Wales.

A Jones Miscellany

The phrase 'Keeping up with the Joneses', which originated in a 1913 American strip cartoon, gathered strength during the decades after World War II, with the new prosperity and subsequent proliferation of snobbery.

☆

The Dow Jones Industrial average Index measures the rise and fall of stocks and shares on the New York and American stock exchanges. It was instituted in 1896 by Charles Henry Dow and Edward D. Jones, former financial journalists who together, in 1882, founded the Wall Street firm of Dow Jones and Co. The British equivalent is the Financial Times Share Index.

☆

'On your Jack Jones' is Cockney rhyming slang for 'on your own'.

☆

Casey Jones (1864–1900) is the legendary hero commemorated in the famous ballad of the same name for his heroism as the engineer on the 'Cannonball Express'.

☆

There are no Jones-related towns or major geographic features in the United Kingdom. The only towns bearing this name are in the United States where there are 19, including 9 Jonesboros and 6 Jonesvilles. A portion of the Atlantic Ocean's floor is known as Jones Bank, and Canada has a Jones Sound.

Related Names

Other surnames which are related as to root, derivation or usage include:

Keller	Kellie	Killie	McKelly
Kelley	Kellye	MacKelly	O'Kelly

Normally the surname Kelly comes from the Gaelic O'Ceallaigh. Apart from this fact the origins of the name Kelly – at least in Ireland, where it is most numerous – are obscure. One possible derivation is from the Gaelic word 'ceallach' which means 'conflict, strife or war'. If this is so, Kelly would be a nickname, the original Kelly probably achieving renown as a great fighter.

Kellys are found all over Ireland – and indeed, with emigration, all over the world. (From Boston and New York to Sydney, the local telephone directories have pages of Kellys.) The main family clan of the Kellys is native to mid-Galway and south Roscommon, but other separate family clans have their origins in Leix, Wicklow, Meath and Derry.

Kellys also come from the Isle of Man and Scotland – but almost all of these are due to early emigration. Exceptions are rare, but nonetheless these do exist. In Scotland the name Kelly is sometimes a place name, being given to natives of the town of Kelly in Angus and to those from the village of Killie in Fife. These places get their names from the Scots Gaelic or the Cornish words for 'woods'. It is also just possible that the Irish Kellys – at least in part – derive their name from a similar source in Irish Gaelic. In this case the Irish name could also be a place name, rather than the more heroic nickname. Kelly is also an old surname in Devon. In the Pipe Rolls for Devon in 1194 one Warin de Kelly is listed, named after the Devon village, and this is the first note of a Kelly in English records.

A Kelly Miscellany

In 1888 James Kelly, the Liverpool wife-murderer, escaped from Broadmoor, the celebrated top-security prison for mental patients in Berkshire. He did so by making a passkey from a corset spring. After his escape he lived in Paris, then in New York for many years, eluding all attempts to recapture him. Finally, he returned in 1928 to the gates of Broadmoor and asked for readmission. This was granted, and he died an inmate in 1930. No one else has ever escaped and remained free from Broadmoor for anything approaching this period.

☆

Helen Adams Keller (1880-1968) became blind, deaf and dumb as a baby. By sheer persistence and with the devoted help of Anne Sullivan, she overcame these overwhelming handicaps to graduate *cum laude* from Radcliffe College, Cambridge (US). She became an inspiration to many similarly handicapped, and her autobiography, *The Story of My Life* (1902), remains widely read.

☆

The sixteenth-century alchemist's assistant, Edward Kelley, claimed that he could confer with the angels by use of the magic crystals belonging to his master, John Dee. Kelley eventually persuaded his master to adopt a community of wives.

☆

HMS *Kelly* was the first command of Lord Louis Mountbatten (1900–79). Later to become Viceroy of India, Earl Mountbatten earned the undying respect of his men as a result of his bravery at the time of the engagement during which HMS *Kelly* was finally sunk. He knew the name of every man on board, and refused rescue before his wounded shipmates had been assisted.

☆

The first full-length film, *The Story of the Kelly Gang*, was made in Australia in 1906.

☆

The United Kingdom has towns called Kelly and Kelly Bay. Other countries with name-related towns include Australia (Kelly), the US (3 Kellys), South Africa (Kelly's View) and Ireland (Kelly's Grove). There are Kelly rivers in Alaska and Australia and Kelly lakes in Angola and Canada, as well as Kelly Hills in Australia.

✳✳✳✳✳✳✳✳✳✳✳✳✳✳✳✳✳✳✳✳✳✳✳✳✳✳✳✳✳✳✳✳✳
✳   **KING**   ✳
✳✳✳✳✳✳✳✳✳✳✳✳✳✳✳✳✳✳✳✳✳✳✳✳✳✳✳✳✳✳✳✳✳

Related Names
Other surnames which are related as to root, derivation or usage include:

Kingdom	Kingett	Kingman	Kingsbury
Kinge	Kinggett	Kings	Kingsford

Kingshott	Kingsman	Kingson	Kington
Kingsland	Kingsmill	Kingston	Kingwell
Kingsley	Kingsnorth	Kingstone	

The surname King has two origins. One is the Old English word Cyng, 'a king', which was used in Old English times as a personal name and may have given rise to a surname. The other, and by far the more common, is a nickname 'king' found in many villages in medieval England. Experts believe that the most common designation of the name was for men who governed the rituals of harvest-time in medieval villages. Sometimes these rites were celebrated with annual pageants and masques, where the same parts were often taken by the same individual year after year. Thus he who played the part of the king often found the name attached to him.

Alternatively the nickname may have been an ironic reference to the overbearing, swaggering manner of someone in the village. Or it may have been used as an occupational name for someone in the King's service – i.e. a servant of the King, a King's messenger, or sometimes simply a tax collector.

In extremely rare cases, it is thought that the name King was given to an illegitimate offspring of royal descent. However, many authorities doubt whether this ever happened.

The surname King has many related names. Most of them are place names – given to someone who came from a particular place. The best known of these are Kingsbury (places in Middlesex and Somerset), Kingsford (Hampshire and Suffolk), and Kingston (the official name of Hull, and the town in Surrey).

Variants on the name King appear in many of the early records, but perhaps the earliest reference to the name as we know it is in the Pipe Rolls for Cambridgeshire. There in 1177 one Geoffrey King is mentioned.

A King Miscellany
Martin Luther King (1929–68) was the black American civil rights leader whose example did more to advance his people's rights than any other of his generation. In 1964 he was awarded the Nobel Peace Prize, but just four years later was killed by an assassin's bullet.

☆

British botanist Francis Ward Kingdon (1885–1958) discovered and began cultivation of the Himalayan blue poppy. In half a century of pioneering expeditions he made 25 journeys to the eastern Himalayas.

☆

Unconventional Louisiana governor Huey Long was nicknamed 'The Kingfish' by his poverty-stricken adulatory followers, to signify his supremacy in their affections.

☆

American politician John Alsop King persuaded the 1855 state convention of the Whig Party to adopt 'Republican' as the party's name. It has remained that ever since.

☆

William Mackenzie King (1874–1950) was Canada's Prime Minister a remarkable three times during his 30 years as head of the Liberal Party.

☆

President Charles King of Liberia was elected into office in 1928 by a massive 600,000 majority. It was an amazing feat in a country whose electorate was then just 15,000.

☆

King takes pride of place when it comes to name-related towns, cities and geographic features. In all, 106 towns and cities in the United Kingdom are King-related. These range from Kingarth to Kingswelton and include 9 Kingstons and 7 Kingswoods. The US has 45 such towns and cities, Canada has 4, Australia 10, New Zealand 2, and South Africa 5. Kingston is Jamaica's capital. Numerous geographic features bear the generic name or are named for specific kings (King George's Reservoir, King Edward River, King Lear Mountain, King Leopold range, etc.)

```
******************************
*              LEE           *
******************************
```

Related Names
Other surnames which are related as to root, derivation or usage include:

Atlee	Lea	Lees	Ley
Lay	Leabrook	Legh	Leys
Laye	Leagh	Leigh	Lye

The surname Lee is a variant of Lea. This is a place name coming

198

from the Old English word 'leah', which means 'wood, glade, clearing, field or pasture'. The related surnames Legh and Leigh are usually from the Middle English form of the word, 'legh' – though they do occasionally derive from the older source. However, contrary to appearances, these latter Leighs (and Leghs) are not closer derivations of the Old English source than the Lees and Leas. 'Lea' is the dative of the Old English 'Leah', and was used after prepositions such as 'at' or 'in'. It was common practice to refer to someone who lived by a particular place as living 'at' it – as, for example, in John at Lee. Thus we get the name Atlee.

Other variations on the name come from the Old English 'laege' meaning 'fallow', and 'laes' meaning 'meadow'. These include Ley, Leys, Laye, Lye, Lees, and such obvious rural compounds as Leabrook.

Early references to Lee abound in the records from the twelfth century onwards, and are found all over England. One of the earliest is to an Ailric de la Leie, who appears in the early Charters for Norfolk covering the years 1148–66.

A Lee Miscellany

Gypsy Rose Lee (1904–70) was the greatest strip-tease artist of them all, bringing wit, style and grace to this profession unmatched since Salome. After retiring she wrote the best-selling autobiography *Gypsy*, and then wrote two further best-sellers *The G-String Murders* (1941) and *Mother finds a Body* (1942). During World War II she returned to the stage to strip for war-bonds.

☆

The Lee Commission was appointed by the British Government in 1923 to consider the racial composition of India's higher government services. As a result of its recommendations, when India became independent in 1947 over half of the 1,000 members of these services were Indians with long experience.

☆

Lee's Professor is the holder of one of three chairs at Oxford.

☆

England's Prime Ministers, past and present, owe a debt of gratitude to Arthur Hamilton Lee – he left them his estate, Chequers, for use as a country house.

☆

Poet and novelist Laurie Lee based books like *Cider with Rosie* and *As I Walked Out One Midsummer Morning* on his deep love and understanding of rural Gloucestershire, where he grew up.

199

☆

Manfred B. Lee is better known by his pseudonym, Ellery Queen. Together with Frederic Dannay, he wrote murder mysteries which often featured a break just before the end, inviting the reader to see if he could solve the crime before the fictional detective announced the solution.

☆

Lees seem to have a predilection for achieving fame on the stage. Amongst the best known of these are Christopher Lee, maestro of the Hammer horror films, Bruce Lee the great Kung Fu hero, and Vivien Leigh, one-time wife of Laurence Olivier, who played Scarlett O'Hara in *Gone With The Wind*.

☆

Robert E. Lee was the only general in history to have been offered the command of both armies in a war. He turned down the offer of the Union command and went on to become the legendary leader of the Southern Army during the American Civil War.

His family produced several other outstanding military commanders. Robert's father, Henry 'Light-Horse' Lee, was a close aide to George Washington, and Henry's eldest son, also called Henry, distinguished himself in the War of 1812.

☆

English clergyman William Lee (1550–1610) invented the first knitting machine. The woman he was courting showed far more interest in knitting than in his attentions, and this was his solution.

☆

A total of 25 towns and cities in the United Kingdom are related to this name including 5 towns called Lee, 2 Leeds, and 2 named Lees. While Canada is Lee-less the United States has 26 name-related towns and cities. Denmark also has a town called Lee. The name is geographically common.

✳✳✳✳✳✳✳✳✳✳✳✳✳✳✳✳✳✳✳✳✳✳✳✳✳✳✳✳✳✳✳✳✳✳✳
✳ **LEWIS** ✳
✳✳✳✳✳✳✳✳✳✳✳✳✳✳✳✳✳✳✳✳✳✳✳✳✳✳✳✳✳✳✳✳✳✳✳

Related Names
Other surnames which are related as to root, derivation or usage include:

Leuis	Lewison	Lewys	Louis
Lewisohn	Lewse	Llewelyn	Lowis

The surname Lewis began life as a first name. It means 'renowned or famous in battle', and its original form was first found in Germany where it is now found in the form Ludwig. When the name crossed to France as Lowis or Louis, it soon became popular. This popularity increased through the centuries, as we can see from the fact that France had no fewer than eighteen kings called Louis, one of whom even became a saint. As the name Louis spread beyond the borders of France it changed once more. In Italy it became Luigi, and by the time it came to England with the Norman invasion it had become Lewis.

In this form the name gradually spread across the entire country, although being originally a foreign name it never achieved the same popularity as it achieved in France. Why, then, are there now so many people called Lewis? The answer to this question lies in their distribution.

The name has existed for many centuries throughout all the English counties, and in Wales is extremely common. The theory which best accounts for the proliferation of the Welsh Lewis is that it is in fact an attempted anglicisation of the Welsh name Llewelyn. (In times of persecution, when Wales was only a princedom under repression, many Welshmen found it expedient to change their name to a more English form.) This theory may sound rather far-fetched, but it would appear to be confirmed by the earliest reference we have to the name Lewis. In the 1413 records the Alderman of Brecon is given as 'Llewelyn ap-Madoc, alias Lewis Rede'. By then Lewis was certainly a widespread and popular name and over 100 years later it crops up in Shakespeare, a distinction shared by very few of the more popular British names. Among these few are two other predominantly Welsh names: Thomas and Griffith.

There are several names which derive directly or indirectly from Lewis. The best known of these are Leuis, Lowis, Lewse – all being simply variations in spelling dating from the times before spelling was formalised. (Lewison, from 'son of Lewis', is also popular.) However, the similar-looking name of Lewes is not a variation of Lewis. It is a local name, deriving from the town in Sussex, and means 'hills or mounds', referring to the Downs among which the town lies.

Another origin of the name Lewis results from the eastern European pogroms of the nineteenth century. During this time many Jews crossed over to England and on arrival decided to anglicise their names. A number of refugees with the name Levinsky changed it to Lewin, Levin or Lewis.

Owing to its popularity in Britain and France – two of Europe's major colonising nations – the name Lewis (or Louis) has spread around the globe. Over the centuries it has been particularly popular in the United States. Here we find it in St Louis, in Louisville, and even in the State of Louisiana (which, under French colonial rule – before the famous Louisiana Purchase in 1803 – stretched from the coast of the Gulf of Mexico up into the Mid-West, to within a few hundred miles of the Great Lakes).

In America, because of this early pervasive French influence, the French spelling of Louis is still more popular than the Anglo-Welsh Lewis (e.g. Louis Armstrong), so much so that its popularity as a first name in this French form has even spread back across the Atlantic, but this time to England.

A Lewis Miscellany
The American explorer Meriwether Lewis (1774–1809) led the great overland journey to the Pacific coast, thus opening up the north-west to a flood of settlers. Despite encounters with grizzly bears, Indians, rattlesnakes and near-starvation Lewis's only brush with death came when a hunting companion mistook him for an elk and shot him in the leg. As a reward for his explorations he was appointed the first governor of Louisiana but died soon after in mysterious circumstances.

☆

The first machine-gun was invented by the American Isaac Newton Lewis (1858–1931). The American military brass proved uninterested in his new invention so he took it to Europe in 1913 where the Lewis Gun played a vital part in the last stages of World War I. Over 100,000 were manufactured for the Allied armies by the Birmingham Small Arms Company.

☆

Many people with the name of Lewis have achieved fame as writers. The first American to win the Nobel prize was Sinclair Lewis, whose best-seller *Main Street* swept him to fame. C. Day Lewis (1904–72) was one of the 'Thirties Poets' of Auden's generation. He later became Poet Laureate. The controversial writer-artist Percy Wyndham Lewis founded the English modernist movement called Vorticism, which created a furore prior

202

to World War I. The prolific scholar-writer C.S. Lewis is best remembered for his *Screwtape Letters*.

☆

Several jazz greats are called Lewis. George Lewis was a veteran of the Old New Orleans style and John Lewis, the composer-pianist, recorded with Charlie Parker and Dizzy Gillespie.

☆

The United Kingdom has a Lewisham (along with South Africa), a Lewis, a Lewiston and a Butt of Lewis. A total of 22 United States towns and cities are Lewis-related. Both Australia and the US have Lewis Ranges and the name is geographically common.

✳✳✳✳✳✳✳✳✳✳✳✳✳✳✳✳✳✳✳✳✳✳✳✳✳✳✳✳✳✳✳✳✳✳✳
✳   **MacCARTHY**   ✳
✳✳✳✳✳✳✳✳✳✳✳✳✳✳✳✳✳✳✳✳✳✳✳✳✳✳✳✳✳✳✳✳✳✳✳

Related Names
Other surnames which are related as to root, derivation or usage include:

Craddock	Cradick	MacCartie	McCarthy
Cradduck			

The Irish surname MacCarthy comes from the Gaelic Mac-Carthaigh. This surname originates from the first name Carthach, which means 'loving'. As well as being the thirteenth most popular name in Ireland, it is also the most popular 'Mac' name. The MacCarthys have played a heroic part in Irish history throughout the ages, and are one of the leading family clans of Munster.

This simple explanation of the origin of MacCarthy omits a number of complicating but interesting variations en route. MacCarthy also means 'son of Craddock' – a form of the name Carthach (or Carthaigh) – and an earlier form of Craddock was Caratacus. This renowned Ancient British name is perhaps more recognisable as the Welsh Caradoc. Caratacus (or Caradoc) was a famous British chieftain of the Catuvellauni, who resisted so nobly against the Romans between 37–43 AD. Finally, around 50 AD, he was captured and together with his family he was shipped to Rome in chains. Here, amongst other

203

indignities which befell him, Caratacus had his name Latinised to Caractacus (and as such he appears in the popular song).

The name which derives most directly from Caradoc is the Welsh surname Craddock. In its early form this name appears in the 1177 Pipe Rolls for Hereford, where one Caradoc is listed.

It was over a century later that MacCarthy (or 'son of Craddock') began to appear. The earliest mention of this name is of one Douenald Roth' Mackarthi in the Patent Rolls for 1285.

A MacCarthy Miscellany

McCarthys have played a large part in post-war American politics. Infamous US Senator Joseph McCarthy (1908–57) captured national headlines in the early 1950s with his sensational claim that Communists had infiltrated the highest levels of government, especially the State Department. Although he never actually produced the name of one 'card-carrying Communist', the witch-hunt whipped up a national hysteria that destroyed many careers. McCarthy's power finally declined after a lengthy 1954 televised hearing in which top civilians and military brass were cross-examined in front of an audience of millions. McCarthy, always a heavy drinker, finally died a broken alcoholic.

Another US Senator, Eugene McCarthy (b. 1916), made a bid for the 1968 presidential nomination against the incumbent, Lyndon B. Johnson. Though unsuccessful, he mobilised political idealism and anti-Vietnam War sentiments. As such he was influential in Johnson's decision not to seek re-election.

☆

A descendant of Blarney Castle's fifteenth-century builder, Cormac MacCarthy gave the English language a new term for slippery eloquence – 'blarney' – when he put off Queen Elizabeth I's demands for his allegiance with 'fair words and soft speech'.

☆

Governing comes naturally to the MacCarthys. Sir Charles MacCarthy was Governor of the Gold Coast until he was killed in the Ashanti in 1824. MacCarthy's Island, originally a site for freed slaves, off the West African coast is named for him. In the eighteenth century a MacCarthy was Governor of Madras, and in the nineteenth century Sir Charles Justin MacCarthy was Governor of Ceylon.

204

A MacCarthy – Colonel Daniel E. – was the first American soldier to set foot in France in 1917.

☆

Geographic and urban namesakes are all but non-existent. There is one town called McCarthy in Alaska.

✳✳✳✳✳✳✳✳✳✳✳✳✳✳✳✳✳✳✳✳✳✳✳✳✳✳✳✳✳✳✳✳✳✳
✳   **MacDONALD**   ✳
✳✳✳✳✳✳✳✳✳✳✳✳✳✳✳✳✳✳✳✳✳✳✳✳✳✳✳✳✳✳✳✳✳✳

Related Names
Other surnames which are related as to root, derivation or usage include:

Donald	MacConnell	MacDonnell	McDonald
Donaldson	MacDonell		

The surname MacDonald means 'descendant of Donald' and comes from the Scots Gaelic Mac Dhomhnuill. The origin of the first name Dhomhnuill was a nickname meaning no less than 'world ruler'. Not being a backward modest people, the Scots adopted this name in large numbers, and it soon became one of the most popular first names in the land, being held by several kings and one saint (in the ninth century). The abbreviation Don also became widespread, though the formal Donal is more an Irish usage.

According to George Black, the greatest expert on Scottish names, strictly speaking there is no such name as MacDonald, (because the Gaelic Mac Dhomhnuill really means 'son of a *particular* Donald'). This holds true for all the 'Mac' names.

The MacDonalds are one of the major Scottish clans, whose chieftains are descended directly from Donald, son of Reginald (Old Norse Ragnaldr), second son of the great Somerled (Old Norse Sumarlithr), Lord of the Isles, so the line is ultimately Scandinavian. The Scots Gaelic name for the clan is Clann Domhnuill. The clan can claim to be the most numerous and widespread of all the Scottish clans. However, not all clan members are of pure descent – through the centuries the Clan MacDonald absorbed several minor family clans and 'broken' men (who had left or 'broken from' their own clans).

A popular verbal variant of the original MacDonald is the

name MacConnell, which is found particularly in Ulster. Another popular variant name is MacDonell. Yet these are the tip of the iceberg compared with the many variations in the ancient records which tried to transliterate from the original Gaelic. These range from Maconhale (1588) through McConnil (1564) to M'Donnyle (1326). Fortunately, most of these variants have now become absorbed into the more standard forms. The earliest reference to the name in any form in the records is in the Dublin lists for 1257, where one Robert Dovenald appears.

A MacDonald Miscellany

McDonald's hamburger chain, the largest restaurant group in the world, was founded by brothers Maurice and Richard McDonald whose parents emigrated to the United States from County Mayo.

☆

Alistair MacDonnell, called 'Pickle the Spy', was a Scottish chieftain of dubious integrity employed by Highland leaders on a secret mission to Charles Stuart, Pretender to the English throne. When captured by the English, he promptly switched his allegiance and agreed to spy on the Prince.

☆

MacDonalds have had a way of getting to the top in politics. Ramsay MacDonald, an illegitimate child who grew up in poverty and left school at the age of 12, overcame these handicaps to become Britain's first Labour Prime Minister. Two John MacDonalds have been Prime Ministers of Canada: Sir John A. MacDonald, as Canada's first Prime Minister, is known as 'the father of Confederation', while Prime Minister John Sandfield Macdonald, unlike Sir John, violently opposed federation.

☆

Scottish-born Sir James Ronald Leslie Macdonald, soldier and explorer, first made a geographical exploration of British East Africa (now Kenya and Uganda), and later mapped the Lake Victoria area.

☆

MacDonalds have been notable for getting into tight spots, then extricating themselves with great skill. After his crushing defeat at Culloden, Bonnie Prince Charlie was helped by Flora Mac-Donald (1722–90) to escape from the Hebrides dressed in her maid's clothes. The British briefly imprisoned, then pardoned, her.

Jacques-Alexandre MacDonald (1765–1840) had a brilliant career as one of Napoleon's top generals (his winter crossing of the Alps was favourably compared to Napoleon's own crossing of the St Bernard Pass). Arrested for anti-Bonapartist plots, he was regarded as so indispensable that he was pardoned and recalled to duty when France was threatened by Austria. He went on to be a Marshal of Empire and member of the Legion of Honour.

☆

Sir Hector MacDonald (1853–1903) distinguished himself in the Afghan War, the Boer War and the Sudan where, as a major-general in command of Egyptian troops, he became a national hero and was voted Parliament's thanks.

☆

When foreign legations in Peking were besieged by thousands of marauding Chinese during the Boxer Rebellion of 1900, British diplomat Sir Claude Maxwell Macdonald was in command.

☆

The sixteenth-century Irish chieftain of Scottish descent, Sorley Boy MacDonnell, was tricked by the English into battling it out with his rival Shane O'Neill over disputed lands in Ulster. When O'Neill retaliated vigorously, MacDonnell was defeated. Twenty-two years later Sorley Boy was confirmed in his possessions by Elizabeth I and became Constable of Dunluce Castle.

☆

There are no MacDonald towns or major geographic features in the United Kingdom. Around the world there are 2 towns named McDonald in the US and a MacDonald Downs in Australia. Both countries also have McDonald lakes while Australia and Canada have MacDonald Ranges. There is a MacDonald Island in the Indian Ocean and a MacDonald Rock in the Pacific.

****
*   **McKAY**   *
****

Related Names
Other surnames which are related as to root, derivation or usage include:

| Mackay | Mackey | Mackieson | McKie |
| Mackaye | Mackie | McKee | |

The surname McKay is of Scots origin, coming from the Scots Gaelic MacAoidh which means 'son of Aodh'. The original meaning of the first name Aodh remains uncertain, but the most probable translation is 'fire'. This would thus have been a nickname, referring probably to the temperament (or possibly the complexion or hair colour) of the holder. Another possible translation of Aodh is 'inspiration'. This original first name is another possible origin for some instances of the popular first names of Hugh and Hugo.

The McKays originally came from the far north of Scotland, and from Inverness-shire. The origin of the main northern McKays is obscure, but they may well have come from the legendary Clann Morgan. The Inverness-shire McKays usually write their name in Gaelic as MacAi. This further complicates the origin of the name, for MacAi in Scots Gaelic is a form of MacDhai, which translated as 'Davidson' (the Scots Gaelic Dhai being similar to the popular Welsh first name 'Dai').

As is usual with names that have been translated from the Gaelic through the ages, there have been countless variations on this name in the records. These range from Mackhe (1538) to Macky (1513) and M'Akie (1559). This variation gave rise to the ancient Stirlingshire name of Mackie, and thus Mackieson. This popular form means 'son of the son of—'. The more common Macpherson is not the same – this comes from the Gaelic Mac an Phearsain, meaning 'son of the parson'.

The earliest mention of any version of McKay comes in the 1098 Manx records. Here one Cucail Mac Aedha is mentioned. However, it is not until 1326 that we find the more recognisable name Gilchrist M'Ay, who is listed by George Black, the eminent expert on Scottish names.

A McKay Miscellany

The American colloquialism 'the real McCoy' (meaning 'genuine', 'best of its kind') originated through a mix-up over a brand of whisky called McKays exported to the US in the 1880s. The company slogan was confused with the name of an American boxer named McCoy.

☆

Scotsman James Mackay explored the Missouri River and pushed on to the Pacific coast, drawing up the map later used by the famous Lewis and Clark expedition.

☆

The enormous multi-national company International Telephone and Telegraph (IT&T) was founded by Clarence Hungerford MacKay (1874–1938) who supervised the completion of the first trans-Pacific cable between the United States and the Far East (1907).

☆

The largest clipper ship ever built, the *Great Republic*, 4,555 tons, was produced by master Boston shipbuilder Donald McKay (1810–80). Not only did he make them big; he made them fast. His boatyard's ship *Lightning* had a top speed of 21 knots and established a long-standing record of 436 nautical miles in 24 hours.

☆

The only two towns named McKay are in Australia and the United States. Australia has a MacKay Lake, Canada has 2 (one spelled MacKay) as well as a McKay river. Australia has a MacKay mountain and a McKay mountain range.

****
*   **MACKENZIE**   *
****

Related Names
Other surnames which are related as to root, derivation or usage include:

Kenny	MacCoinneach	MacKinnie
Kinney	MacCoinnig	McKenzie

The surname Mackenzie is of Scots origin and comes from the Scots Gaelic MacCoinnich, which means 'son of Coinneach'. This obsolete first name derives indirectly from the Gaelic word 'cann' meaning 'fair, bright or comely'. Thus, this first name originated as a nickname, describing the appearance or personality of the original holder. (The equivalent Irish Gaelic roots of this word may in some rare cases have given rise to the Irish name Kenny – though this is certainly not the main derivation.)

Mention of the name Mackenzie goes back as far as 1264, when one Makbeth Makkyneth attended the pleas held at Dull in Angus during 1264. This name may seem a long way from the Mackenzie we know, but being originally a Gaelic name, Mackenzie (or MacCoinnich) was translated into English when it was written down in the records. Because Gaelic and English are by no means parallel in pronunciation, this led to a large number of different spellings in the records. These range from M'Hunzie (1684) to M'Kenzoch (1586) and Makkunze (1513). Most of these variants have now died out, so that the name is almost invariably spelt Mackenzie – an unusual uniformity in a Gaelic-derived Scottish name.

A Mackenzie Miscellany

Sir Edward Montague Compton Mackenzie (1883–1972), with over 100 novels and plays to his credit, is well known as one of Scotland's (and indeed Britain's) most prolific writers, with an output that topped one work per annum. What is less well known is that he was one of the founders of the Scottish Nationalist Party.

☆

British missionary John Mackenzie (1835–99) was a dedicated champion of the rights of native Africans in nineteenth-century South Africa, and was instrumental in the British Government's move to set up Bechuanaland as a protectorate to combat Boer racialism.

☆

The polygraph machine, popularly known as the 'lie detector', was the brainchild of British physician Sir James Mackenzie. When used in police work, the assumption is that a guilty suspect's respiration, blood pressure and pulse rate will increase due to nervousness when he lies.

☆

Mackenzies have made a name for themselves in distant lands. Sir Alexander Mackenzie (1755–1820) traced the course of the 1,100-mile Canadian river which now bears his name to its delta the Arctic Ocean, the first known trans-continental crossing of North America above Mexico. Bishop Charles Frederick Mackenzie (1825–62) headed the Church's mission in the Zambezi River region of Central Africa and scandalised settlers by insisting that black converts had equal rights in all church affairs.

☆

Canada's first Liberal Prime Minister was Alexander Mackenzie. After emigrating from Perth he swiftly rose to his new homeland's highest political office, holding the post from 1873–78. He refused a knighthood three times.

There are no towns, cities or major geographic features related to this name in the United Kingdom. Canada has 2 towns named Mackenzie, 2 McKenzie lakes, Mackenzie mountains and the famed Mackenzie river. The United States has 3 towns named McKenzie and a McKenzie river. New Zealand has the Mackenzie Plains while Australia has a river called Mackenzie.

✳✳✳✳✳✳✳✳✳✳✳✳✳✳✳✳✳✳✳✳✳✳✳✳✳✳✳✳✳✳✳✳✳
✳   **MacLEAN**   ✳
✳✳✳✳✳✳✳✳✳✳✳✳✳✳✳✳✳✳✳✳✳✳✳✳✳✳✳✳✳✳✳✳✳

Related Names
Other surnames which are related as to root, derivation or usage include:

MacIlwaine	Maclean	McLane	McLean
MacLane	McLaine		

The surname MacLean is of Scottish origin and means 'son of the devotee of (Saint) John'. The intrusive '-L' in the middle of the name is all that remains of the Scots Gaelic word 'gillie', which means 'servant, lad or follower'. This we see more clearly in the Scots Gaelic version of McLean, which is Mac Gille Eoin. Eoin is the main Gaelic version of John, and is now more usually found as Iain, a highly popular Scots first name. The original first name John comes from the Hebrew Jochanaan, which means 'God is gracious'. (For further details of history and origin of the first name John, see entry for Johnson.)

The origins of the Clan McLean are clouded in spurious legends. However, it seems almost certain that the clan had two separate origins. The collective clan is known today in Gaelic as Clann 'ic 'ill Eathain.

The earliest mention of this name comes at the end of the thirteenth century, when one Gilmore Maclyn is listed as having paid homage to the King in 1296. As is usual in names translated from the Gaelic, there is a large variety of different spellings to be found in the records. These range from MacGillane (1526) to M'Gillean (1436) and M'Illclyane (sixteenth century). Most of these variations have now died out or have reverted to the standard McLean or MacLean. However, the version McLane is well known in America.

211

By a curious oddity, the name MacLean is also found frequently in Prussia. These MacLeans refer to themselves as the 'MacLeans of Coll' and are almost certainly of mercenary origin, though a persistent local legend has it that these MacLeans helped John MacLean, son of the laird of Dowant, to build the Swedish city of Gothenberg in the mid-seventeenth century. (In so doing, the canny Scot also accumulated a fortune, and was enrolled by Queen Christina of Sweden in 1649.)

A MacLean Miscellany

The last surviving participant in the Charge of the Light Brigade was Sir Fitzroy Donald Maclean (1835–1931). He also achieved the distinction of being the longest-lived baronet on record.

☆

One of the most consistent best-selling authors of all time is the Scottish-born adventure writer Alistair MacLean (b. 1922), many of whose books have been made into action-packed films.

☆

It is a little-known fact that the American Civil War both began and ended in the same room: the front parlour of Major Wilmer McLean's house in Virginia. After the peace treaty was signed, souvenir-hunters stripped the house of all its furniture. A speculator later bought the house and dismantled it brick by brick, with the idea of re-erecting it in Washington as a tourist attraction. Unfortunately, he went bankrupt in the process, and the dismantled house has never been reassembled.

☆

There are no towns, cities or major geographic features related to this name in the United Kingdom. Canada has one town named McClean, the United States has 4 (including McLean, Virginia, home of the CIA) and a McLeansboro. Australia has a MacLean and South Africa a MacLeantown. The only major geographic feature is Canada's McLean Lake.

✳✳✳✳✳✳✳✳✳✳✳✳✳✳✳✳✳✳✳✳✳✳✳✳✳✳✳✳✳✳✳✳✳
✳   **MARTIN**   ✳
✳✳✳✳✳✳✳✳✳✳✳✳✳✳✳✳✳✳✳✳✳✳✳✳✳✳✳✳✳✳✳✳✳

Related Names

Other surnames which are related as to root, derivation or usage include:

Kilmartin	Martens	Martinsmith	Martyn
Martell	Martenson	Martinson	Martyns
Marten	Martins	Marton	

The surname Martin derives from the popular first name. The first name Martin has ancient origins which start at the same source as the first name Mark. Both these first names derive from the Latin name Martius, which means 'of Mars'. Mars was a pagan god of war, and thus Martius was a common name for a warrior. Strictly speaking, Martin is a diminutive of Martius.

Martin owes its popularity as a Christian name to the fourth-century Saint Martin, who was originally a soldier but finally ended up as Bishop of Tours in France. His best-known act was tearing his cloak in two and giving one half to a beggar.

Occasionally, the surname Martin derives from a place name. There are in fact villages called Martin or Marten in six English counties; and from this source the surname would mean 'a person from Martin (or Marten)'. The place name means 'a place near a mere or lake'.

The most widespread variations on Martin are Marten, Martyn and Martell. The last of these is a double diminutive (though occasionally it is an occupational name coming from the same Old French word, which means a hammer). The name Martinsmith, which looks occupational, is actually a corruption of the medieval Martinsmough, 'Martin's brother-in-law'. The same development is seen in Hudsmith (Hud's – i.e. Hugh's – brother-in-law), while the original form remains in Watmough, 'Walter's brother-in-law', and Hitch-mough, 'Richard's brother-in-law'. Martinson or Martenson, as well as Martins or Martens, are also derivatives of Martin. In other languages the name appears as Martine, Martines, Martinez, Martineau, Martinelli, Martini, Martino and Martinuzzi.

The first name Martin appears in its Latinised form Martius in the Domesday Book records for 1066. However, the surname does not appear until a century later, the first mention being in the Red Book of the Exchequer for Cambridgeshire. Here in 1166 Walter and Helewis Martin are listed.

A Martin Miscellany

Martin brothers have on several occasions made major names

for themselves in the decorative arts. In the eighteenth century Robert, Julien, Guilliaume and Étienne-Simon Martin invented and perfected the application of a special lacquer for furniture and furnishings. Known as *vernis-Martin*, this was extensively used at Versailles.

☆

Admiral Sir William F. Martin was renowned in the Royal Navy for having his men arrested ('pinched') for even the slightest offence. Ever since, any Martin joining the Navy picks up the nickname 'Pincher'.

☆

Simon Manfritie de Borton (1210–85) ascended the papal throne in 1281 calling himself Martin IV, under the mistaken assumption that there had already been Popes Martin II and III. His entire short reign was marred by similar ineptitudes, and he was driven from Rome by a popular uprising in 1285.

☆

Glen Luther Martin (1886–1955) was a pioneer aviator and aircraft manufacturer. He made the first flight over the ocean, a short hop from Newport Beach to Santa Catalina Island. Later he formed a large aeroplane manufacturing company, which was responsible for producing such epoch-making craft as the B-26 bomber and the PBM Marina flying boat. Both of these played a major part in the World War II bombing of Germany.

☆

Martins are members of the swallow family. The mud martin is so named because it makes its nest of sticks, straw and mud. Martens are weasel-like carnivores found in Canada, the northern US, Europe and the Far East. The soft, thick fur of these creatures is much valued.

☆

In all, 8 towns in the United Kingdom are Martin-related. There are 17 in the United States including 5 Martins and 5 Martinsburgs. South Africa has a Martindale while New Zealand has a Martinborough. Because of the Saint Martin connections, related town and geographic names are widespread and notably prevalent in Latin-language areas.

Related Names

Other surnames which are related as to root, derivation or usage include:

Mellard	Millers	Millward	Molineux
Meller	Millerson	Millwood	Mullard
Mellers	Millier	Milne	Muller
Millar	Millman	Milner	Mylne
Millard	Mills		

Not surprisingly, the surname Miller was originally an occupation name – for one who grinds (or mills) the corn. The earliest forms of this name are Mulnare (1275), Milner and Mylnere.

The original Milner, or Miller, has many related names. Common examples of these are Millward (the ward or keeper of the mill), Milne (usually meaning 'dweller or worker at the mill'), Millers (a derivative of Miller) and Millman.

There are also a number of names which would at first sight appear to be related to Miller, but come from completely different sources. Examples of these are Millican, Millikin (which derive from Milligan, which in turn comes from the Irish name Mulligan), and Millicent (which originates from a German first name meaning 'work-strong' and which came over to England with the Norman Conquest). Interestingly, Molineux, which looks at first sight to be from a different source, is a French name meaning 'miller' and is ultimately related to Miller by etymology.

The popular and widespread name Mills has two possible derivations, one of which is related to Miller. On the one hand it could be from 'dweller by the mills' (plural); on the other it could represent the first name Miles (now more common as Myles).

Owing to its early rural origins, the name Miller is extremely widespread, being one of the few English names which is common to all counties throughout the land. It is also the twentieth most popular Scottish name and, more surprisingly, was recently found to be sixth most popular in the United States – though many of these will have been anglicised from European versions of this occupational name or from similar-sounding more complex European names, or simply adopted by people whose names proved too long and/or too complex for everyday English use – as in many Polish or Greek names.

The name Miller began to appear early in the English records – though its earliest appearance was in a variation of the original Milner form. One John le Mulnare is mentioned in the Subsidy Rolls for Worcester for 1275. Only 21 years later the Miller form appeared in the Subsidy Rolls for Sussex, where one Ralf Muller is listed.

A Miller Miscellany

Miss Marple and Hercule Poirot are the creations of Agatha Mary Miller (1891–1976), better known as Agatha Christie. Worldwide sales of her 77 detective novels are in the tens of millions. Dame Agatha is unique in being the only modern playwright to have had three West End plays running concurrently, including *The Mousetrap* which has run for a record-breaking number of years.

☆

Other Millers have also been notably successful as twentieth-century literary figures. Henry Miller (1891–1980) is famous for his sexually explicit novels *Tropic of Cancer* and *Tropic of Capricorn*, written and published in Paris and banned in the UK and US until the early Sixties. The major American dramatist Arthur Miller's best-known work *Death of A Salesman* won a 1949 Pulitzer Prize.

☆

Famous English comedian Joseph Miller (1684–1738) was ironically dubbed 'The Father of Jests', since he was something of a dullard and the butt of contemporary jesters. A 'Joe Miller' was a popular nineteenth-century term synonymous with any joke, as in 'I don't see the Joe Miller of it'.

☆

The most popular Allied band leader during World War II was Glenn Miller (1904–44). The plane carrying him to entertain the troops at Christmas-time vanished over the sea and was never found. The 'Glenn Miller sound' goes on to this very day.

☆

The United Kingdom has towns named Miller, Mill and Miller's Dale, South Africa has a Miller and Australia a Millaroo. The United States has 6 name-related towns while the Bahamas has a town called Millars and New Zealand has Miller's Flat and Millerton. Surprisingly few major rivers bear the name. Australia has a Miller river and a Miller's creek while the United States has a Millers falls.

```
******************************
*              MITCHELL              *
******************************
```

Related Names

Other surnames which are related as to root, derivation or usage include:

Meickle	Michelson	Micklejohn	Mitchinson
Michael	Michie	Mitchel	Mitchison
Michaels	Michison	Mitchelson	Mutch
Michel	Mickle	Mitchenson	

The surname Mitchell has two separate derivations. In the first it comes from the first name Michel, the Norman form of Michael. Michael is a name of great antiquity and comes from the Hebrew, where it means 'Who is God?'. The Archangel Michael appears in the Book of Revelations, where he overcomes Satan and the powers of evil. This role has made him the patron saint of soldiers. The first name Michael started to become popular in Europe around the twelfth century, probably as a result of its 'rediscovery' during the Crusades to the Holy Land. It has always been particularly popular in Ireland, to such an extent that it is now often used in the form of Mick, as a (fairly derogatory) nickname for an Irishman. Michael is presently one of the most popular first names in the United States.

The second derivation of Mitchell is as a nickname from the Middle English word 'muchel' (in the North, 'mickle') which means 'big', hence Micklejohn, 'big John'. The word survives today as 'much' in such place names as Much Haddington.

The original name Mitchell has many variations. Mitchel and Mitchelson are the most frequent, and Mitchenson and Mitchinson are both versions of Mitchelson. Other surnames from the same source are Michael and Michaels.

References to the name Michel began to appear in the records of the early thirteenth century. The earliest reference to it as a surname is in the Curia Regis Rolls for Northumberland. Here in

217

1205 the name Gilbert Michel is mentioned. That example almost certainly comes from the first-name derivation.

A Mitchell Miscellany
One of the greatest best-sellers of all times, *Gone With The Wind*, was written by Margaret Mitchell (1900–49). This romantic chronicle of the American Civil War sold over one million copies within six months of publication. The film version, starring Vivien Leigh as Scarlett O'Hara and Clark Gable as Rhett Butler, was for many years the longest movie ever released.

The Scottish-born explorer Sir Thomas Livingstone Mitchell (1792–1855) began his adventurous career as an aide-de-camp to the Duke of Wellington in Spain. Later he explored uncharted regions of New South Wales in Australia, eventually laying out over 200 new towns and villages.

The many retail cooperatives throughout Britain and the US owe their existence to Lancashire-born John Thomas Whitehead Mitchell. He was the key figure in shaping the policies of the 1863 Cooperative Wholesale Society, basing the return of members' dividends on their total purchases. Radical Socialist Beatrice Webb later successfully championed his ideas.

☆

Mitcheldean, Mitchell and Mitchel Troy are name-related towns in the United Kingdom. Canada and Australia each have one Mitchell while the United States has 4 such towns and Ireland has a Mitchelstown. There are 2 Mitchell rivers in Australia, one in Canada and 2 Mitchell lakes in the United States. Australia has a Mitchell Point.

✳✳✳✳✳✳✳✳✳✳✳✳✳✳✳✳✳✳✳✳✳✳✳✳✳✳✳✳✳✳✳✳✳
✳   **MOORE**   ✳
✳✳✳✳✳✳✳✳✳✳✳✳✳✳✳✳✳✳✳✳✳✳✳✳✳✳✳✳✳✳✳✳✳

Related Names
Other surnames which are related as to root, derivation or usage include:

Atmore	Moorcock	Moorehead	Moorgate
Moor	Moorcroft	Moorey	Moorhead

Moorhouse	Moorwood	Morecraft	Morland
Mooring	Morcombe	Moreland	Morley
Moorman	More	Moreman	Morton
Moors			

The surname Moore has two distinct derivations. In one it originated from the first name Moor, whose origins are of great antiquity. This comes from the Old French Maur, which in its turn derives from the Latin first name Maurus. (There was even a Saint Maurus in the sixth century.) The first name Maurus originally meant 'moor' (as in Othello the Moor) and was given to a native of North Africa. These were very rarely black people – like Othello – but were usually Arabs or Berbers. However, the name Maurus soon came to be used as a nickname for anyone with a dark complexion, meaning 'darkie' – almost certainly with racialist undertones. Thus this derivation of the name Moore came to England with the Normans in the eleventh century (see also Morris.)

The other derivation of the surname Moore is from the Anglo-Saxon word 'mor' meaning 'heath'. It is thus a place name, being given to someone who lived at or on a moor, heath or fen. The earliest forms of the name were preceded by 'at' or 'de' (e.g. Harry at Moore) with the additional 'e' because of the dative case.

There are many names related to, or variations of, the original Moore. Common examples of these are Moorhouse (house or home in the fen or moor, also a frequent place name in the northern counties of England), Moorehead (dweller at the top edge, or head, of the moor, also local name from places in Northumberland and West Yorkshire), Moorcroft (croft, or cottage, on the moor), Moorman, Moorwood (dweller in or by the wood on the moor). The name Morton also derives from this source – being short for Moorton, meaning farm on the moor. However, two very similar names have different derivations. The surname Moorcock is sometimes derived from a diminutive of the first name More: Morcoc. However, it also derives on occasions from 'son of Maurice', or as a nickname from the bird, the moorcock. The name Moorson, more commonly Morson, comes from 'son of Morris'.

The name Moore is widespread throughout Britain and Ireland. However, in Ireland the name occasionally derives as an anglicised version of the Irish name O'More. This comes from the Irish Gaelic O'Mordha, which originates from the Gaelic

219

first name 'Mordha' meaning 'majestic'.

The earliest mention of the surname Moore is in the 1185 Records of the Templars for Lincolnshire. Here one Johannes filius More is listed.

A Moore Miscellany

Sir Thomas More (1478–1535) was a statesman, scholar, author – and finally a martyr. Today he is best remembered as the hero of the film *A Man for All Seasons*. This depicts his friendship with Henry VIII, and their final quarrel, when Thomas More refused to support Henry's divorce from Catherine of Aragon. For this Henry had him imprisoned, and later beheaded. Thomas More's saintliness of character soon became universally renowned. He was subsequently canonised by the Catholic Church while to this day there is a Thomas More room in the bounds of the Kremlin.

Several Moores have distinguished themselves in the arts. One of the most notable of these was Yorkshire sculptor Henry Moore (1898–1986). Another was America's greatest female poet of the twentieth century – Marianne Moore (1887–1972). Her many prizes included a Pulitzer, the National Book Award, and the Gold Medal of the National Institute of Letters.

The United Kingdom has 19 Moore-related towns. These range from Moorby to Moortown (2). Jamaica has a Moore Town while Canada has a Moore's Mills and a Moores, and Australia a Moor-lands and a Moorooka. In all, 21 US towns and cities relate to the name. Moore-related names for geographic features are common.

✳✳✳✳✳✳✳✳✳✳✳✳✳✳✳✳✳✳✳✳✳✳✳✳✳✳✳✳✳✳✳✳✳✳✳
✳   MORGAN   ✳
✳✳✳✳✳✳✳✳✳✳✳✳✳✳✳✳✳✳✳✳✳✳✳✳✳✳✳✳✳✳✳✳✳✳✳

Related Names

Other surnames which are related as to root, derivation or usage include:

Morgans   Morganson   Morganton   Morgen

The surname Morgan is extremely ancient. Though it is known to be of Celtic origin, its meaning remains uncertain. The name

220

itself derives from a Celtic first name which was rendered as Morcant in Old Breton, Old Welsh and Cornish; and as Morgunn in Pictish. One possible meaning of the name is 'sea-bright', in which case it would have been a nickname referring to the appearance or personality of its original holder.

The name Morgan is most frequently found in South Wales, where it is related to the Country of Glamorgan. Here the name was originally Ap-Morgan, meaning 'son of Morgan', (as in Ab-Evan, 'son of Evan', which became Bevan). However, the name also occurs often in Scotland, where it is known to have originated from Aberdeenshire and amongst the Mackays of Sutherland. There is even a Clan Morgan in Scotland and this clan title was used by the Mackays of the Reay country.

Other origins include ancient Brittany and Cornwall as well as England, where the name gave rise to the related Morgans, which is short for Morganson.

Morgan was the name of the early British monk who travelled to Europe and started the first Christian heresy. In Europe his name was Graecised to Pelagius – hence the Pelagian heresy, which denies original sin.

The surname Morgan appears in many forms in the early records. The earliest references are to the Latinised form Morganus, which occurs in the Pipe Rolls for Gloucestershire in 1159, and also in the Pipe Rolls for Salop in 1166. However, this form was probably used only for official records. The more vernacular form of Morgund is listed in Scottish records between 1204 and 1211. In 1214 the Curia Regis Rolls for Berkshire list a John Morgan.

A Morgan Miscellany

The most notorious pirate of the Spanish Main was Sir Henry Morgan (1635–88). For over a decade he terrorised the Caribbean. Such was his power that at one time he commanded a fleet of 36 ships, with over 2,000 buccaneers, and at one stage actually seized control of Jamaica from the Spanish as well as Cuba. He later retired and died a respected planter in Jamaica.

☆

Whimsical fairy Morgan le Fay is variously depicted in Arthurian romance as a magical healer, mistress of Avalon and later as a malign sorceress constantly plotting the death of Arthur and dreaming up evil schemes to discredit the Knights of the Round Table. As late as the nineteenth century the famous mirages seen

221

in the Strait of Messina were popularly believed to be *Fata Morgana* (the Fairy Morgan) a name still used to describe them.

☆

A morganatic marriage is one between a male of royal birth and a woman of lesser rank, with the provision that any children resulting from the union will not inherit their father's station or property.

☆

Morgan horses, once the most popular breed in the US, are stylish, all-purpose steeds especially suited for riding. A horse named Justin Morgan (after its owner) was the early-nineteenth-century father of the breed with an eclectic pedigree that, among other strains, combined thoroughbreds and Arabians.

☆

Anglican clergyman William Morgan's 1588 translation of the Bible into Welsh became the written language taught to the Welsh people for the next 200 years and thus standardised the language.

☆

The United Kingdom has one name-related town, Morgan's Vale. Australia has a Morgan and a Morganville while Russia has a Morgana. In the US there are 15 name-related towns including the exotically designated Morganza. There are Morgan mountains in Australia and the US and a Morgan's Bluff in the Bahamas as well as a Morgan's Bay in South Africa and a Morgan Island in Antarctica.

✳✳✳✳✳✳✳✳✳✳✳✳✳✳✳✳✳✳✳✳✳✳✳✳✳✳✳✳✳✳✳✳✳
✳   **MORRIS**   ✳
✳✳✳✳✳✳✳✳✳✳✳✳✳✳✳✳✳✳✳✳✳✳✳✳✳✳✳✳✳✳✳✳✳

Related Names
Other surnames which are related as to root, derivation or usage include:

Fitzmaurice	Morcock	Morrish	Morrissey
Fitzmorris	Morison	Morrison	Morson
Marin	Morrice	Morriss	Morys
Maurice	Morrisey		

The surname Morris is a variation of the name Maurice, which was, and still is, a popular first name. The first name Maurice came to England with the Norman Conquest and derives from the Old French name Meurisse. This name in turn came from the Latin first name Mauritius (like the island) which originates from the word Maurus, meaning a Moor (as in Othello the Moor, an inhabitant of North Africa, usually of Berber or Arab origin – see also Moore). Thus this name was originally given to a Moor. However, it was also often used as a nickname for anyone of swarthy or dark complexion.

The name Maurice spread all over Europe. There was even a St Maurice who was martyred in Switzerland in AD 286. (The fashionable ski resort of St Moritz is named after him.) When the name came to England, it gave itself to that most English of rural pastimes, the Morris Dance. Ironically, this originally meant 'Moorish Dance'.

The name Morris is found all over the land, but is most common in Wales, the Welsh border country and the southern counties of England. The variation Morrish is found in Somerset and Devon. This is a corruption of the more French Maurice, just as the French word liquorice is now often corrupted to liquorish. Other related names are Morrison (most common in the northern counties of England, and in Scotland), Morrice, and Fitzmaurice (son of Maurice).

The earliest mention of the surname Morris in the records is one of Fulco Julius Mauricii (this being the Latin version of the name, with Julius meaning 'son of'). He appears in the records of the Templars for Lincolnshire in 1185. The slightly more recognisable Ricardus Julius Morys appears in the 1297 Subsidy Rolls for Yorkshire.

A Morris Miscellany
The English artist, poet and social reformer William Morris (1834–96) revolutionised Victorian taste with his designs for furniture, fabrics and wallpaper – which remain influential in interior design to this day.

☆

A key figure in the development of the British motor industry was William Richard Morris (1877–1963), who later became Lord Nuffield. He started his business in a bicycle repair shop, and later set up his factory at Cowley, Oxford. The Morris Oxford car was his greatest popular success.

☆

Liverpool-born American patriot Robert Morris was dubbed

'the Financier of the American Revolution' for his private role in procuring supplies and borrowing money to keep Washington's army going through the most crucial years of the revolution. Later he loyally served the fledgling nation by securing loans to help it through early financial crises. But by 1798 disastrous land speculations had eaten up his personal fortune, and he was arrested and clapped into a debtor's prison, where he stayed for 3½ years. He later died in obscurity, a broken man.

☆

The sole name-related town in the United Kingdom is Morriston while Canada has a Morris and a Morrisburg. A total of 24 United States towns and cities are Morris-related. Name-related geographic features are rare. Australia has a Morris mountain and there is a Morris Island off the coast of South Carolina in the United States.

✻✻✻✻✻✻✻✻✻✻✻✻✻✻✻✻✻✻✻✻✻✻✻✻✻✻✻✻✻✻✻✻✻✻✻
✻ **MURPHY** **✻**
✻✻✻✻✻✻✻✻✻✻✻✻✻✻✻✻✻✻✻✻✻✻✻✻✻✻✻✻✻✻✻✻✻✻✻

Related Names
Other surnames which are related as to root, derivation or usage include:

MacMurphy	Morphey	O'Morchoe	O'Murphy
Morchoe	Murphey		

The name Murphy is easily the most widely held surname in Ireland and as such appears in large numbers wherever Irishmen have emigrated. It has also long been found in Scotland, but it is not indigenous there, its presence being due solely to early immigration.

There were three original family clans (or septs) of this name, in Wexford, Roscommon and Cork, where there are still more Murphys per head of population than anywhere else. Once upon a time the forms MacMurphy and O'Murphy (both meaning 'son of Murphy') were widespread, but the prefixes have generally been dropped. The MacMurphys were originally found mainly in Armagh and Tyrone.

The name Murphy came from the Irish Gaelic O'Murchadha which derives from the first name Murchadh, meaning 'sea warrior'. It is thus possible that some, but certainly not all, of the

224

original Murphys may have been of Viking origin.

An early form of the name Murphy is Morchoe (or O'Morchoe). This is still in use, and the chief of the O'Murphys is called O'Morchoe.

Unlike most names derived from the Gaelic, Murphy has few variants. The alternative spelling Murphey is still found, but it is in no way as popular as Murphy.

The name Murphy does not appear in early English records, and the name did not come to England in any significant numbers until the great Irish immigration of the eighteenth century.

A Murphy Miscellany

In 1952 amateur hypnotist Morey Bernstein put a young housewife Virginia Tighe (b. 1923) into a deep trance. Thus began one of the strangest controversies of the twentieth century. Tighe proceeded to recount in great detail her former life as an Irishwoman named Bridey Murphy, born in Cork in 1798. She supplied details of that time and place no modern young American could be expected to know, such as slang expressions and the title of a book which, it turned out, had been published in Ireland but not in the US. Bernstein's account of his experiment, *The Search for Bridey Murphy*, instantly became a best-seller, with 170,500 copies in print within two months. However, *Life* magazine, through its own investigations, revealed that in childhood, one of Mrs Tighe's neighbours had been a Mrs Corkell, maiden name Bridey Murphy. That revelation, plus other inconsistencies in Bridey's recollections, cooled the public's interest but the episode raised questions that have yet to be satisfactorily answered.

☆

Murphys have made a major impact on medicine. American doctor William Murphy shared a Nobel Prize with two others for his discovery that raw liver cured pernicious anaemia, while American surgeon John Benjamin Murphy was a pioneer in the study and treatment of peritonitis, and invented the Murphy Button (1892), a device for linking severed intestinal ends thus enabling important advances in gastrointestinal surgery. Artificial lung collapse (by the injection of nitrogen, instrumental in the treatment of tuberculosis) was another Murphy innovation.

☆

Marie Louise Murphy (1733–1814) rose from being a draper's daughter to become Louis XV's mistress. Madame de

Pompadour stage-managed the whole affair by arranging to have the King meet Marie Louise while she posed at Versailles as the Virgin for a portrait of the Holy Family. When the king tired of her she was replaced in his affections by her sister, Marie Brigette.

☆

Irish-born Arthur Murphy was an eighteenth-century all-rounder. As publisher of the *Gray's Inn Journal* he got to know Dr Johnson, later writing an *Essay on Johnson*. When he encountered financial reverses he took to the stage, so success-fully that he was able to pay off his debts; then he began both to write and produce plays on his own. After entering Lincoln's Inn in 1757 he was called to the Bar and practised law success-fully while finding time to publish a highly regarded translation of Tacitus.

☆

Few related place and major geographical feature names attach to Murphy. The United States has 3 towns called Murphy, one Murphys, and one Murphysboro as well as a Murphy Lake, while Antarctica has a Mount Murphy.

****
*　　　　　　　**MURRAY**　　　　　　　*
****

Related Names
Other surnames which are related as to root, derivation or usage include:

Kilmorey	Merry	Murie	Murrihy
MacGilmore	Moray	Murrey	Murry
MacIlmurray	Morrey	Murrie	O'Murry
MacMurray	Morrie		

The surname Murray is a place name deriving from the county of Moray (as in Moray Firth) in Scotland. As such it is a Scots Gaelic derivation from the ancient British place name, whose exact meaning remains unknown. It is also the English spelling for a wide variety of Irish surnames ranging from O'Muirighte to Mac Gille Mhuire.

The Irish Murrays are mainly in the north, and their presence is due almost entirely to the Cromwellian land settlements and other immigrations from Scotland.

A witness to the Royal Charter to the Abbey of Holyrood in 1203 was one William de Moravia – the first Murray on record. The Moray (or Murray) origin of this name is confirmed by the appearance in the records 50 years later of one Malcolm de Moravia, who witnessed a charter by the Earl of Strathern.

Some modern Murrays living in England may well have a different origin. These almost certainly derive from the Middle English name Murie (more recognisable in its root form Merry). This was originally a nickname, describing an obvious quality of character. These Murrays are sometimes spelt Murrie. Other widespread variations on Murray include Murrey, Morrey and Murry.

A Murray Miscellany

The Murray Fracture Zone is a long submarine mountain range stretching nearly 2,000 miles across the Pacific Ocean from northern Hawaii to the shores of south-western California. It is named after Sir John Murray (1841–1914), the Ottawa-born pioneer in the science of oceanography.

☆

One of the most influential English literary figures in the early decades of the twentieth century was John Middleton Murry. His close and often stormy relationship with the novelist D.H. Lawrence was depicted in thinly disguised form in Lawrence's novel *Women in Love*, which was later made into a controversial film by the flamboyant film director Ken Russell.

☆

Australia's principal river is the Murray River. It flows through some 1,000 miles of south-eastern Australia and was named after the Colonial Secretary, Sir George Murray. The Murray Valley is the main wheat-growing and sheep-farming area in south-western Australia. This valley also has a disease named after it, Murray Valley encephalitis, a form of brain tissue inflammation which was once prevalent in the area. The disease is also known as Australian X disease, and is transmitted by bird migration.

☆

The American astronomer Bruce Murray masterminded the data-finding equipment for the Mariner 10 space rocket which provided us with revolutionary new knowledge about the planet Mercury.

There are no name-related towns or major geographic features in the United Kingdom. Both Canada and the US have Murray-villes while the US also has 4 towns called Murray and a Murray City. Australia has a Murray Downs and a Murrysboro, while Bermuda has a Murray's Anchorage. Murray rivers are common outside of the United Kingdom while Australia's Murray range and the Pacific Ocean's Murray Deep are world famous.

```
******************************
*            O'BRIEN         *
******************************
```

O'BRIEN

Related Names
Other surnames which are related as to root, derivation or usage include:

Brian	Bryan	O'Briain	O'Bryan
Brien	Bryant	O'Brian	O'Bryen

The surname O'Brian comes from the Irish Gaelic O'Briain, which means 'son of Brian'. Brian is an ancient Celtic name of uncertain origin – but the most likely explanation is that it means 'hill'.

The family clans of the O'Brians have great importance in Ireland. This is mainly due to their illustrious predecessor, the great Brian Born, King of Leinster and Munster, who fought the Vikings at the Battle of Clontarf.

The O'Brians were originally found mainly in Munster, but are now numerous all over Ireland, and indeed wherever Irishmen have immigrated. It is not unexpected to find the name O'Brian occurring frequently in London, Boston, or Sydney, but a little-known fact is that one of the great wines of France – Chateau Haut Brian – is in fact derived from the Irish O'Brian. (The O'Brians are not the only Irish to have distinguished themselves in this most French of preserves – witness the Hennessys of Cognac fame.)

In some cases the Irish O'Brian is derived from O'Byrne (see Byrne), derived from O'Biorain. Also, during the centuries of British persecution in Ireland, many Irish O'Brians found it prudent to anglicise their name to Bryan, Bryon or Bryom: compare the case of the Byrnes, above. In other cases it is a derivation of the first name Brian, which in this instance came to England with the Norman Conquest, being found in Latinised form in the Domesday Book, and giving rise to a number of variant English surnames such as Bryant and Byrne. Thus the Irish who switched from O'Brian to Bryan were really doing little more than completing a circle of variations.

An O'Brien Miscellany

The O'Briens have produced several Irish literary figures during the twentieth century. The novelist Edna O'Brien (b. 1932) is famed for her romantic portrayals of her childhood in remote County Clare; the humorist Flann O'Brien (1911–66), whose real name was Brian O'Nolan, is best remembered for his hilarious novel *At Swim-Two-Birds*.

Special effects genius Willis O'Brien gave birth to one of the screen's greatest stars, King Kong. His brilliant stop-animation techniques reached a peak with the climactic battle with aircraft atop the Empire State Building – one of the most memorable scenes in cinema history. O'Brien's handiwork was unsurpassed 43 years later, when Dino De Laurentiis, employing the latest technology, resurrected the giant ape. A laudable attempt, the second ape wasn't a patch on the strangely charming original.

Place and major geographic feature names related to O'Brien are rare. The United Kingdom has none. Ireland has 2 towns – O'Briensbridge and O'Briens Town, while Canada has one town called simply O'Brien.

✱✱✱✱✱✱✱✱✱✱✱✱✱✱✱✱✱✱✱✱✱✱✱✱✱✱✱✱✱✱✱✱✱✱
✱   **O'NEILL**   ✱
✱✱✱✱✱✱✱✱✱✱✱✱✱✱✱✱✱✱✱✱✱✱✱✱✱✱✱✱✱✱✱✱✱✱

Related Names

Other surnames which are related as to root, derivation or usage include:

McNeal	Neale	Nelson	Nigel
McNeil	Neel	Niall	Nihill
McNell	Neill	Nielsen	Niles
Neal	Nell	Nielson	O'Neil

The surname O'Neil comes from the Irish Gaelic, which is spelt the same. It means 'son or descendant of Neil (or Neal)'. This first name was originally Nial, and came from the Old Irish 'niadh', meaning 'champion'.

This first name has been popular in Ireland since earliest times. During the Viking invasions its popularity spread throughout the Norse world. In Iceland it became Njal (as seen in *The Story of Burnt Njal*), and in France it became Nel (or Nele). Here it was later Latinised to Nigellus (meaning 'black') which gave over to the variant Nigel.

Various forms of the name appear as a first name in the Domesday Book. Consequently, it soon gave rise to many variant surnames – such as Nelson and Nielson (which developed on its own in Scandinavian from the same first-name source).

The main family clan of the Irish O'Neills are the illustrious O'Neills of Ulster. Here they originated in Tyrone, being descended from the legendary Niall of the Nine Hostages. Other family clans originated further south in Waterford and Carlow – though the name still remains most numerous in the Ulster counties of Tyrone, Antrim and Down. It is Ireland's tenth most popular name.

Widespread variations on the surname O'Neill range from Neal to Niles, and from Nihill to Nigel. Again, these are largely of Norman origin.

The first mention of any surname related to O'Neill appears in the Domesday Book records for Berkshire in 1086, where one Willelmus filius Nigelli is listed. After this many variations appear in England, but it is unlikely that any of these are of Irish origin until the eighteenth century or even later.

An O'Neill Miscellany

Shane's Castle, perched on County Antrim's Lough Neagh, is the ancient stronghold of the O'Neill clan. Thirty feet up the main tower's south wall there is a sculpture known as the Black Head of the O'Neills. According to ancient legend, the family will come to a tragic end if the head is ever destroyed. The O'Neills also have a banshee in the form of a beautiful young woman who paces back and forth wringing her hands and singing a haunting lament. Her appearance is said to herald the death of any member of the family unlucky enough to hear her wailing.

☆

Hugh O'Neill (c. 1540–1616), the second Earl of Tyrone, was an Irish rebel. Known in his time as 'The Great Earl', he led several Roman Catholic uprisings against the English rule. Confirmed in his title by James I but under threat of arrest because of a dispute over lands, he fled to Europe in 1607 in an unsuccessful attempt to raise an army. This 'flight of the earls', as it is known, marked the end of Gaelic Ulster, which was then anglicised.

☆

The iconoclastic English educator, A.S. Neill (1883–1973), established the experimental boarding school, Summerhill, in the early 1920s. His ideas on liberal education have considerably influenced subsequent development in education at all levels.

☆

Towns and major geographic features which relate to O'Neill are extremely rare. The United States has one – O'Neill Nebraska.

✳✳✳✳✳✳✳✳✳✳✳✳✳✳✳✳✳✳✳✳✳✳✳✳✳✳✳✳✳✳✳✳✳✳✳
✳   **PARKER**   ✳
✳✳✳✳✳✳✳✳✳✳✳✳✳✳✳✳✳✳✳✳✳✳✳✳✳✳✳✳✳✳✳✳✳✳✳

Related Names
Other surnames which are related as to root, derivation or usage include:

Duparc	Parkerhouse	Parkhouse	Parkman
Park	Parkes	Parkhurst	Parks
Parke	Parkhill		

Parker is an ancient occupational name. It probably first came to this country with the Norman Conquest, though it possibly existed here prior to 1066. The surname Parker derives from the Old French word 'parquer' ('parchier'), which means 'park keeper' or 'ranger'. The Old French word derives in turn from a Germanic original meaning 'a park, enclosure, or thinly wooded land kept for beasts of the chase'.

    There are several related surnames, such as Parkman, and Parkhouse (place name for a dweller in a house in a park), and Duparc (Norman, meaning 'of the park').

231

Variations on the name Parker include Park, Parke, Parks and Parkes. Park and Parkes are, strictly speaking, place names (i.e. a dweller in a park). However, as often as not they probably indicated someone who worked in a park, and were thus occupational names.

The first reference to the surname Parker is in the Domesday Book records for Somerset where, in 1086, one Anschetel Parcher is listed.

A Parker Miscellany

When someone can't mind his own business, he's colloquially labelled a 'nosey parker'. The original was sixteenth-century English clergyman Matthew Parker, Archbishop of Canterbury under Queen Elizabeth I, whose critics dubbed him 'Nosey Parker' because he kept poking his nose into church matters that weren't his concern.

☆

One man stood between Abraham Lincoln and assassin John Wilkes Booth – an alcoholic policeman named John Parker, the only guard posted outside the President's box at Ford's Theater. Half-way through the evening's performance he wandered off to get a drink, with consequences that changed the course of American history.

☆

Comanche leader Quanah Parker, son of a chief who had married a white woman captured in childhood, led a year-long Texas rebellion of 700 warriors against the full might of the US cavalry before agreeing to settle on a reservation in 1875. He went on to become a powerful mediator between his people and the whites, spending his last 30 years as a successful businessman while still retaining his Indian culture and beliefs.

☆

British Admiral Sir Hyde Parker sent a withdrawal signal to the Baltic Fleet during the 1801 Battle of Copenhagen. His subordinate, Horatio Nelson, whose small ships had done most of the fighting, put his telescope to his blind eye so he could honestly claim he hadn't received the order, then went on to win the battle.

☆

Scottish explorer Mungo Park (1771–1806) was the first European to explore the Niger and several other interior regions of Africa.

The United Kingdom has no towns or major geographic features which are related to the name Parker. Canada has a town called Parkerview while the United States has 10 related-name towns and cities (including 5 called Parker) as well as the famous Parker Dam. Australia has a Parker hill, a Parker range and Parker Point while Hong Kong has a Parker mountain.

✳✳✳✳✳✳✳✳✳✳✳✳✳✳✳✳✳✳✳✳✳✳✳✳✳✳✳✳✳✳✳✳✳✳✳
✳   **PATTERSON**   ✳
✳✳✳✳✳✳✳✳✳✳✳✳✳✳✳✳✳✳✳✳✳✳✳✳✳✳✳✳✳✳✳✳✳✳✳

Related Names
Other surnames which are related as to root, derivation or usage include:

Fitzpatrick	Paton	Patricks	Pattison
Pater	Patrick	Pattinson	Patton
Paterson			

The surname Patterson derives from a first name and means 'son of Patrick'. The first name Patrick has a long history and goes back to Roman times, where it comes from the Latin word 'patricus', meaning 'nobleman'. The word 'patrician' comes from the same source, and the popular girl's name Patricia is the feminine form.

    The popularity of the first name Patrick in this country originated largely from the fifth-century saint of the same name. St Patrick almost certainly came originally from Scotland, but he is famous mainly for having brought Christianity to Ireland. For this deed he is now patron saint of Ireland, and his name is easily the most popular first name there. The diminutive of the name has even become the vernacular nickname for an Irishman – Paddy.

    In Scotland, the first name Patrick became synonymous for a while with Peter, and it may well be that some Scottish Pattersons originate from this other first name (Peter comes from the Greek 'petros' meaning 'rock'). Scotland also tends to spell Patterson differently from the English form. The English form almost invariably has two t's.

    There are several variant surnames arising from the same original source as Patterson. The best known of these are

Pattison (the form used south of the Scottish border, especially in Cumbria), Patton and Paton (which are from a double diminutive of Patrick, with an added Old French suffix), and the obvious Patrick.

The origins of the surname Patterson become much more apparent in the early versions found in the records – one of the earliest of which is William Patrison. He is mentioned in the 1446 records for Aberdeen.

A Patterson Miscellany

Australian poet Andrew 'Old Banjo' Paterson made a memorable contribution to the nation when 'Waltzing Matilda' appeared in a 1917 collection of his verse. Set to music, it quickly became Australia's unofficial anthem.

☆

Scots-born stone-cutter Robert Paterson (1715–1801) earned his nickname 'Old Mortality' when he abandoned his wife and five children to devote forty years to the task of repairing and erecting headstones to martyrs.

☆

South African novelist Alan Paton was an early protestor against the iniquities of apartheid. His best-selling *Cry, The Beloved Country* (1948) was a moving examination of his homeland's racial problems.

☆

Financier William Paterson founded the Bank of England in 1694. King William III approved his plan for a national bank when merchants raised £1,200,000 from shareholders and loaned it to the King at 8 per cent interest. William then granted the Bank a Royal Charter.

☆

General George Smith Patton (1885–1945) was the hell-for-leather commander of the US 3rd Army which drove the Nazis back across France in 1944.

☆

The only related place name in the United Kingdom is Patterdale in Cumbria. South Africa has one town called Patersen, the United States has 2, along with 5 Pattersons and one Pattisen. Australia has a Patersen river and a Patersen range while mountains in Canada's Yukon and in California are named Patterson. New Zealand has a Patterson Inlet while the New Hebrides has a Pattersen Passage.

```
****************************************
*               PHILLIPS               *
****************************************
```

Related Names

Other surnames which are related as to root, derivation or usage include:

Filkin	Philip	Philp	Phipps
Fill	Philips	Philpot	Piaf
Filpot	Philipson	Philpott	Potkin
Phelps	Phillip	Philps	Pott
Philbin	Phillipson	Philson	Pottell
Philcox	Phillpot	Phips	

The surname Phillips derives from the first name Philip. The 's' is short for 'son', so strictly speaking Phillips means 'son of Philip'.

The first name Philip comes from the Ancient Greek and means 'lover of horses'. (The prefix 'phil-' means 'lover of', as in philosophy (lover of wisdom) and philanthropy (lover of one's fellow men)). The first name Philip achieved wide popularity throughout Christendom owing to the apostle Philip. However, this first name rapidly went out of fashion in England during the reign of Elizabeth I, when our national enemy was Spain. In those days the King of Spain was Philip II, and with England under the threat of the Armada the name Philip became about as popular in England as Adolf is at present. The first name Philip remained under a cloud for several centuries after this, and did not really revive in popularity until the start of the reign of the second Queen Elizabeth, the popularity of the Queen's husband causing the name to come into fashion again. Prince Philip, being descended from the Greek royal family, was named after European royalty, where the name has always been popular.

The surname Philip (or Phillips), on the other hand, did not suffer such dramatic changes in fortune. Phillips, like any name derived from a widespread first name, has a whole host of related names (compare the surnames for Robert, David and John). The surname Phelps (originally as Philps) derives from an abbreviated form of Philip, as does the more obvious but rarer Philson. Phipps is the same. Philpot (and thus Filpot) derives from the once popular diminutive, Philip-ot, a French

235

diminutive form. (In this way Mary gives us the name Marriot, and nowadays in France Charlie Chaplin ('Charlie') is still commonly known as 'Charlot'.)

Other derivative surnames from the first name Philip include Fill, Filkin, and Philcox. In some cases even the original first syllable has been dropped, thus we get (by way of Philpot) the surnames Pott, Potkin, and Pottell – though in some cases these surnames have alternative entirely separate derivations.

The first name Philip first arrived in England during the twelfth century, coming by way of France in the French form Philippe. From this time on it appears regularly in the records as a first name. The earliest reference to the surname comes in the 1275 Hundred Rolls for Norfolk, where one Henry Philip is listed.

A Phillips Miscellany

Tuberculosis was one of the scourges of the nineteenth century. The Scottish physician Sir Robert William Phillip played a major role in its prevention and cure, and founded Europe's first TB dispensary at Edinburgh in 1887. By the time of his death in 1939, the dread disease had been brought under control.

☆

The Phillips Curve, named after A.W. Phillips, is a graphic representation of the economic relationship between the rate of unemployment and the rate of change of wages. It indicates that wages tend to rise faster when unemployment is low.

☆

The Phillips Collection is a small but outstanding collection of late-nineteenth- and early-twentieth-century American and European paintings. The museum, in Washington DC, was founded in 1918 by Duncan Phillips.

☆

In 1891 Anton Frederik Philips founded Philips Electric in Holland, now one of the world's largest firms for the manufacture of electrical appliances and lighting equipment.

☆

In 1687 the English colonial administrator Sir William Phipps (1651–95) headed an expedition to the Caribbean in search of sunken treasure and came back with £300,000 of Spanish gold. With his newfound wealth he bought himself a knighthood, and eventually rose to become Royal Governor of Massachusetts. He was later recalled to England, however, to face charges of misgovernment, but died before his trial.

☆

The United Kingdom has no towns or major geographic features which are related to this name but those with the name of Phillips need not feel downhearted. An entire country is their namesake – the Philippines. Canada has a Philipsburg, South Africa a Philipstown and a Philippolis, Belgium a Philipville, Holland a Phillippine and Germany a Philippsburg. Some 14 United States towns and cities are Phillips-related. Geographic features with the name are common and include Australia's famed Phillips range.

```
**********************************
*              PRICE             *
**********************************
```

Related Names
Other names which are related as to root, derivation or usage include:

Prise	Pryse	Reese	Rice
Pryce	Rees	Rhys	

The surname Price originated in Wales. It is a corruption of the name Ap-rhys, meaning 'son of Rhys'. Another similarly derived Welsh name is Bevan, which comes from a corruption of Ab-Evan. Rice is better known in the form Rees or Rhys, and the first name Rhys is thought to derive from the Old Welsh, meaning 'ardour'.

The surname Price is found all over Wales and in the Welsh border counties, as are the previously mentioned names to which it is clearly related.

Occasionally, the surname Price has an English origin. The word 'pris' came to England with William the Conqueror and the Normans in 1066, then, as a word for the price of goods. In the thirteenth century it became an occupational name given to a pricer or fixer of prices (with 'fixer' in the original sense of the word – no deviousness is implied).

Popular variations on this name are Pryce, Prise, and Pryse. It is also often found in double-barrelled form with the widespread Welsh names Jones and Thomas, as in Price-Jones and Price-Thomas. The surname Thomas derives from the first name,

237

which comes from the Ancient Aramaic word meaning 'twin' (for further details see Thomas). The surname Jones is short for 'son of John'. The first name John comes from the Hebrew meaning 'God is gracious' (see Johnson).

The first mention of the Welsh form of Price comes in the 1393 Archives for the City of London, where one Jorwerth ap Reys is listed. However, the Anglo-Norman name appears even earlier, in the 1297 Accounts for the County of Cornwall, where one Robert Price is mentioned.

A Price Miscellany

Prices have made a name for themselves in the arts. Vincent Price (b. 1911) has been a superstar of horror movies and thrillers since the early Thirties. He also has a second career as an art critic, and owns a remarkable collection of Impressionist paintings. Leontine Price (b. 1927) was the first black American soprano to achieve superstar status in the world of international opera. Her appearance in the 1950's revival of *Porgy and Bess* is now remembered as a classic. English character actor Dennis Price appeared in such notable films as *Kind Hearts and Coronets* and *I'm All Right, Jack* and was the unflappable Jeeves in *The World of Wooster*. In fact, Dennis Price's real name is Dennistown Franklyn.

☆

One of the great master-buildings designed by America's greatest twentieth-century architect, Frank Lloyd Wright (1868–1959), is the Price Tower in Bartlesville, Oklahoma. It was erected in 1956 and incorporates many of his revolutionary 'organic' ideas.

☆

The National Laboratory of Psychical Research was founded in 1937 by Harry Price. He advertised in *The Times* for objective observers to witness psychical phenomena. Countless inexplicable 'phenomena' have been, and continue to be, investigated by this society, though their authenticity continues to be doubted by the sceptical.

☆

The early American architect Bruce Price designed some of North America's most distinctive buildings. His most memorable works include the imposing Gothic-style Chateau Frontenac hotel in Quebec City, Montreal's Royal Victoria College, and several dormitories at Yale University. He also laid out New

York's Tuxedo Park, and designed many of the houses there.

☆

Bonamy Price, professor of political economy at Oxford in the late nineteenth century, helped mould economic thinking of the day in books such as *The Principles of Currency* and *Chapters on Practical Political Economy*.

☆

The United Kingdom has one name-related place, Price Town, while Canada has one town called Price and the United States has 3 so named as well as a Pricetown. Australia and the United States have Price rivers, while Canada boasts a Price Island in British Columbia.

✳✳✳✳✳✳✳✳✳✳✳✳✳✳✳✳✳✳✳✳✳✳✳✳✳✳✳✳✳✳✳✳✳✳
✳   **REID READ**   ✳
✳✳✳✳✳✳✳✳✳✳✳✳✳✳✳✳✳✳✳✳✳✳✳✳✳✳✳✳✳✳✳✳✳✳

Related Names
Other surnames which are related as to root, derivation or usage include:

Reade	Red	Reed	Reide
Reader	Redd	Reede	Reidy
Readett	Rede	Reeder	Ridding
Reading	Reditt	Reedman	Riding
Readman	Redman	Reeds	Rufus

These surnames have two distinct origins. The most usual derivation is from the nickname 'reed' or 'rede', which is Middle English for red. Thus the name would be given to someone with a ruddy complexion or red hair. This latter fact, together with its prevalence in East Anglia, the north-eastern counties of England, and Scotland (where it is spelt Reid), suggests that some of the original holders of this name were of Norse origin – though the name has long been widespread throughout the land.

The Old English word 'read' – 'red' also occurs in some place names, as perhaps in the Cumbria Redmayne which might mean 'red stone'. It appears as a personal name Reada, 'the red one', in Reading (Berkshire), 'the place where the people called after Reada live'. But not all examples of Reading as a surname necessarily allude to the Berkshire surname. Some may derive

239

from places called Reading (in Kent), Reddings (Worcestershire), Redding Wood (Herefordshire), and so on. There was an Old English word 'ried' – 'a clearing' – giving rise to place names Read and Reed, from which some surnames would be derived.

Finally, there is a third possible origin, an Old English word 'hreod' – 'reed', which gives us the place names Readett, Reditt etc. – 'reed-bed', and the occupational surnames Reader, Reeder, Readman, Reedman, and Redman – 'reedman, reed-cutter, thatcher'.

The surname Read is one of the oldest in the records. The first mention of the nickname derivation appears before the Norman Conquest in the earliest Kent annals. Here Leofwine se Reade is mentioned in the records for 1016–20. After the Norman Conquest, this form of Read (and sometimes the alternative variation) often became Latinised to Rufus (as in William Rufus, William the Conqueror's son).

The earliest mention of the place-name derivation is in the 1160 records for Sussex where one Alwin de Larede is mentioned.

A Reid Miscellany

Reids have made a notable contribution to the fine arts on two continents. Sir George Reid, Scottish landscape and portrait painter, headed the Royal Scottish Academy during 1891–1902. His paintings hang in museums in London, Edinburgh, Oxford, Aberdeen, Glasgow, Liverpool and Manchester. He is also noted for his book illustrations. Canadian George Andrew Reid's career was remarkably similar. Born in Canada in 1860, he served as president of his country's Royal Academy and later headed the Ontario College of Art.

☆

Henry Fielding Reid was an American seismologist who developed the 'elastic rebound' theory explaining earthquake mechanics (1911).

☆

Down-to-earth eighteenth-century philosopher Thomas Reid displayed one of the Scotsman's most basic qualities when he opposed the empirical scepticism of Locke and Hume with his 'philosophy of common sense'. His approach accepted the existence of things and didn't try to make subjective mental phenomena of them. Similarly, his system's morality was based

240

on an intuitive perception of ethics. Such views led to professorships at both Aberdeen and Glasgow.

☆

American army physician Walter Reed (1861–1902) conducted decisive experiments that proved typhoid germs are transmitted by the mosquito. His findings led to the elimination of yellow fever in Havana during the Spanish-American War, and later in Panama during the building of the Canal.

☆

Because Reid has so many spelling variations (Reed, Read, Ried) and because two roots are involved ('red' and 'reed') this name is notably hard to relate properly to geographic features and place names. Given the most comprehensive interpretation of the name some 6 United Kingdom towns and cities are related – Read, Reading, Reading Street, Reed, Reedham and Reedness. Canada has a Readlyn, Australia a Reedy Springs and 2 Reids, Jamaica a Reading, while the United States has 18 name-related towns and cities. Rivers, lakes, and other topographic features with variations on the name are relatively common and include Fiji's dangerous Reed Reef.

REILLY

Related Names

Other surnames which are related as to root, derivation or usage include:

Orailly	O'Riley	Riley	Ryley
O'Reilly	Reily		

Reilly is a widespread Irish surname which comes from the Irish Gaelic O'Raghallaigh which means 'descendant of Raghallach' ('the valiant or prosperous one'). Thus it is derived from an ancient Gaelic first name, and was probably given originally to a warrior (who would have become prosperous through booty).

The Reillys are an important family clan, which now has many subdivisions all over Ireland. However, the Reillys are still most numerous in County Cavan, where the main band of the clan is thought to have originated. The prefix 'O' is now being more frequently adopted in the anglicised form. This

241

means 'descendant of' and is similar to the Scottish (and Irish) 'Mac-' – 'son of' – and to Anglo-Norman 'Fitz-', and Welsh 'Ap-'/'Ab-', though this last does not usually appear in the original form, as more frequently it has been absorbed. The most widespread example is in the Welsh surname Bevan, which derives from Ab-Evan.

The earliest record in English sources is in the Calendar of Patent Rolls, which shows a reference to one William Orailly in 1451, though in Ireland the name certainly goes back much further than this. The anglicised forms Riley and Ryley are borrowed from a native English surname based on a common place-name type (Devon, Lancashire, etc.) meaning 'clearing where rye grows'.

A Reilly Miscellany

Edward O'Reilly compiled one of the first Irish-English dictionaries in 1817.

☆

Hugh Reilly (1630–95) accompanied James II into exile and wrote *Ireland's Case Stated Briefly*, the only printed account of the state of Catholics in Ireland for a century.

☆

Irish-born nineteenth-century newspaper editor and author Henry O'Reilly made a notable, if unusual, contribution to his adopted homeland when he contracted with inventor Samuel Morse to erect telegraph lines from Pennsylvania to the Great Lakes. He had strung over 8,000 miles of line before falling out with Morse, which event led him to abandon the project.

☆

Hard-fighting US marine Lieutenant General William Riley, whose decorations included the Silver Star, the Purple Heart and the Croix de Guerre, proved to be an equally able diplomat when handed the tricky assignment of supervising United Nations military observers in potentially explosive post-war Palestine. The commission he headed tactfully settled over 1000 Arab-Israeli disputes and dealt with 65 cease-fire violations between 1948 and 1950.

☆

Only one place name, Riley Hill, and no major geographic features in the United Kingdom relate to this name. It is equally rare elsewhere. The United States has 4 towns named Riley and a Rileyville and there's a Reiley Peak in Arizona.

Related Names

Other surnames which are related as to root, derivation or usage include:

Dick	Hicks	Hix	Richman
Dickens	Hickson	Reckett	Rick
Dickenson	Higgins	Ricard	Rickard
Dickson	Higginson	Rich	Rickeard
Dixon	Higgs	Richard	Rickett
Heacock	Higman	Richards	Ricketts
Hick	Hiscock	Riche	Rickman
Hickin	Hitch	Richer	Ricks
Hickman	Hitchcock	Richett	Rickson
Hickmot	Hitchison	Richey	Ritchard
Hickox	Hitchmough	Richie	Ritchie

The surname Richardson derives from one of the most popular first names in the land. The name Richard was brought to England by the Normans in 1066, and its origins are Germanic. It began life as the name Richard which, in Old German, means 'powerful – brave'.

Richard was popular right from the start and appears as a first name many times in the Domesday Book, usually Latinised to Ricardus. It was further popularised out of admiration for the valiant efforts of Richard I (known as 'The Lionheart'). Even the exploits of the next two Richards (especially the notorious hunchbacked Richard III) failed to dim its popularity.

Naturally, Richard soon began to spawn a whole number of diminutives and variations. Dick was one of the first and is still the most common – as is seen in the phrase 'every Tom, Dick and Harry'. The variation Dick gave rise to the surnames Dickens, Dickenson and Dickson.

Richard, in its standard form, gave rise to the surnames Richard, Richardson and Richards. The surname Richards – 'descendent of, dependent of, Richard' – is most common in Cornwall, South Wales and the Midlands. Richardson, on the other hand, is common all over the country, with the exception of the West Country. The name is most popular in the north.

Other derivatives of the first name Richard (most of which

have died out) gave rise to such widespread surnames as Hick, Hitch, Richie, Richey, and Rick (Ricks and Rickson), also Rich (though this is sometimes derived from a nickname), Richett (from the Old French diminutive Richot), and Rickman (which means 'servant of Richard'). Hud, sometimes a pet name for Richard, is more usually used for Hugh (see Hughes). Hitchmough and Hickmot both mean 'Richard's brother-in-law.'

The earliest mention of a form of this name as a surname is the Hundred Rolls of 1276 for Oxford. There one Thomas Richard is mentioned.

A Richardson Miscellany
Versatile British physicist and psychologist Lewis Fry Richardson (1881–1953) first applied mathematical techniques to predict the weather reasonably accurately. He died in Kilmun, Argyllshire, one of the wettest spots on Scotland's west coast.

☆

I.A. Richards (b. 1893) English literary critic and semantics expert, was co-arthur of *The Meaning of Meaning*. Despite the seeming circularity of the title, it is one of the most influential books ever written on the symbolism of language.

☆

Richardson's Number is the parameter used to predict the occurrence of fluid turbulence.

☆

Richardson and its related names have been held by some of literature's most lasting figures. Samuel Richardson (1689–1761) is the founder of the English domestic novel. As a young man he was so proficient as a letter writer that others employed him to compose their correspondence. This led to his first successful book *Familiar Letters*, a how-to guide to letter composition. Novels, starting with *Pamela, or Virtue Rewarded*, all in epistolary form, followed and all were vastly popular. Charles Dickens (1812–78) possibly the best-loved author of all time, drew on his impoverished childhood to write novels that exposed the hypocrisies and evils of Victorian England. All were first published in monthly instalments. The phrase 'a Dickensian childhood' has since entered the language.

☆

In the United Kingdom one place name relates directly to this surname – Richards Castle. Canada has towns called Richard,

Richards Landing and Richardson Station while the United States has 6 related-name towns. Geographic namesakes are common and include mountains in Canada, Australia and New Zealand, the Richards Deep in the Pacific and Richardsbreen glacier in Norway.

****

ROBERTS   ROBERTSON

****

Related Names
Other surnames which are related as to root, derivation or usage include:

Dobbs	Hopkins	Robbett	Robin
Dobkins	Hopkinson	Robbie	Robins
Dobson	Nobbs	Robbins	Robotkin
Hobbins	Robart	Robers	Robson
Hobbs	Robarts	Roberson	Ropkins
Hobday	Robb	Robert	*see also*
Hobkins	Robbens	Robeson	Robinson
Hobson			

The surnames Roberts and Robertson come from the first name Robert.

This first name derives originally from the centuries-old German name Rodbert, which is a combination of two Old German words. These are the word 'hroth' which means 'fame' and the word 'berht' which means 'bright'. Thus the original Roberts were 'fame-bright', meaning in the literal sense much the same as our modern word 'illustrious'.

When this name spread to France it became transformed to Robert, and as such it was imported to England by the Normans in 1066. Robert soon became very popular. The first name Robert and the surname form both appear frequently in the Domesday Book. From the earliest records this name also appears in several variations, the most common being Robin which by the thirteenth century had started giving rise to variations of its own. Nowadays it is often impossible to tell which of these variations spring from the original Robert, and which from Robin. They range through Rob, Dob, Hob, Bob and Nob. In Scotland the variants, Rab, Rabbie and Robbie (as in the poet Rabbie Burns) soon appeared.

This host of variations gave rise to numerous surnames, all of which derive from the same source as Roberts and Robertson. The most common of these are Robinson (see under appropriate heading), Robbins, Robson, Robeson, Dobkins, Hobkins, and even Dobbs and Dobson. All of these mean 'son or dependant of Robert' (through a variation or diminutive). Other related names in common use include Robbett and Robb.

The earliest mention of a form of Roberts (or Robertson) used as a surname is in the Domesday Book records for Kent in 1086, where Willelmus filius Roberti is mentioned.

A Roberts Miscellany

English livery-stable owner Thomas Hobson (1554–1631) of Cambridge earned himself a place in history with his habit of insisting customers take the horse that happened to be nearest the door. This led to the expression 'Hobson's Choice', i.e. 'this or none'.

☆

Scottish choral conductor Hugh Robertson (1874–1952) founded Glasgow's noted Orpheus Choir in 1906.

☆

Legendary cricketer Sir Jack Hobbs (1882–1963) was one of the greatest batsmen England ever produced. His feats include making 3,636 runs, including 12 centuries, in test matches against Australia, and a record number of 197 centuries in first-class cricket including, in 1926, the highest score at Lords (316).

☆

William Dobson (1610–46) succeeded Van Dyck as portrait painter to Charles I.

☆

When Sir Robert Peel founded metropolitan London's police force in 1829, constables were at first called 'Peelers', as they still are in Ireland (the term was first applied to the force Sir Robert founded in Ireland when he was Chief Secretary for that country). This was quickly superseded by the still-common term 'Bobbies', from his first name.

☆

Five United Kingdom towns are related to this name: Robertson (2), Robert Hill, Robertsbridge and Roberttown. Canada has 3 Robertsvilles while the United States has 6 name-related cities and towns. Ireland has a Robertstown, Liberia a Robertsfield and a Robertsport and India a Robertsganji. Geographic namesakes are widespread.

```
********************************
*              ROBINSON              *
********************************
```

Related Names
Other names which are related as to root, derivation or usage include:

Dobbs	Hobkins	Robbens	Robins
Dobkins	Hobson	Robbins	Robison
Dobson	Hopkins	Robers	Robson
Hobbins	Robart	Robeson	*See also*
Hobday	Robb	Robin	Robertson

Robinson is a patronymic, in other words a name derived from the father's name. (Though inevitably, as the name was handed down, the original father became a great-grandfather and so on.) This habit of handing down names was particularly prevalent amongst the Vikings. (Even today, Ericson and Anderson feature far more prominently in the Stockholm telephone directory than Smith and Jones in the London counterpart.) For this reason it used to be assumed that all names ending in '-son' were of Viking origin – especially as many of these named originated from the north of England in the area occupied by the Vikings. Research has shown however that names ending in '-son' occurred in English before the Viking invasions, and also originated later in southern areas untouched by the Vikings.

In England, before Henry IV's reign, a son did not necessarily take on his father's name (whether by calling himself '-son' or simply by adopting the father's surname). But from this time on the practice became almost universal. (One of the last recorded instances of this *not* happening is in the 1431 records, which mention one Robertus de Lynly, filius Thomas Johnson.) In southern Lancashire, to facilitate tenure of land, daughters were occasionally named after their fathers, with the addition of '-daughter' to the original name. These awkward names quickly fell out of use, however.

Robinson (or occasionally Robison) thus derives from 'son of Robin'. Robin itself is a diminutive of the French name Robert, popular in Normandy and England in medieval times. This French name had in turn originated from the Old German name of Rodbert, derived from 'hroth' which means 'fame' and 'berht' which means 'bright'. So the name Robert would represent a parental wish for the child's 'fame-bright' future.

After the Norman Conquest, Robert quickly became a popular name in England. It appears frequently in the Domesday Book, and has been amongst the dozen most popular first names in England ever since. The main surprise here is that England has never had a king called Robert. Scotland, on the other hand, has had several. The most famous of these was Robert the Bruce, the scourge of the English at the Battle of Bannockburn. (This may well account for the lack of Kings called Robert in England.) The naming of kings has always been a serious business, with past history and superstititon often playing no small part. (No King of England would want to take on the name of his victorious Scottish counterpart.)

Despite its simplicity (or perhaps because of the popularity of those who held it) the name Robert soon spawned innumerable derivatives and nicknames. Rob, Nob and Dob were amongst the earliest – and today's more popular Bob only came on the scene several centuries later. Rab and Rob were evolved in Scotland and Northern Ireland. Robin is a diminutive of the nickname Rob, and quickly became so popular that by the middle of the thirteenth century there were more Robins than there were original Roberts. Though England may never have had a King Robert (or Robin), one of its most popular heroes is Robin Hood.

The earliest Robinson to appear in the records is one John Robynson. He is listed in the Court Rolls of the Manor of Wakefield for 1324.

A Robinson Miscellany

Londoner Henry Crabb Robinson (1775–1867) was a famous controversialist of his day, noted for giving lively Sunday morning breakfast parties that attracted literary guests like William Blake, Charles Lamb, Coleridge and the Wordsworths.

☆

The modern garden owes much of its style to British landscape designer William Robinson (1838–1935). A passionate believer in the natural garden, he launched and won a vigorous life-long campaign against the rigidly formal architectural gardens popular in his early career.

☆

Noted Canadian-born US-based illustrator and political cartoonist Boardman Robinson was strongly influenced by French political cartooning in his student days. His own trenchant World War I cartoons brought him world-wide fame. He also illustrated classics like *Moby Dick* and *The Brothers Karamazov*, and created the murals in New York's Rockefeller Center and Washington DC's Department of Justice.

☆

Wildly inventive illustrator W. Heath Robinson (1872–1944) specialised in drawings of incredibly complex machines which served no useful purpose. Since then any elaborate or overwrought piece of equipment has become known as a 'real Heath Robinson'.

☆

There are no related geographic or place names in the United Kingdom. Both Australia and South Africa have towns called Robinson, while there are 2 such towns in the United States and in Canada. The US also has towns called Robin and Robinette, while Canada has a Robinsonville and a Robinvale. Australia has the Robinson range of mountains. The name is geographically fairly common.

```
******************************
*              ROSS          *
******************************
```

Related Names
Other surnames which are related as to root, derivation or usage include:

Roos   Rosce   Rose

The surname Ross has several variations, none of which is predominant. One derivation is from the Norman French name Roce, from Old German Rozzo, which originated from personal names containing the Old German word 'hroth' – 'fame'. This word also gives us the first syllable of the name

249

Robert (see Roberts/Robertson). So in this case Ross comes from a Norman first name of Germanic origin, and as such would have first arrived in England at the time of the Norman Conquest

The other derivations are from a variety of place names all containing the Celtic element 'ros' or 'rhos' – 'a heath, a promontory or an isthmus'. Thus Ross would mean 'from Ross'. There are places called Ross in Herefordshire and Northumberland; there is a Scottish county of Ross. There are places called Roos in Yorkshire and Roose in Lancashire, both of which could give rise to the local surname Ross, as well. Other place names containing Ros-, Rose- and Rhos- occur in Wales, Scotland, Brittany, Ireland and Cornwall.

Another source of the name Ross is the small village of Rots in Calvados (Normandy). By this derivation the surname came across the Channel with the Normans in 1066.

The first mention of Ross as a surname appears in the Pipe Rolls of 1197 for Kent, where one Johannes filius Rosce is mentioned. The name in this instance almost certainly comes from the Norman word for fame.

A Ross Miscellany

A Ross became chief of the Cherokee Indians in 1828. John Ross, also known as Kooeshoowe (1790–1866), was the son of a Scottish father and an Indian mother. For years Ross bravely resisted the encroachment of the white man and his laws on Cherokee territory, but despite all his attempts it was largely a losing battle.

☆

As every US schoolchild knows, Betsy Ross (1752–1836) stitched the first American flag, at the request of George Washington. Recent historical opinion, however, has begun to doubt the authenticity of Betsy's patriotic feat.

☆

The first man to discover the magnetic north pole (1831) was Sir James Clarke Ross (1800–62). This famous explorer also sailed the coasts of Antarctica, many parts of which are named after him.

☆

The Nobel Prize-winning pathologist, Sir Ronald Ross (1857–1932), was a professor of tropical medicine. Best known for his investigations into malaria, he made the discovery that the disease is transmitted by the *anopheles* mosquito.

☆

Fur trader and pioneer Alexander Ross left Scotland to join John Jacob Astor's 1810 expedition to the unexplored wilds of Oregon. He later helped found Astoria, Fort Walla Walla and the Red River Settlement, and left vivid accounts of his adventures in books such as *Fur Hunters of the Far West*.

☆

One United Kingdom geographic feature, Rossall Point, and 9 towns and cities are related to this name, including 3 towns named Ross and Ross-on-Wye. South Africa has a Rossing while Canada has a Rossendale, Rossland, Rossport, Rossway and Rosswood. Australia and Senegal each have a Ross while Ireland has 8 Ross-related towns including Rosslare. In the United States there are 9 such towns. Geographic features named for Ross are all over the globe. There are Ross Islands in Antarctica and in Burma as well as a veritable flood of lakes and rivers and masses of mountains.

✳✳✳✳✳✳✳✳✳✳✳✳✳✳✳✳✳✳✳✳✳✳✳✳✳✳✳✳✳✳✳✳✳✳
✳   **RYAN**   ✳
✳✳✳✳✳✳✳✳✳✳✳✳✳✳✳✳✳✳✳✳✳✳✳✳✳✳✳✳✳✳✳✳✳✳

Related Names
Other surnames which are related as to root, derivation or usage include:

Mulrine	Muroyne	O'Mulryan	O'Ryan
Mulryan	O'Mulrigan	O'Riain	

The surname Ryan comes from the Irish O'Riaghain or O'Riain, respectively meaning 'descendant of Riaghan' and 'of Rian'. Closely related are the names O'Mulrigan (anglicised from the Irish O'Maoilriaghain) and O'Mulryan (anglicised from the Irish O'Maoilriain). These latter Irish surnames mean 'descendant of Maol-riaghain or Maol-riain'; the Maol-names mean 'follower of Riaghan' or 'of Rian'. The meaning of the name O'Maoilriaghain is disputed, but the most likely explanation is that it means 'devotee of St Iain' (Iain being the Gaelic for John), or perhaps 'Iain the Chief'.

    The first name John is one of the most ancient in popular use. It derives from the Hebrew name Jochanaan (or Johanan) which means 'God is gracious'. The Crusaders introduced the Latin form Johannes into Europe, and the name quickly spread. In each country it developed its own variations, from Jan in Holland to Jean in France. In England it became John, and in Scotland it became Jock (as well as Iain). The Welsh version is Evan (giving rise to the popular surname), and the Irish version is Sean (pronounced Shawn) indicating its similarity to the French Jean.

The Ryans are one of the great Irish family clans (or septs), and the name is found all over Ireland. It is most frequent in County Tipperary, where it is four times more popular than the other two best-known names from this county (O'Brien and Mahon). Variations on the original Mulryan are still found in Galway and Leitrim in the form of Mulrine and Muroyne. O'Riain is the more usual Leinster form.

Occasionally the name Ryan derives from an entirely different source. Here the origin of the name as we know it is Ruane. This comes from the Irish Gaelic 'O'Ruadhain', which derives from the Gaelic word 'ruadh' meaning 'red'. Thus the first holders of the name would have been given it as a nickname, alluding either to their ruddy complexion or to their red hair. In the latter case an original 'ruadh' might well have been of Norse origin. Many of the Ryans in County Mayo derive their name from the Ruane source.

A Ryan Miscellany
Dr James Ryan (1891–1970) was, with Eamon de Valera, a founder of the Irish political party, Fianna Fail, whose name means 'Army of Destiny'.

☆

In ancient Arthurian legend and romance, Ryance, King of Wales, Ireland and The Isles, cut the beard off every knight he vanquished and made the beards into a cloak. Finding himself one short, he sent a messenger to King Arthur, demanding his beard and threatening to come and take it if necessary. Arthur refused and dispatched two knights who overcame Ryance and brought him back a prisoner.

☆

There are no name-related towns in the United Kingdom (but there is a Ryan lake and Loch Ryan) and few Ryans anywhere. The United States has 2 towns named Ryan and a Ryan Park township.

Related Names

Other surnames which derive from one or other of two roots include:

Scot	Scotter	Scutt	Scutts
Scotson	Scotts		

The surname Scott is a location or nationality name, and is the best-known example of this type of naming in the land. Naturally, one would expect the original bearers of the name to come from Scotland, and this is frequently the case – though the name has always been found most frequently in Northumberland. (A location name was most often given to someone only after he had left his place of origin – and naturally the highest concentration of people of Scottish origins would have occurred in early times just south of the border.)

However, by one of the quirks of fate, the first Scots people (long before the origin of the name) came originally from Ireland. Nowadays, the descendants of these early Hibernian immigrants are mainly found in the Highlands and the Hebrides. Most lowland Scottish people are of English origin, whereas the inhabitants of the Orkneys and the Shetlands are almost exclusively of Norse descent. This fact is not so surprising when you consider that to this day the nearest railway station to Lerwick, the main town in the Shetland Islands, is Bergen in Norway.

The surname Scott would thus originally have referred to the Gaelic origin of its holder, at least in Scotland. Just south of the border, where the name is most frequent, the name would have simply been given to someone who came from Scotland. However, the name Scott is also numerous all over England, especially in the eastern countries and in the south-west (particularly Devon). Here the original Scots may well have been settlers, or the name may have been given as a nickname – to someone considered Scottish in appearance or manner. Speculation upon the actual attributes alluded by this nickname lead one into the minefield of racialism – but one can be certain that originally the nickname would not have been sympathetic. In years gone by, rural communities tended to be insular and biased against foreigners (a trait which has not completely vanished), and for many years in previous centuries Scotland was at war with England.

The close names of Scutt and Scotter, which appear in the West Country (almost exclusively in Dorset), are usually of different origin. This is an occupational name of Old French origin, meaning 'scout' or 'spy'. However, here there are oral difficulties. Many of the original Scutts have changed through the years to Scott, and vice versa.

According to the great authority on Scottish names, Black, the surname Scott first appears in the Selkirk records which cover the years around 1124. Here one Uchtred filius Scot is mentioned.

A Scott Miscellany

Reginald Scott (1538–99) is credited with the introduction into England of hop-growing and therefore deserves a grateful nod from the nation's ale fanciers. He was also an author, although his works were not always well received: James I ordered his *The Discoverie of Witchcraft* (1584) burned.

☆

The Gothic Revival triumphs of London's St Pancras Station and the Albert Memorial are the work of the architect Sir George Gilbert Scott (1811–78). Sir George's grandson, Sir Giles Gibert Scott (1880–1960), carried on the family's architectural tradition; his contributions include Liverpool's Anglican cathedral and the new Waterloo Bridge in London.

☆

Sir Peter Scott (1909–89), ornithologist son of Captain Robert Falcon Scott, was well known for his paintings of wild fowl and illustrations for wildlife books. He was instrumental in setting up the British Wildfowl Trust at Slimbridge, and was Chairman of the World Wildlife Fund.

☆

Barbara Ann Scott (b. 1928) became the first North American to win a world championship in figure skating. That 1947 victory made her a national heroine in Canada.

☆

The combination of the nation and the explorer have led to exceptional use of this name both for places and for geographic features. Apart from the name Scotland itself, 19 UK towns contain the name. These range from Scotch Corner to Scotton. Canada has 7 name-related places, Australia a Scottsdale and

South Africa a Scottburgh. The United States has 25 Scott-related places including a ghost town in Death Valley called Scotty's Castle, 3 towns called Scott and 2 Scotlands. Name-sake geographic features are widespread.

```
************************************
*                SMITH             *
************************************
```

Related Names
Other surnames which are related as to root, derivation or usage include:

Arrowsmith	Kovac	Smither	Smithwick
Brownsmith	Lefèvre	Smitherman	Smithy
Coppersmith	Smid	Smithers	Smyth
Faber	Smisson	Smithfield	Smythe
Goldsmith	Smit	Smithies	Smythman
Greensmith	Smithe	Smithson	Whitesmith
Haddad			

Entire books have been written about the great English name of Smith. In origin this is an occupational name and comes from the Old English word 'smith' meaning 'a metal-worker'. In this form it has remained unchanged for over 1,000 years, apart from the spelling variations of Smyth or Smythe. However, occasionally the name Smythe will in fact be a location name, deriving from Smithy. Thus it would mean 'dweller at the smithy'.

The surname Smith has also frequently become double-barrelled, as for example in Robinson-Smith. The partner name in this case would have its own entirely separate derivation; it would usually be adapted from an indirect female line. Other variations on this name derive from specific trades – such as Brownsmith (meaning 'copper or brass-smith'), or Greensmith (for 'coppersmith' – the green referring either to the patina of copper, or to the colour of the flame when it is worked), Arrow-smith and Goldsmith. London's borough of Hammersmith is named after a forge – a 'hammer-smithy'.

Besides being easily the most popular name in England, Smith is also the most popular in Scotland, and in the United States (where the name will frequently have been anglicised from foreign sources, such as the German Schmidt). In Wales, however, Smith comes second to its greatest rival, Jones.

Besides the previously mentioned German form, there are also many other foreign versions of Smith. Some of the most widespread of these are Lefèvre (the French form), Kovac (in Slavonic languages), Hadded (in Hebrew), or Faber (from the Latin). Once again, these are only the simple forms and, like our English Smith, they also have their compound forms. The lesser-known examples are the French Orfèvre (goldsmith) and the German variation Messerschmidt (knifesmith).

Early examples of the name Smith were sometimes Latinised in the records to Faber. This name appears in the records from the 1066 Domesday Book onwards. However, the surname Smith has appeared in all records from the earliest times and pre-dates the Domesday Book. The first reference comes in the Annals for Durham in AD 975, where one Ecceard Smith is mentioned.

A Smith Miscellany

One enterprising branch of the Smith family has blazoned the name on hundreds of British high streets. W.H. Smith (1792–1865) took over his father's small news-stand in 1816 and later, helped by his son (also named William Henry (1825–91)) expanded the business into the largest such enterprise in Great Britain. The younger W.H. became an MP in 1868 and served as, amongst other things, First Lord of the Admiralty (1877). He was affectionately nicknamed 'Old Morality' by *Punch* and was the butt of the famous line, 'Now I am the ruler of the Queen's Nav-ee' in Gilbert and Sullivan's 1878 operetta *HMS Pinafore*.

☆

Fiery-tempered British general, Sir Harry Smith (1787–1860), was Governor of Cape Colony and High Commissioner of South Africa from 1847 to 1852. During his colourful career he took part in the Peninsular War, witnessed with horror the burning of Washington DC during the War of 1812, and fought at Waterloo. Transferred to Cape Colony during the Cape Frontier War, he made a historic ride, galloping the 600 miles from Cape Town to Grahamstown in under six days, to tell terrified colonists that help was on the way. It is his wife whose memory is recalled by the town of Ladysmith in Natal.

☆

The massive Smithsonian Institution in Washington DC was founded by the bequest of over £100,000 'to the United States of

America for the increase and diffusion of knowledge among men' by English scientist James Smithson (1765–1829), illegitimate son of Hugh Percy, Duke of Northumberland. He apparently made the bequest out of bitterness, writing, 'My name shall live in the memory of man when the title of the Northumberlands are extinct and forgotten.'

☆

One of the best-known of all Smiths was Sydney Smith (1771–1845). Lord Macaulay called him the 'Smith of Smiths', Abraham Lincoln quoted him frequently, Charles Dickens named a son after him, and even Queen Victoria found him amusing. Clergyman, wit and essayist, Smith was lauded in his lifetime as the greatest master of trenchant ridicule since Jonathan Swift and Voltaire, although he lacked their vitriol. For a quarter of a century he deflated pomposity and exposed hypocrisy as he fought for parliamentary reform and for emancipation of Catholics. Eventually made a canon of St Paul's, he invented the still-common expression for a misfit: 'a square peg in a round hole'. This master of quotable quotes once summed up his life by saying he had spent it like a razor, 'in hot water or a scrape'.

☆

The geographical centre of the United States lies in Smith County, Kansas.

☆

Joseph Smith (1805–44), founder of the Mormon Church, claimed that an angel had presented him with golden plates and a book written in hieroglyphics which he translated with the aid of magic stones and had published as *The Book of the Mormon*. Having led his followers from New York State to Illinois, Smith claimed personal divinity and ruled with an iron hand until his plans to introduce polygamy caused violence and led to his arrest. While in goal he was killed by an angry mob.

☆

London's major meat market, Smithfield, was long famous for its cattle sales. In the time of Mary Tudor it was the place where heretics were burnt at the stake. It takes its name from the Old English word *smethe*, meaning 'smooth'.

☆

Donald Alexander Smith, Baron Strathcona and Mount Royal, served as High Commissioner for Canada from 1896 and at one time controlled both the Great Northern and the Canadian Pacific railways.

257

English-born Assyriologist George Smith (1840–76) achieved world-wide fame in 1872 by his translation of fragments of Chaldean tablets in the British Museum which described The Flood. Public interest ran so high that a London paper financed an expedition to search for the missing fragment. On the fifth day of digging Smith found it – an almost miraculous stroke of luck. His *Chaldean Account* was a nineteenth-century best-seller.

☆

Smith-related places and geographic features are popular but not nearly as dominating as the surname itself. The United Kingdom has 6 towns with related names – Smith Green, Smithsfield, Smithincott, Smithston, Smithstown and Smithy Houses. Canada has a Smith, a Smithers and a Smithtown; Australia a Smithton; South Africa a Smithfield; and there's a Smith in Argentina. The United States has 26 related-name towns – all are relatively small. Related-name geographic features are common.

STEWART

Related Names
Other surnames which are related as to root, derivation or usage include:

Steuart	Stewardson	Stiward	Stuart
Steward	Stewartson		

The surname Stewart (or Stuart) is a variation of the name Steward. This name is thus an occupational name, and as such it derives from the Old English word meaning 'steward or keeper of a household'. The changing of the final 'd' in the original to the more usual 't' is typical of Scottish usage, and accounts for why the name is so widespread in that country. Stewardson and Stewartson are occasional variations.

After the Norman Conquest, the rank of steward became synonymous for 'an official who controls the domestic affairs of a household' and became similar to chamberlain, though stewards were frequently more exalted in the hierarchy. For instance, the Lord High Steward of Scotland was the first officer of the Scottish kings and had the doubtful privilege of leading the Scots army into battle. Despite this hazardous occupation, a steward soon rose to the highest position in the land. Robert the Steward became King Robert II of Scotland in 1371 and founded the House of Steward (now known as the Stuarts, the French form of the word, adopted by Mary Queen of Scots).

In Scotland, steward (or stewart) was also often another name for a magistrate. For this, and the more domestic occupational reason, the name became very widespread in Scotland. Thus, only in the rarest of cases would the family name Stewart indicate royal descent (and most of these are already traced in the records).

The first mention of the surname occurs in the early records for Devon covering the years 1100–30, where one Rogere se Stiwerd appears.

A Stewart Miscellany

'Bonnie Prince Charlie', the Young Pretender, is one of the great heroes of Scottish history. As Charles Stuart (1720–88) he laid claim to the English throne and led the Scottish clans in the great '45 rebellion. His loyal highlanders rallied round him and he marched south, reaching as far as Derby – only to be defeated at the Battle of Culloden. After this massacre he fled to France disguised as a woman. He finally died, a drunkard, in Rome.

☆

Frances Teresa Stewart (1647–1702) was the favourite of Charles II, her legendary beauty giving her the edge over her many rivals, such as Nell Gwynne. Known as 'La Belle Stewart', she was considered by Samuel Pepys as the greatest beauty of her time, and was immortalised when she posed for the image of Britannia on the coin of the realm.

☆

The Australian town Alice Springs was formerly known as Stuart.

☆

Scottish-born explorer John McDouall Stuart made six expeditions into the Australian interior between 1858 and 1862, finally reaching the Indian Ocean.

☆

'Walking Stewart' was the baldy apt nickname bestowed upon John Stewart (d. 1822), an intrepid English wanderer who travelled on foot through Hindustan, Persia, Nubia, Abyssinia, the Arabian desert, Europe and the US.

☆

The US Stuart tank, an M3 mounting a 37-millimetre gun, saw heavy action during World War II, playing a major role in the Italian Campaign and the post-D-day offensive.

☆

Five towns in the United Kingdom are related – Stewartby, Stewarton (2), Stewartstown and Stuartfield. Canada has 5 as well, the United States has 9, but Australia and New Zealand have none. Both New Zealand and Chile have Stewart Islands while Australia has numerous mountains, points and bluffs named Stewart or Stuart. Name-related bodies of water and other topographic features are also common. Canada alone has 2 rivers named Stewart and 2 named Stuart.

```
**********************************
*              SULLIVAN              *
**********************************
```

Related Names

Other surnames which are related as to root, derivation or usage include:

O'Sullivan

This popular Irish surname comes from the Gaelic O'Suileabhain meaning 'descendant of Suilebhain'. The exact meaning of the Gaelic Suileabhain is uncertain, but it is thought to mean 'black-eyed' for the first syllable is undisputably derived from the word 'suil' meaning 'an eye' – as in the similar surname O'Sullaghan which derives from the Gaelic O'Suileachain meaning 'quick-eyed'. The last part of the name may derive from some obsolete forename whose origins are now lost in the mists of time. There is speculation that it has a descriptive meaning which would compound with 'eye'. The most likely meanings of the name according to this interpretation are 'black-eyed', 'one-eyed' or 'hawk-eyed'.

Sullivan (or O'Sullivan, which means 'son of or descendant of Sullivan') is the most numerous name in Munster, and indeed

260

the third most popular in all Ireland. The first O'Sullivans came from South Tipperary, but were driven north in the path of the Anglo-Norman invasions. They soon established themselves as the leading family clan in Munster.

This name does not appear in the early records (which are largely English and cover the mainland). The Sullivans first came to England and Scotland in appreciable numbers during the great emigrations of the nineteenth century. Here they can be found to this day in large numbers, especially in Liverpool, Glasgow, Manchester and London. However, the heaviest concentrations of O'Sullivans still crop up in Ireland. One of these is in the small seaside village of Waterville in Kerry on the far south-west coast of Ireland. Here, there are so many O'Sullivans in the village that at one time every shop and bar in the main street was called 'O'Sullivan's.'

A Sullivan Miscellany

To this day, the most popular of all light operas remain those written by Gilbert and Sullivan, *The Mikado, HMS Pinafore* and *Trial by Jury* being their most-performed works. Sir Arthur Seymour Sullivan (1842–1900) was the musical half of the partnership and also composed several successful symphonies and concertos in his youth. He also wrote that epitome of Victorian parlour songs, 'The Lost Chord'.

☆

Perhaps the greatest of all American prize-fighters was the celebrated John L. Sullivan (1858–1918). 'The Great John L.' could not only knock out all comers with his fists, he could also drink all comers under the table. He earned over $1 million in his career, and his flamboyant personality contributed to his legendary status. Ironically, later in life, reformed by his second wife, he ended up lecturing on the temperance circuit.

☆

Cartoon character Felix the Cat was the creation of the Australian newspaper cartoonist, Pat Sullivan (1887–1933), who emigrated to the US.

☆

Places and geographic features incorporating the name Sullivan are relatively rare. Only the United States has towns which are so named – 5 called Sullivan and one Sullivanville. Canada has a Sullivan lake as well as 2 named O'Sullivan, also a Sullivan Bay. Off the coast of Burma there is a Sullivan Island.

Related Names
Other surnames which are related as to root, derivation or usage include:

Tailer	Tailor	Taylerson	Taylour
Taille	Tayler	Taylorson	

The surname Taylor is an occupational name from the trade we today spell as tailor. The name derives from the Middle English word 'tayler' or 'tailor'. Through the centuries the convention has gradually been established that the surname is spelt with a 'y' and the name for the trade is spelt with an 'i' – though this is not invariably the case. The Middle English word comes originally from the Old French word 'tailleur', meaning 'cutter'. This Old French source has given rise to several types of 'cutter'. The best-known one has given us the surname Talboys, which has nothing to do with youth or height. This comes from the Old French 'taillebois', which means 'cutter of wood'.

The surname Taylor is thus of Norman origin and came to England with William the Conqueror. Incidentally, it also gave the lie to the exclusiveness of Norman names. Taylor does not sound as Norman as, say, the more numerically exclusive de la Tour, but it is just as old and just as French.

There are several well-known variations on the most usual spelling – Taylor. They range through Tailer, Tayler or Taylour to Taylorson and Taylerson.

References to the surname Taylor start appearing in the records from the twelfth century on. One of the earliest of these is in the Pipe Rolls for Somerset. In the records for the year 1182 one William le Taillur appears. Here the Norman origin and the occupational derivation are well illustrated.

A Taylor Miscellany
Scottish dramatist Tom Taylor adapted over 100 works for the stage. One of them, *Our American Cousin*, was the play Abraham Lincoln was watching when he was assassinated.

☆

In 1948 Sir William Francis Kyffin Taylor became, at 93, the oldest person ever raised to the peerage.

☆

Thespian Joseph Taylor was an Englishman mentioned in Shakespeare's *First Folio* as one of the 26 actors who took principal parts in all those plays. Legend has it that the Bard himself coached Taylor in the role of Hamlet.

☆

The Taylor Standard Series is the method used to discover which characteristics of a ship's hull govern its water resistance. Its inventor, David Watson Taylor, became a rear admiral in the US Navy and designed the first plane to fly the Atlantic (1919).

☆

Coventry-born Edward Taylor (d. 1729) is considered to be colonial America's finest poet but, at his request, the best of his verse was not published until over 200 years after his death.

☆

British mathematician Brook Taylor (1685–1731) is noted for his great contributions to the development of calculus – he postulated 'Taylor's Theorem'.

☆

John Henry Taylor (1871–1963) was one of 'the great triumvirate' (with Harry Vardon and James Braid) which won the British Open (golf) Championship 16 times between 1894 and 1914 (Taylor won five times). Later he was a founder and the first chairman of the British Professional Golfers' Association.

☆

A.J.P. Taylor (b. 1906), prolific English historian, wrote the celebrated study *Origins of the Second World War* which is considered the definitive work on the subject.

☆

There are no Taylor-related places or major geographic features in the United Kingdom. Canada has a town called Taylor. The United States has 10 such towns as well as 5 Taylorsvilles, a Taylors, a Taylor Bridge and a Taylor Springs. South Africa boasts a town called Tayler's Pan while New Zealand has one delightfully named Taylor's Mistake. Virtually all of the foregoing, except the UK, have other geographic features named Taylor.

Related Names

Other surnames which are related as to root, derivation or usage include:

MacThomas	Thompkin	Tomas	Tomkinson
Thomason	Thompkins	Tombleson	Tomlin
Thomasson	Thompsett	Tomblin	Tomlinson
Thomaston	Thompstone	Tombling	Tompkin
Thomazin	Thoms	Tombs	Tompkins
Thomerson	Thomsen	Tomison	Tompsett
Thomkins	Thomson	Tomkin	Tomsett
Thomkinson	Tomalin	Tomkins	Tomson
Thomlinson	Toman		

The surnames Thomas and Thompson both derive from the first name Thomas. The first name is one of the most ancient still in popular use, deriving from the ancient Aramaic where it meant 'twin'. Its popularity in Western Europe stems from the Apostle of the same name, though in fact his real first name was Judas, and Thomas was only his nickname (given to distinguish him from Judas Iscariot).

In early days Thomas was not one of the great popular names, largely because of its link with 'Doubting Thomas' – an unwise connotation in times when heretics were drawn and quartered. However, the fortunes of this name revived in England after 1170, when Thomas à Becket (who was later canonised) was murdered in Canterbury Cathedral at the instigation of his erstwhile friend, King Henry II. In fact, there are two other English saints called Thomas – St Thomas of Hereford, and Sir Thomas More (the hero of *A Man for all Seasons*) who was executed by King Henry VIII for refusing to admit the King as head of the Church.

The first name Thomas soon became the most popular in the land – witness its use in the phrase 'every Tom, Dick and Harry'. It also became synonymous for anything male (thus we get the words Tomcat and Tomboy) and to this day it is the popular name for an English soldier (Tommie).

The first name Thomas, besides giving rise to the identical surname, also gave rise to many derivations from nicknames and variations. Thus we get Tomkin, which gave rise to Tomkins and Tomkinson. It is easy to see (in terms of English pronunciation) how the middle 'p' crept into these variant surnames – as in Thompkins. This also accounts for the 'p' in Thompson. Scottish pronunciation did not find a need for the intrusive 'p' and consequently we find the spelling Thomson chiefly in Scotland.

The first name Thomas appears frequently in the Domesday Book, but it is nearly 200 years before we find the first use of the name as a surname. This is in the Hundred Rolls for Wiltshire in 1275, where one Walter Thomas is mentioned. Early in the next century the first Thompsons start appearing in the records. The first mention of the Scottish variation is in the records for Carrick in 1318, where one John Thomson is listed.

A Thomas Miscellany

Scottish engineer Robert William Thomson was well ahead of his time. In 1845 he patented the pneumatic tyre, but nearly 50 years passed before Dunlop revived his invention for use in bicycles.

☆

Newspaper magnate Roy Thomson (1894–1978), first Baron of Fleet, was the Canadian-born owner of the world's largest publishing empire. In 1953 he moved to the UK and successively bought *The Scotsman, The Sunday Times* and *The Times* itself.

☆

Scottish biologist Sir Charles Wyville Thomson (1830–82) led the famous *Challenger* expedition, the first important attempt at deep-sea exploration (1872–76). He discovered many life forms previously believed extinct, sometimes as far down as 650 fathoms.

☆

The deadly Thompson sub-machine gun (popularly known as the 'Tommy Gun') was the co-invention of American Army engineer John Taliaferro Thompson (1860–1940).

☆

Sir Benjamin Thompson (1753–1814), later Count Rumford, was a physicist, administrator and founder of the Royal Institution of Great Britain. His contributions to society include the cultivation of the potato, the invention of the kitchen range and a drip coffee pot, and the exposition of 'Count Rumford's

Principle' concerning the cure of smoking chimneys.

☆

M. Thomson was one of over fifty pseudonyms used by the French writer and philosopher, François Marie Arouet, better known as Voltaire.

☆

The youngest recorded university entrant was William Thomson, later Lord Kelvin, who entered Glasgow University in October 1834, aged 10 years, 4 months.

☆

The English geologist Herbert Henry Thomas (1876–1935) established that the bluestones at Stonehenge had been transported 200 miles from the Prescelly Mountains in Wales where they had been quarried.

☆

Physicist Sir Joseph John Thomson (1856–1940) established in 1897 that cathode rays were moving particles, later called electrons. This led to the discovery of isotopes and a greater understanding of atomic structure.

☆

The world is full of Thomas/Thomson/Thompson-related places and geographic features. The United Kingdom alone has 21 towns ranging from Tomatin to Thomshill. Canada has 5 towns, the United States 28, Australia 3 and South Africa 2. Other places are spread all over the earth from Tomas Barron in Bolivia to Thomson Village in Singapore. Name-related lakes, rivers, mountains and islands are also common.

✳✳✳✳✳✳✳✳✳✳✳✳✳✳✳✳✳✳✳✳✳✳✳✳✳✳✳✳✳✳✳✳✳✳✳
✳   **TURNER**   ✳
✳✳✳✳✳✳✳✳✳✳✳✳✳✳✳✳✳✳✳✳✳✳✳✳✳✳✳✳✳✳✳✳✳✳✳

Related Names
Other surnames which are related as to root, derivation or usage include:

Tourneour	Turnor	Turnpenny	Turnur
Turnehare	Turnour		

Turner has several derivations, dating from antiquity to comparatively recent times. All of these derivations are occupational – in other words, stemming from some form of work or activity.

In earlier times, when society was less complex, a man *was* what he did. Common examples of this are the names Archer, Shepherd, Hornblower and Goldsmith.

The earliest derivation of Turner (or Turnour, or Turnor) is from the Old French word 'tournour'. This means 'one who turns or fashions objects of wood, metal, bone, etc. on a lathe'. The reason there are so many Turners today is because in medieval times there was a great variety of objects which could be 'turned'. Most frequently these were measures for wine and ale, or round pieces of wood for chairlegs. The lathes used by these turners bore little relation to the one you'll find in a modern workshop, though the principle was the same. The ancient lathe almost certainly evolved originally from the potter's wheel – although it's thought unlikely that the names Turner and Potter were ever synonymous. In medieval times there was little call for rounded chairlegs, except amongst the gentry at The Hall.

The turners were a sub-branch of the trade of cabinet-makers, which included many carpentering skills whose practitioners took on the name of their skill. Hence the Turners were closely related (by trade at least) to the Carvers, Dishers (fashioners of wooden dishes) and Arkwrights (chest makers).

A secondary derivation of Turner is from the Old French word 'tournoieur' which meant 'one who takes part in a tourney or tournament'. However, it's likely that only very few modern Turners derive their name from this fine medieval pastime.

The last but probably the most intriguing derivation of the name Turner comes from the old word 'turnehare'. In medieval times this was the man who ran after the hare and he literally 'turned' it into the path of the waiting hunters. Needless to say, these Turners (or Turnehares) had to be fast runners, and soon the name became synonymous with what we would term a sprinter. The name may also have had derogatory connotations. A Turnehare (the opposite of a Turnbull) was someone who only had sufficient courage to turn a hare (or perhaps run away like a hare). Turnpenny was a nickname for a miser.

The earliest Turner in the records is one Warner le Turnur, who appears in the 1180 Pipe Rolls for London.

A Turner Miscellany

The Worshipful Company of Turners, founded in England in

1604, is still a thriving guild of makers of lathe-turned wooden articles.

☆

English soldier Sir Tomkyns Hilgrove Turner (1766–1843) brought the Rosetta Stone back from North Africa's Alexandria. Dating from the time of Ptolemy V (*c*. 195 BC), it is covered in inscriptions in Ancient Greek and both demotic and hieroglyphic Egyptian. His ability to decipher it unlocked the secrets of other inscriptions and led to an intensive study of Egyptian antiquity. The stone is now displayed in the British Museum.

☆

Sixteenth-century botanist William Turner (1520–68) introduced scientific botany into England. The many plants he named include hawkweed and goatsbeard.

☆

Joseph Mallord Turner (1775–1851) is generally acknowledged to be one of England's greatest landscape painters. His impressionistic use of light and colour is world-famous. Celebrated and wealthy in his time, he died a virtual recluse leaving over 20,000 watercolours and drawings, and 300 paintings to the nation.

☆

One town in the United Kingdom is a namesake – Turner's Hill. Australia has a town named Turner while the United States has 6 towns so named as well as a Turners Falls, Turnercrest, Turnersville and Turnerville. Given the popularity of the surname remarkably few geographic features are Turners. Australia does have a mountain and a river which are so named.

✳✳✳✳✳✳✳✳✳✳✳✳✳✳✳✳✳✳✳✳✳✳✳✳✳✳✳✳✳✳✳✳✳✳✳✳
✳   **WALKER**   ✳
✳✳✳✳✳✳✳✳✳✳✳✳✳✳✳✳✳✳✳✳✳✳✳✳✳✳✳✳✳✳✳✳✳✳✳✳

Related Names
Other surnames which are related as to root, derivation or meaning include:

Fuller	Tucker	Walkare	Walkere

The surname Walker comes from the Old English 'wealcere', which is another name for a fuller. A fuller or walker was a person who trod cloth in a trough in the fulling process, which is

268

mentioned in the fourteenth-century poem *Piers Plowman* where it is said:

> Cloth that cometh fro the wevying (i.e. weaving)
> Is nought comely to were
> Tyl it be fulled under fote.

Thus the stamping and pressing practised by the walker or fuller required much the same attributes as a modern-day grape presser in Spain or France.

The surnames Fuller and Tucker derive from the same profession.

The name Walker is popular all over England, but is found in greatest concentration along a band stretching up from Nottingham and Derby through West Yorkshire to Durham. However, in the Durham region and in Northumberland the name Walker may occasionally be a place name, originally being given to a person who came from Walker in Northumberland. This name is a derivation of 'marsh by the (Roman) wall'. This derivation comes out more clearly in the close name Waller, which in one variation comes from being a location name for 'a dweller at the wall'.

The first mention of the surname Walker is in the Documents for the Abbey of Bec, where in the 1248 records for Warwickshire one Richard le Walkere is mentioned.

A Walker Miscellany

The Walker Cup is a golf trophy awarded to the winner of a competition between amateur men's teams from the United States and the British Isles. Held every other year since 1922, the venue alternates between the two countries.

☆

One of the earliest American feminists was Mary Edwards Walker (1832–1919). She attracted attention to the cause by wearing men's clothes, and later served as a nurse during the American Civil War. In 1897 she established a women's colony known as 'Adamless Eden'.

☆

There are 8 towns in the United Kingdom which are name related – Walker, Walker Fold, Walkerburn, Walkeringham, Walkerith, Walkering, Walker's Green and Walkerton. Canada also has a Walkerton, while the United States has 13 Walker-related towns including 7 Walkers. Both South Africa and Australia have Walkervilles. Walker-named geographic features are common and include Walker Coy Island in the Bahamas.

269

```
************************************
*              WALSH               *
************************************
```

Related Names

Other surnames which are related as to root, derivation or meaning include:

Brannagh	Wallis	Walsman	Wellish
Brannick	Wallus	Welch	Wellsman
Walch	Walshe	Welchman	Welsh
Waleys	Walshman	Wellis	Welshman
Wallace	Walsingham		

The surname Walsh is a location name, more recognisable in the rarer form Welsh. Walsh derives from the Old English words 'walh', 'wealh' and 'welise', all of which mean 'a man from Wales'. However, the original meaning was much wider than our geographical interpretation and covered anyone who was a Briton, Celt, Welshman, or even just a foreigner. Just as once the word Gaul had more than French Gallic connotations, the French still call Wales Pays de Galles, and the native language of Scotland and Ireland is Gaelic.

The name Walsh is now mainly of Irish origin, and in Gaelic is written Breatnach (which means Welshman). This Gaelic name has sometimes been re-anglicised as Brannagh or Brannick – so anyone with these names is, in a way, a Walsh. However, the Irish Walshes have no family clan and are scattered all over the country. Theirs is easily the most numerous name which has no sept (or family clan), being the fourth most popular last name – and this suggests that they may originally have been foreigners, probably of Briton origin.

The surname Walsh has a large number of variations. The most widespread of these are Welch (found chiefly in East Anglia and the West Country), Welshman, Walch and Welchman. Wallace and Wallis are almost certainly the Scottish versions of this name, though here again, a Wallace would probably have been a man of Briton origin, rather than what we would call Welsh.

The surname Walsh has long been widespread in the country, and appears in many early records. The earliest reference to this name yet noted is in the 1273 Wiltshire Assize Rolls where one Henry le Waleis is listed.

A Walsh Miscellany

To 'welsh' on a deal means to fail to keep a promise to fulfil an obligation, notably a bet. The saying first arose in Ireland where emigrating Welshmen kept to themselves and were not trusted.

☆

Welsh rarebit has been a favoured British dish for over 200 years.

☆

Nicholas Welsh (d. 1585) as the Irish Bishop of Ossory had the Protestant service printed in Gaelic, which dramatically increased the number of converts. He was stabbed to death by a parishioner he had condemned for adultery.

☆

Henry le Walleis served a remarkable three terms as Lord Mayor of London (1273, 1281–1283, 1298), while Sir Cullum Welch was Mayor in 1966.

☆

The first pure still life – a partridge, gauntlets and arrows pinned against a wall – was painted in 1504 by Jacobo de Barbari. When this Venetian painter moved to Germany, as a guest and adviser to Dürer, he took on the name Walch.

☆

The United Kingdom has 3 Walsh-related place names, the picturesquely named Walsham Le Willows, Walsham and Walshfort. Canada has 2 towns called Walsh while the United States has but one and no other towns which are related. Curiously few major geographic features are namesakes. Walsh river and Walsh mountains in Canada are exceptions.

✳✳✳✳✳✳✳✳✳✳✳✳✳✳✳✳✳✳✳✳✳✳✳✳✳✳✳✳✳✳✳✳✳✳✳✳
✳ **WARD** ✳
✳✳✳✳✳✳✳✳✳✳✳✳✳✳✳✳✳✳✳✳✳✳✳✳✳✳✳✳✳✳✳✳✳✳✳✳

Related Names

Other surnames which are related as to root, derivation or meaning include:

Hayward	Warder	Wardropper	Watchman
McWard	Wardes	Wardrupp	Weard
Millward	Wardman	Waredraper	Whatrup
Warde	Wardrobe	Watcher	Woodward
Warden	Wardrop		

Ward stems directly from the Old English word 'weard', which means 'one who watches or guards something'. This could be a relatively lowly social position, as in the name de Wardrobe (a variety of chambermaid or room-servant), or a position of comparative power, such as the ward of a castle or an entire estate. In this case the position could often last for many years when, for example, the Lord Mayor of London went off on a Crusade; then the official would be a nobleman in all but name.

To this day the word 'ward' still retains its ancient meaning of guard, guardian or watchman. Someone (usually a minor) who is considered to be in need of protection can still be made a 'ward of court'.

When names described a characteristic or the occupation of the holder, they frequently retained the French 'le' (or sometimes 'la') which was inserted between the Christian name and the surname. Thus we find the names Robert le Rouge (Robert the red in face, or red-haired) and William le Ward. Nowadays the French article has almost entirely vanished, but in earlier times it would often come and go almost at whim. In the records for 1317 we come across one Robert Ward, who was also known on occasion as Robert le Ward, Robert la Ward, and even Robert de la Ward. A wardroper looked after the King's wardrobe, i.e. his stock of robes, ceremonial apparel etc.

There are many variations on the original Ward, denoting particular occupations. Thus Woodward was originally somebody who guarded a wood, Millward guarded a mill, and Hayward guarded enclosed fields from straying cattle. Other guardians which come into the same category as the Wards are Bridgeman (often in the Frenchified form of Ponter), plain Guard (or Garth), Watchman, Wakeman, or Yeoman.

The name Ward is often found in Scotland and Ireland, sometimes in the form McWard. Here the derivation is different from the English version. The root word in this case is the Gaelic 'bhard', which means 'bard, poet or minstrel'. So the Gaelic original would have been a travelling songster.

From earliest times the name Ward was both frequent and widespread. One John Warde is mentioned in the Pipe Rolls for Yorkshire in 1194, while in the Hundred Rolls for 1273 there is a William le Warde in Oxford, a Simon le Ward in Buckinghamshire, and two further le Wardes, one in Hampshire and one in Cambridgeshire.

A Ward Miscellany

The creator of one of fiction's most endearing popular villains, the sinister Chinese criminal genius Dr Fu Manchu, was British-born writer Arthur Sarsfield Ward (1883–1959) who wrote under the pseudonym Sax Rohmer.

☆

Winston Churchill's wartime codename was Colonel Warden. This probably stemmed from the fact that he had been made a Warden of the Cinque Ports.

☆

Pioneering British philosopher/psychologist James Ward (1843–1925) has been labelled the first functional psychologist because of his emphasis on activity of the self. His celebrated article 'Psychology' (1886) appeared in the 9th edition of the *Encyclopaedia Britannica*.

☆

Vanity Fair caricaturist Leslie Ward, using the pseudonym 'Spy', skewered many a notable with his acid-tipped pen in a 40-year career beginning in 1873. Reproductions of his prints sold in the thousands. In 1918 the Establishment honoured this brilliant iconoclast with a knighthood.

☆

Ward-related places and geographic features are common. In the United Kingdom alone 12 towns ranging from Ward Green to Wardy Mill are namesakes. Canada has 3 such towns as does the United States, while South Africa has one named Warden. New Zealand has a town named Ward as well as a Ward mountain and a Ward Island. Bodies of water named for Ward are rare. Canada has a Ward river and South Africa a Warden's Vlei lake.

****
*   **WATSON**   *
****

Related Names

Other surnames which are related as to root, derivation or usage include:

Gaulter	Walter	Waters	Watkins
Gaultier	Walters	Waterson	Watkinson
Gautier	Waterman	Watkin	Watmough

Watt   Watterson   Watts   Wattson
Watters   Wattes

The surname Watson literally means 'son of Wat'. The first name Wat is a diminutive of the first name Walter (as in Wat Tyler, the leader of the Peasants' Revolt during the reign of Richard II). This derivation arose because in medieval times the usual pronunciation of Walter was Water.

The first name Walter derives from the Old German name Waldhari. This is made up of two words – 'wald' meaning 'rule', and 'hari' meaning 'army'. So some original Walters may have been war leaders.

The first name Walter came to England with the Norman Conquest and appears frequently as a first name in the Domesday Book (where it was invariably Latinised to Walterius). Right through to the mid-seventeenth century it was more customary to pronounce this first name Water, and in consequence the popular diminutive Wat (or Watt) gave rise to that surname.

Other variations of names from the first-name source of Walter include Watts (short for Watson) and Watmough ('Walter's brother-in-law'). Waters (short for Walter's son, derived from the early pronunciation of the surname as Waters) is also a derivation from a place name for a 'dweller by the water or stream'.

The surname Watson is widespread throughout the land, but appears most numerously in the north of England and the southern Scottish counties.

The earliest appearance of the name Watson in the records is in the 1324 Rolls for the Manor of Wakefield in Yorkshire, when one Richard Watson is listed.

A Watson Miscellany

Watsons and Watts have excelled in many fields of science. The Scottish inventor James Watt (1736–1819) is generally credited with the invention of the steam engine, for which he was granted a patent in 1769; the watt, a unit of power, is named after him and he also coined the term 'horsepower'; another of his inventions was the duplicating machine, to make quick copies of his records. Another Scotsman, the physicist Sir Robert Alexander Watson-Watt (1892–1973), was knighted in 1942 for his role in the development of radar (Radio Detection And Ranging), a device for locating aircraft, which played a vital part in the defence of Britain against German bombing raids in World War

II. Another, Dr Thomas A. Watson, worked as assistant to Alexander Graham Bell when he made the first trans-Atlantic telephone call in 1915. The American geneticist, James D. Watson (b. 1928), won a Nobel Prize in 1962 for his crucial role in the discovery of the molecular structure of DNA, the vital constituent in the genetic process.

☆

In August 1965 Watts Riot in the Los Angeles ghetto (35,000 inhabitants) was the first big race riot in American history. Five days of burning, shooting and looting left 34 dead, 200 buildings destroyed and led to 3,900 arrests.

☆

Charles Watson-Wentworth, Marquis of Rockingham (1730–82), made a large bet that he could drive a coach and horses at full gallop through the eye of a needle. He then craftily built a 40-foot obelisk with a large opening at the base and won the wager. The 'Needle's Eye Folly' still stands at Wentworth in Yorkshire as a memorial to his ingenuity.

☆

English clergyman Isaac Watts (1674–1748) wrote hundreds of hymns, including 'O God Our Help in Ages Past' and 'When I Survey the Wondrous Cross'.

☆

British-born chemist Richard Watson (1737–1816) was credited with saving the government £100,000 in 1787 with his improvements to gunpowder.

☆

Places and geographic features named for Watson are rare. There are none in the United Kingdom, one each in Canada and Australia (towns called Watson), while the United States has 3 towns so named along with a Watsonton and a Watsonville. No major mountains are so named and only a few bodies of water: Canada's Watson lake and Watson river and Australia's Watson bay.

****
* **WHITE** *
****

Related Names

Other surnames which are related as to root, derivation or meaning include:

Whitaker	Whiteman	Whitmill	Whitting
Whitbread	Whiter	Whitmore	Whittingham
Whitebread	Whiterod	Whitnall	Whittington
Whitecross	Whiteside	Whitnell	Whittle
Whitefield	Whitesmith	Whitney	Whittlesey
Whiteford	Whiteson	Whitson	Whittlock
Whitehair	Whitewax	Whitt	Whittome
Whitehall	Whitewood	Whittaker	Whitton
Whitehead	Whitfield	Whittall	Whitty
Whitehill	Whitford	Whittam	Whitwell
Whitehorn	Whitham	Whittard	Whitworth
Whitehouse	Whiting	Whittemore	Whyte
Whiteing	Whitley	Whitten	Wight
Whiteland	Whitlock	Whitter	Witte
Whitelaw	Whitman	Whittick	Witten
Whiteley	Whitmarsh	Whittin	Witts
Whitelock	Whitmee		

The surname White derives from the Old English word 'Hwit' meaning the colour white. This name would thus have origi- nated as a nickname, given, say, to someone who had a white or fair complexion or hair, and it came to be a Christian name too.

Another, rarer, derivation is from the name Wight. This also is a nickname, but from the Old Norse, and means 'valiant, strong, nimble'. It is possible, but unlikely, that some instances of Wight may have been taken from the place-name form, for someone who came from the Isle of Wight.

Another, very rare, derivation of the surname White is as a place name for someone who came from the village of White. There are two such villages. One is in Cambridgeshire (where the name derives from the Old English for 'a bend in the river'), and the other is in Devon (where the name derives from the Old French for a 'look-out place').

There are innumerable variations of the original name White. The most widespread of these are Whyte, Witt (which as Witte is the Dutch form) and Witts. These gave rise to Whiteson, Whitesmith (an occupational name for a tinsmith, tin being traditionally white), Whiter (an occupational name from the Old English for a whitewasher). And there are numerous surnames such as Whitehall, Whitelaw, etc., which are derived from place names and objects containing White-. Whitebread, however, is a nickname – 'white beard'.

The name White was well established in this country long before the Norman Conquest, and even rose in popularity when the Normans arrived. The first reference to the surname White appears in the pre-Conquest annals for Herefordshire, where one Purcil Hwita was listed in 1038.

A White Miscellany

The Bank of England, in Threadneedle Street, is haunted by a ghost known as the Black Nun, who wanders dismally about the Bank garden, formerly an old churchyard. She is said to be Sarah Whitehead, whose brother Philip was a Bank employee arrested for forging cheques in 1811 and condemned to death. Sarah went mad with grief and for the next 25 years journeyed daily to the Bank looking for her brother. She was buried in the adjacent churchyard, and has reputedly been sighted many times since.

☆

America's highest peak, Mount Whitney in Southern California, is named in honour of geologist Josiah Whitney.

☆

Lord Mayors of London have included many Whites: Richard Whytyngdone (1397, 1406, 1419), William White (1489), Thomas Whyte (1553), John Whyte (1563), Sir Thomas White (1876) and James Whitehead (1888).

☆

Whitworth Standard screw threads are named after Sir Joseph Whitworth, the British mechanical engineer of tool-making fame.

☆

The White House, official residence of US Presidents at 1600 Pennsylvania Avenue, acquired its name when a coat of white paint was hurriedly slapped on to cover scorch marks incurred during the War of 1812, when the British stormed Washington.

☆

White's, the noted gentlemen's club in St James's, London, was established in 1693 as a chocolate-house, and named after its proprietor.

☆

As a colour-related surname White has remarkable representation both in terms of place names and geographic features all over the world. No fewer than 77 United Kingdom towns and cities are namesakes. These range from Whiteabbey to

Whitewreath and include the colourfully named Whitechurch
Canonicorum. Great Britain also has rivers called the
Whiteadder Water and the White Esk, and a White Coomb
mountain. Canada has 13 name-related towns. The United
States has 78, which range from White Bird to Whitewright
and include a number that reflect on life in the midst of the
Indians, such as Whiteface and White Settlement. Australia
has a White Mark and a White Well, New Zealand a White
Rock hill, while South Africa has towns called Whites and
Whitesands. There are many White mountains, being so
named for the presence of year-round snow. White and White
Water rivers are often so called because they run swiftly and
create 'white' water.

****
* **WILLIAMS** *
****

Related Names

Other surnames which are related as to root, derivation or usage
include:

Fitzwilliam	Wilkin	Willey	Willock
Gillam	Wilkins	William	Willocks
Gwilliam	Wilkinson	Williamson	Willot
Wellman	Wilks	Willie	Wills
Wilcock	Willcock	Willies	Willy
Wilcocks	Willcocks	Willis	Wilman
Wilcockson	Willcox	Willison	Wilmot
Wilcox	Willes	Willmet	Wilmott
Wilkerson	Willet	Willmot	*See also*
Wilkes	Willett	Willmoth	Wilson
Wilkie	Willetts	Willmott	

The surname Williams sometimes means the same as William-
son, while it sometimes denotes other dependants – servants,
daughters, wives, and so on. All come from the first name
William. This name is of Old Germanic origin, coming originally from the name Willahelm. This is formed from the words
'wilja' meaning 'will' and 'helm' meaning 'protection'. Thus
the name was probably first given as a kind of talisman of
hoped-for traits.

As the Old German name spread, it became Normanised to Willelm. (In French it also became Guillaume, and as such gave rise to the English name Gillam.) Compare Gaulter, Gautier for Walter, under Watson.

Following the Norman Conquest, William quickly became the most popular first name in the land, only being superseded by John in the middle of the twelfth century. Since then it has remained as one of our most popular first names, and has been the name of four kings. (Only Edward, Henry and George are more popular royal names.)

As one might expect, this popular first name gave rise to a number of diminutives and variations. Most of these have spawned their own variant surnames. Thus the diminutive Wylymot gives the surname Wilmot, and Willet and Willot arise similarly. The diminutive Wilkin gives Wilkins and Wilkinson, and the shortened form Will (for many years the most popular pet version, as in Will Shakespeare) gives us Wills and Wilson.

The name Williams is widespread throughout the land, but has special popularity in Wales. At the end of the nineteenth century one in every fourteen Welsh farmers was called Williams.

The earliest mention of Williams as a surname appears in the Domesday Book. Here in the records for 1086 one Robertus filius Willelmi is mentioned.

A Williams Miscellany

Ellen Cicely Wilkinson (1891–1947) was an English politician, labour organiser and suffragette who led the famous 1936 'Jarrow Crusade' as MP for the northern town of Jarrow, whose shipyard had been closed down in the Depression. Thousands of unemployed Geordies marched to London in a fruitless bid to obtain help from the government. Ellen Wilkinson died in office as Minister of Education, the first woman to hold that post.

☆

William Carlos Williams (1883–1963) was one of America's greatest twentieth-century poets. In an era when Bohemian exile was the rule, Williams was an exception. As a home-town family doctor, his influential verse mirrored this practical streak and his love of everyday events.

☆

Those great 'golden oldie' hits *Your Cheatin' Heart* and *Hey Good Lookin'* were composed by the celebrated American country and western singer, Hank Williams (1923–53). Hank's style has played an influential role in much modern popular music.

☆

The first fighting tank, manufactured by William Foster and Company of Lincoln, was nicknamed 'Big Willie'.

☆

The United Kingdom has one town and one body of water related to this surname: Williamscot and Williams lake. Canada has 4 namesake towns while the United States has 24, including 5 called Williams. Australia also has a Williams as well as a Williamsburg. Geographic features named after Williams are fairly common, with rivers in Canada (2) and Australia as well as mountains in these two countries, while the Bahamas includes a Williams Island.

```
**********************************
*              WILSON            *
**********************************
```

Related Names

Other surnames which are related as to root, derivation or usage include:

Fitzwilliam	Wilkie	Willet	Willmot
Gwilliam	Wilkin	Williamson	Willot
Wellman	Wilkins	Willies	Wills
Wilcocks	Wilkinson	Willis	Wilmot
Wilcox	Wilks	Willison	*See also*
Wilkes	Willcock	Willmet	Williams

The name dates back to the ancient root word 'willahelm' which meant 'a willing man with a helmet' (i.e. protection). This word is largely intact today in the Germanic countries as Willem and Wilhelm. In Normandy it becomes Guillem. By the time of the Norman invasion of our country, this had become today's Guillaume. The name, along with Robert, Richard and John, was widely adopted in preference to Old English first names.

By the twelfth century derivations on William had become the most popular of all first names, accounting for fully 10 per cent of the entire male population registered on one of the rolls. Thus, early on, as efforts were made to distinguish one Will from another, the name was already destined to give rise to many of today's most popular surnames.

By 1324 we were getting close to today's name. That year's Court of Roles at the Manor of Wakefield in Yorkshire records a Robert Willeson. The first recorded Wilson per se was also in Yorkshire: Robert Wilson at Kirkstall in 1341.

Thereafter, during Henry IV's reign from the end of the fourteenth century onwards the '-son' ending was much in vogue. This was notably true in the north of the country.

Ever since, the fairly formal straightforward Wilson has predominated in the north, while in our southern counties less formal pet names gave rise to the diminutives Wilcocks and Wilkin, derived from the Dutch word 'ken' which means 'to know'.

The first record we have of the name in its formative stages is in the Domesday Book of 1086 which refers to a Robertus filius Willelmi (Robert son of William).

A Wilson Miscellany

'A week is a long time in politics' was a saying coined by Harold Wilson (1916–1995), one of Britain's longest-serving Prime Ministers. Earlier in his career he was the youngest Cabinet Minister since Pitt. Another great political Wilson was the American President, Woodrow Wilson (1856–1924). After the Allied victory in World War I, he master-minded the Versailles Peace Conference for which he was dubbed 'the architect of world peace'. During his last years in office he was a bed-ridden recluse and, unknown to the public, the affairs of state were virtually run by his wife.

☆

Wilson's Disease is a hereditary condition leading to degeneration of the brain tissues.

☆

Wilson's Promontory, the southernmost point on Australia's mainland, is named after Thomas Wilson, an English merchant. It boasts over 700 species of plants.

☆

Eighteenth-century English mathematician John Wilson gave his name to Wilson's Theorem, the statement that sets criteria for what are natural prime numbers.

☆

Sir Erasmus Wilson, early nineteenth-century surgeon and noted specialist on skin diseases, spent the vast wealth his practice brought him on charitable bequests and the promotion of Egyptian research. He paid £10,000 to have Cleopatra's Needle brought to London in 1878.

☆

The United Kingdom has 3 towns which are related – 2 Wilsons and a Wilsontown. Canada has one, the curiously named Wilson's Prom, while the United States has 12 of which 9 are Wilsons. Australia has but one – Wilson Cliffs. Canada, the United States and Australia have Wilson lakes and rivers while the US has 3 Mount Wilsons including California's with its world-famed observatory. Australia also has a Wilson mountain.

****
* **WOOD** *
****

Related Names

Other surnames which are related as to root, derivation or usage include:

Atwood	Woodberry	Woodhall	Woodnutt
Blackwood	Woodbine	Woodham	Woodroff
Boyce	Woodbridge	Woodhams	Woodroffe
Dubois	Woodburn	Woodhatch	Woodroof
Garwood	Woodbury	Woodhead	Woodrow
Greenwood	Woodcock	Woodhouse	Woodruff
Underwood	Woodcraft	Woodhull	Woods
Wode	Wooder	Wooding	Woodstock
Wodehouse	Woodeson	Woodland	Woodthorpe
Wodester	Woodfield	Woodlay	Woodville
Wodhams	Woodford	Woodley	Woodward
Woodall	Woodgrange	Woodman	Wooster
Woodard			

Wood is one of many local surnames which derive from a particular geographical feature of a neighbourhood. Other common examples are Hill, Moore, Field, and so on. Until long after the Norman Conquest much of the English countryside was wooded, which accounts for the popularity of the name. An early usage of the name Wood (or Woods) comes in the form 'ate Wode', describing a person who lived 'at the wood'. To the Old English 'ate' was later added the definitive article in the dative form 'then' or 'ten', producing the Middle English 'atten'. This is retained in such names as Attenborough.

In the early years of the Norman Conquest surnames were given more as a form of description than as an actual name as we know it. Thus we find in the 1327 Subsidy Rolls for Somerset one William Wodeward, who was literally keeper or ward of the wood. However, by 1333 he was recorded merely as William in the Wode. Later still his descendants would become simply Wood.

One of the earliest mentions of the name Wood (in its original form) is in the 1273 Hundred Rolls for Oxford. Here there appear two Woods – Arthur ate Wode (at the wood) and Richard de la Wode. The French prepositions show the Norman influence on the language. The extreme Frenchified form still persists in the name Dubois (of the wood) which, despite its foreignness and popularity to this day across the Channel, is in England a name of extreme antiquity. On this side of the Channel the name dates from the centuries immediately following the Norman Conquest. By the thirteenth century these names were becoming increasingly anglicised, and the descendants of Richard de la Wode would almost certainly soon have become Richard ate Wode, and then either Attwood or plain Wood.

By the beginning of the fourteenth century Wood was prevalent as a family name all over England, and by then those with the name often had little to do with any actual woods.

There are numerous surnames derived from the common root Wood, many of them from place names. These include not only the obvious Blackwood, Greenwood, Woodman and Woodward, but also several more obscure forms. Woodard, for instance, derives from 'wood-herd' meaning 'a man who looked after animals in the woods'. (In medieval times pigs were often grazed in woods.) However, not all similar Wood-related names derive from this common source. Some derive from Woader, meaning a dyer who used the dye woad (with which the Ancient Britons used to paint themselves before going into battle). Woad was a very popular blue dye made from a herb known in Anglo-Saxon as 'wad'. The name Wodester (from which we get the fine old Wodehousian name Wooster) also derives from this source. The name Wodehouse (or Woodhouse) meant a man who lived in a house in the woods (not a man who lived in a wooden house, since almost all houses were made of wood in those days). Yet Woodhouse was not a general name. It referred to certain distinct places, located chiefly in West Yorkshire, Derbyshire, Lincolnshire and Nottinghamshire. In rare cases, however, this name derived from the Old English word 'woodwose' which means 'a faun, satyr or troll', and often denoted a 'wild man'. (It is likely that the phrase 'a wild man of the woods' originates from an early popular muddling of these words.)

There is also another similar rare derivation of the primary name Wood. In Old English the word 'wode' (or 'wood') also meant 'mad or frantic'. That is what Shakespeare means when he writes in *A Midsummer Night's Dream* of someone being 'wood within his wood'.

The earliest reference is to one Adam le Wode who appears in the 1221 Assize Rolls for Worcestershire.

A Wood Miscellany

'Wood's half-pence' was named for William Wood, the English ironmaster who purchased the right to coin half-pences and farthings for Ireland in 1722. His excessive profits led to a new Irish tax, prompting satirist Jonathan Swift's *Drapier's Letters* which spearheaded opposition and soon resulted in the patent being revoked.

☆

The creator of the London 'Proms' was Sir Henry Wood (1867–1944). These promenade concerts, intended to bring classical music to a wider audience of young people, are an annual event, running nightly during the late summer, at the Albert Hall. These concerts started in 1897, and were conducted by Henry Wood every year from then on until his death.

☆

The architecture of Georgian Bath is largely the work of John Wood (1704–54). His elegant Palladian designs for the Royal Crescent, Circus and parades were constructed in distinctive yellow Bath stone supplied by his patron, Ralph Allen.

☆

The pay-as-you-earn income-tax scheme was devised by English statesman Sir Kingsley Wood.

☆

British-born composer Haydn Wood is best remembered as composer of the popular song *Roses of Picardy*. He also wrote a string of music-hall hits, before concentrating on serious compositions after his Fantasy String Quartet won an important chamber-music prize.

As a geographic descriptive surname Woods are predictably thick on the ground. The United Kingdom alone has 122 place names which range from Wood Dalling to Woodyates and include such exotics as Woodside of Arbedie and Woodstock Slop. Canada has 17 Wood-related towns, while the United States has 63 including no fewer than 6 Woodstocks. South Africa and Australia each have 2, while New Zealand and Ireland each have 3, and Singapore has a Woodlands. Geographic named features are very common.

****
*   **WRIGHT**   *
****

Related Names
Other surnames which are related as to root, derivation or usage include:

Arkwright	Wheelwright	Wrickson	Wrigson
Cartwright	Wraight	Wrighte	Wrixon
Cheesewright	Wraighte	Wrightman	Wryght
Faber	Wrate	Wrighton	Wrygson
Playwright	Wreight	Wrightson	Wrytte
Sievewright			

The surname Wright is an occupational name from the Old English word 'wyrhta' which means 'a carpenter or joiner'. In early times almost everything was made of wood, and this occupational name covered a huge variety of trades. These we find in the comparatively rare compound surnames Wheelwright, Arkwright (box-maker), Cartwright and Sievewright. Later, the word 'wright' became synonymous with 'worker', and in many of the records this name is Latinised to Faber. (This also happened to many people called Smith, which see.) As the meaning of 'wright' came to spread to all trades, many compounds were formed for skills which involved no connection with wood – amongst these are Playwright, and the lesser known Cheesewright (which remains as a rare surname).

The word 'wright' has long been in common usage in England. In literature, we find Chaucer using it in the fourteenth century. He mentions a man who 'was a well good wright, a carpenter'. However, the surname Wright appears even earlier.

Other common variations on the original name are Wrighte, Wraight(e), Wrate and Wreight.

One of the earliest references to the name is found in the Feet of Fines records for Sussex in 1214 where a Patere le Writh is mentioned.

A Wright Miscellany

The Wright Brothers – Orville (1871–1948) and Wilbur (1867–1912) – have gone down in history as the designers of the first heavier-than-air flying machine. Their 745lb wheel-less biplane powered by a 12hp motor first took to the air on 17 December 1903 at Kill Devil Hill near Kitty Hawk, North Carolina. Airborne for 12 seconds, it travelled about 10 feet above the ground with Orville strapped into the driving seat, for 120 feet before taking a nose dive. Nicknamed Wright Flyer I, it now hangs in the Smithsonian Institution in Washington.

☆

British physician Sir Almroth Wright was noted for his work in developing an anti-typhoid inoculation.

☆

Two Wrights have been Lord Mayors of London: Edmund Wright in 1640 and Thomas Wright in 1785.

☆

The United Kingdom has one related place name – Wrightington Bar, while Canada has 3 (one Wright and 2 Wrightsvilles) and the United States has 7 ranging from Wright to Wrightwood. Australia has a Wright lake; Canada has a Wright mountain; and the United States has a Wrightson mountain.

✳✳✳✳✳✳✳✳✳✳✳✳✳✳✳✳✳✳✳✳✳✳✳✳✳✳✳✳✳✳✳✳✳
✳   **YOUNG**   ✳
✳✳✳✳✳✳✳✳✳✳✳✳✳✳✳✳✳✳✳✳✳✳✳✳✳✳✳✳✳✳✳✳✳

Related Names

Other surnames which are related as to root, derivation or usage include:

Yong	Younger	Youngmay
Yonge	Younghusband	Youngs
Youngblood	Youngman	Youngson
Younge		

The surname Young derives from the Old English 'geong', meaning 'young', and from the Middle English word 'yong', or 'yung'. Initially this name could have been given as a nickname, either with reference to its bearer's appearance or, more usually, to distinguish the bearer from his father, who may well have had the same name. In this sense 'yung' would mean 'junior'. This is similar to the modern American use of the word junior (as in, for example, Kurt Vonnegut Jnr). Very occasionally the word is used to distinguish two brothers.

There are many variations on the surname Young. The most frequent of these are Youngs (son of Young), Younge, Yonge and Younger. A frequent compound variation is the name Younghusband. This is an occupational name and has nothing to do with marriage. Here 'husband' is used in the sense which remains in our word 'husbandry'. Thus Younghusband means 'young farmer'. Youngman is also an occupational name and means 'young servant', or simply 'servant'. To this day, this term is still used occasionally in London clubs to waiters (who are often far from young), and this sense remains in the French word for a waiter, which is 'garçon' meaning 'boy' or 'young man'. Another widespread variation is the predictable Youngson, whose meaning is self-evident. The variant Younger occasionally has a less obvious meaning. This is when the name derives from the Middle Dutch word 'jonghheer', which means 'young nobleman' (much like the similar German word 'Junker').

This name is one of the oldest to appear in the records, and references to it go back well before the Norman Conquest. The earliest mention of a name stemming from this meaning is in the Anglo-Saxon Chronicle in the records for Essex. Here, in 744, one Wilferth seo Iunga is mentioned.

A Young Miscellany

The Young–Helmholtz theory explains colour vision as resulting from separate retina fibres for red, green and blue light. The theory is named after Thomas Young (1773–1829) and, of course, Hermann Ludwig Ferdinand von Helmholtz (1821–94). Young also established the wave theory of light, and assisted in deciphering the Rosetta Stone.

☆

Jazz great Lester 'Pres' Young got an early start: at the age of 10 he became a drummer in his father's New Orleans Show.

Switching to the saxophone at 13, he made his name when he started playing with the legendary trumpeter, Joe 'King' Oliver, in Kansas City, later joining Count Basie's band for 10 years. His unique, sparse but buoyant sound triggered a bitter controversy which ranged through the jazz world for 15 years. Young's long-term love affair with Billie Holiday led to a series of recordings still regarded as masterpieces.

☆

US astronaut John Young joined Virgil Grisson on the first two-man space flight, Gemini 3. Seventeen years later he orbited the moon on the final check-out of the Apollo systems before the successful Apollo 11 flight.

☆

Sir Francis Younghusband (1863–1942), born in India, was a key member of the 1902 expedition which opened Tibet to the Western world. The main purpose of the expedition was to begin trade negotiations; when the first attempt was unsuccessful, the team undiplomatically slaughtered some 600 Tibetans, occupied the capital, Llasa, and forced the concession of a trade treaty on the Dalai Lama. A grateful England knighted Younghusband.

☆

The United Kingdom has one related place name, Young's End, while Canada has 2 (Young and Youngstown) and the United States has 10 including 5 Youngsvilles. Australia has a town called Young, and so does Uruguay. The name is common for geographic features and sometimes refers to the geologic age of the mountain or body of water so named.

Appendix

Useful names and addresses, telephone numbers and hours of opening (all liable to change with the passage of time).

Be aware of local Bank Holiday variations.

Registries

England and Wales
The General Register Office
St Catherine's House
10 Kingsway
London WC2B 6JP
Tel: 0171 242 0262
Open: Monday–Friday 8.30am–4.30pm
Closed: Saturday, Sunday, Bank Holidays.
No entrance fee.
Certificates: personal application £6
           postal application £11.50 (no search)
                  £15.50 (with search)

Postal applications to:
OPCS GRO
Smedley Hydro
Southport
Merseyside PR8 2HH

Scotland
General Registry Office
New Register House
Edinburgh EH1 3YT
Tel: 0131 334 0380
Open: Monday–Thursday 9.00am–4.30pm
     Friday 9.00am–4.00pm
Closed: Saturday, Sunday, Bank Holidays.

Glasgow Office:
General Registrar
Marriage Suites
22 Park Circus
Glasgow G3
Tel: 0141 249 4500

Search fees: daily £12 or £16, weekly £60
monthly £185, yearly £1,250
Appointment necessary.
Certificates: personal application £10
postal application £12

Eire
General Registry Office
James Joyce House
8–11 Lombard Street
Dublin 2
Eire
Tel: 00 353 1 671 1000
Open: Monday–Friday 9.30am–4.30pm
Closed: Lunch daily 12.30pm–2.15pm, Saturday, Sunday,
Bank Holidays.
Search fees: daily IR£12
one search for five years IR£1.50
Photocopies: IR£1.50
Certificates: IR£5.50

Northern Ireland
Oxford House
49/55 Chichester Street
Belfast BT1 4HI
Northern Ireland
Tel: 01232 235211
Open: Monday–Friday 9.00am–4.30pm
Closed: Lunch daily 1pm–2.15pm, Sunday, Bank Holidays
No entrance fee charged

Isle of Man
General Registry
Finch Road
Douglas
Isle of Man
Tel: 01624 673358
Open: Monday–Saturday 9.00am–4.30pm
Closed: Lunch daily 1pm–2.15pm, Sunday, Bank Holidays

The Channel Islands
The Librarian
The Société Jersiaise
9 Pier Road, St Helier
Jersey, Channel Islands
Tel: 01534 75940
Open: Monday–Saturday 10.00am–4.00pm winter
                              10.00am–5.00pm summer
            Sunday 1.00pm–4.00pm

Registrar General
States Building
Royal Square
St Helier
Jersey, Channel Islands
Postal enquiries recommended.

Registrar General
Royal Court House
St Peter Port
Guernsey, Channel Islands
Postal enquiries ONLY.

Principal Probate Registry
Somerset House
Strand
London WC2R 1LP
Tel: 0171 936 6000
Open: Monday–Friday 10.00am–4.30pm
Closed: Saturday, Sunday, Bank Holidays
Copying facilities.
No entrance fee.

Other useful addresses

Public Record Office
Chancery Lane
London WC2A 1LR
Tel: 0181 876 3444
Open: Monday–Friday
          9.30am–5.00pm
Closed: Saturday, Sunday,
          Bank Holidays,
          first two weeks in
          October
Reader's ticket required –
   no charge.
Copying service.

Public Record Office
Ruskin Avenue
Kew
Richmond
Surrey TW9 4DU
Tel: 0181 876 3444
Open: Monday–Saturday
          9.30am–5.00pm
Closed: Sundays,
               Bank Holidays
Reader's ticket required –
   no charge.
Copying service.

Public Record Office of Northern Ireland
66 Balmoral Avenue
Belfast
Northern Ireland

National Archives (Ireland)
Bishops Street
Dublin 8
Eire
Tel: 00 353 1 478 3711
Open: Monday–Friday 10.00am–5.00pm
Closed: Saturday, Sunday, Bank Holidays

Registry of Deeds (Ireland)
Henrietta Street
Dublin 1
Eire

British Museum Library
Great Russell Street
London WC1B 3DG
Tel: 0171 636 1544
Recorded information: 0171 580 1788
Reader's Ticket required – no charge.

National Museum of Wales
Cathays Park
Cardiff CF1 3NP

National Library, Dublin
Kildare Street
Dublin 2
Eire
Open: Monday 10.00am–9.00pm
        Tuesday/Wednesday 2.00pm–9.00pm
        Thursday/Friday 10.00am–5.00pm
        Saturday 10.00am–1.00pm
Tel: 00 353 1 661 8811

Mid Glamorgan County Library
Coed Parc, Park Street
Bridgend CF31 4BA

National Library of Wales
Aberystwyth
Dyfed SY23 3BU
Tel: 01970 623816

National Library of Scotland
George IV Bridge
Edinburgh EH1 1EW
Tel: 0131 226 4531

Genealogical Office (Ireland)
Kildare Street
Dublin 2
Eire
Personal Consultancy Service
Monday–Friday 10.00am–12.30pm
2.00pm–4.00pm
Fees: IR£20.00 per hour
Tel: 00 353 1 661 8811 ex. 402

Borthwick Institute of Historical Research
St Anthony's Hall
York YO1 2PW
Tel: 01904 624315
Open: Monday–Friday 9.30am–5.00pm
Closed: Lunch daily 1.00pm–2.00pm, Saturday, Sunday,
Bank Holidays, two weeks in August
Copying facilities.
Appointment necessary.

Guildhall Library
Aldermanbury
London EC2P 2EJ
Tel: 0171 606 3030
Open: Monday–Saturday
9.30am–5.00pm
Closed: Sunday,
Bank Holidays
Copying service.
No entrance fee.

British Red Cross
Archives and Historical
Exhibition
Guildford
Surrey
Tel: 01483 898595
Appointment necessary

India Office Library
197 Blackfriars Road
London SE1 8NG
Tel: 0171 928 9531
Open: Monday–Friday
9.30am–5.45pm
Saturday
9.30am–1.45pm
Closed: Sunday, Bank Hols
Copying facilities.
Day pass – no charge.

Newspaper Library
Colindale Avenue
London NW9 5HE
Open: Monday–Saturday
10.00am–4.45pm
Closed: Sunday, Bank Hols,
1 week in October
Copying facilities.
Reader's Ticket required.
No charges.

St Brides Printing Library
Bride Lane
London EC4Y 8EE
Tel: 0171 353 4660
Open: Monday–Friday 9.30am–5.30pm
Closed: Saturday, Sunday, Bank Holidays
Copying facilities.
No charge.

Manx Museum
Kingswood Grove
Douglas
Isle of Man IM1
Tel: 01624 675522
Open: Monday–Saturday
    10.00am–5.00pm
Closed: Sunday and Bank Hols

Morpeth Chantry Bagpipe
    Museum
Bridge Street
Morpeth
Northumberland NE61 1PJ
Tel: 01670 519466

Museum of Mining
Chatterley Whitfield Colliery
Tunstall
Stoke on Trent
Tel: 01782 813337
Open: Daily 10.00am–4.00pm
Entrance fee.

Museum of Chartered
    Insurance Institute
20 Aldermanbury
London EC2V 7HY
Tel: 0171 606 3835

Baptist Union
129 The Broadway
Didcot
Oxon OX11 8XB
Tel: 01235 512007

Huguenot Library
University Library
Gower Street
London WC1
Tel: 0171 380 7094

Catholic Central Library
17 Francis Street
London SW1P 1DN

Catholic Family History Society
Secretary: Mrs Barbara Murray
2 Winscombe Crescent
Ealing
London W5 1AZ
Annual subscription: £6

Jewish Museum
Woburn House
Tavistock Square
London WC1H 0EP
Tel: 0171 388 4525

Mormon Branch Library
LDS Chapel
401 Holywood Road
Belfast BT4 2GU
Northern Ireland
Tel: 01232 768250

Presbyterian Historical Society and
  United Reform Church History Society
86 Tavistock Place
London WC1H 9RT
Tel: 0171 837 7661

Society of Friends Library
Friends House
Euston Road
London NW1
Tel: 0171 387 3601

Society of Genealogists
14 Charterhouse Buildings
Goswell Road
London EC1M 7AB
Tel: 0171 251 8799
Open: Tuesday, Friday, Saturday 10.00am–6.00pm
        Wednesday, Thursday 10.00am–8.00pm
Closed: Monday, Bank Holidays (and Friday previous),
        one week in February
Search fees: £3.00 per hour
            £7.50 for 4 hours
            £10.00 per day
No fees to members.

Professional Researchers

Association of Genealogists
  and Record Agents
  (AGRA)
The Secretary
29 Badgers Close
Horsham
West Sussex RH12 5RU

Association of Professional
  Genealogists (APG)
4321 M Street N.W.
Suite 236
Washington DC 20007
USA

Paul Gorry
Gorry Research
12 Burrow Road
Sutton
Dublin 13
Eire
Tel: 00 353 1 393942

Stephen T J Wright
4 Rose Glen
Chelmsford CM2 9EN
Tel: 01245 259965

Mrs Sandra Speedie
57 Dunellan Road
Milngavie
Glasgow G62 7RE
Tel: 0141 956 7050

Regnal Table

Monarch		Years of Reign	
William I	25 December	1066 – 25 September	1087
William II	26 September	1087 – 4 August	1100
Henry I	5 August	1100 – 25 December	1135
Stephen	26 December	1135 – 18 December	1154
Henry II	19 December	1154 – 2 September	1189
Richard I	3 September	1189 – 26 May	1199
John	27 May	1199 – 27 October	1216*
Henry III	28 October	1216 – 19 November	1272
Edward I	20 November	1272 – 7 July	1307
Edward II	8 July	1307 – 24 January	1327
Edward III	25 January	1327 – 21 June	1377
Richard II	22 June	1377 – 29 September	1399
Henry IV	30 September	1399 – 20 March	1413
Henry V	21 March	1413 – 31 August	1422
Henry VI	1 September	1422 – 3 March	1461
Edward IV	4 March	1461 – 8 April	1483
Edward V	9 April	1483 – 25 June	1483
Richard III	26 June	1483 – 21 August	1485
Henry VII	22 August	1485 – 21 April	1509
Henry VIII	22 April	1509 – 27 January	1547
Edward VI	28 January	1547 – 26 June	1553
Lady Jane Grey	27 June	1553 – nine days	
Mary I	6 July	1553 – 24 July	1554
Philip & Mary	25 July	1554 – 16 November	1558

*King John regnal years were calculated from Ascension day each year.

Elizabeth I	17 November	1558 – 23 March	1603
James I	24 March	1603 – 26 March	1625
Charles I	27 March	1625 – 18 May	1649
	Commonwealth Interregnum 1649–1660		
Charles II	30 January	1649 – 5 February	1685
James II	6 February	1685 – 11 December	1688
Interregnum	12 December	1688 – 12 February	1689
William III & Mary	13 February	1689 – 27 December	1694
William III	28 December	1694 – 7 March	1702
Anne	8 March	1702 – 31 July	1714
George I	1 August	1714 – 10 June	1727
George II	11 June	1727 – 24 October	1760
George III	25 October	1760 – 28 January	1820
George IV	29 January	1820 – 25 June	1830
William IV	26 June	1830 – 19 June	1837
Victoria	20 June	1837 use of regnal years discontinued	

Index

References to actual names are in italics.

300

309

311